THE JEWISH BRIGADE

MARVANO

COLORIST: BÉRENGÈRE MARQUEBREUCQ
TRANSLATOR: MONTANA KANE
LETTERER: SYLVAIN DUMAS

DEAD RECKONING

ANNAPOLIS, MARYLAND

Para Amber. Te deseo todo lo mejor en tu vida. Un abrazo muy fuerte.

Published by Dead Reckoning
291 Wood Road
Annapolis, MD 21402

1-LA BRIGADE JUIVE - COMPILATION
1 - Vigilante
2 - TTG
3 - Hatikvah
© Marvano 2013–2016
All rights reserved

Library of Congress Cataloging-in-Publication Data

Names: Marvano, illustrator, author. | Marquebreucq, Bérengère colourist.

Title: The Jewish Brigade / Marvano ; colorist, Bérengère Marquebreucq.
Other titles: Brigade Juive. English
Description: Annapolis, Maryland : Dead Reckoning, [2021] | English
    translation of the French: La Brigade Juive - Compilation.
Identifiers: LCCN 2021014880 (print) | LCCN 2021014881 (ebook) | ISBN
    9781682477236 (paperback ; alk. paper) | ISBN 9781682477250 (epub) |
    ISBN 9781682477250 (pdf)
Subjects: LCSH: Great Britain. Army. Jewish Brigade—Comic books, strips,
    etc. | World War, 1939–1945—Participation, Jewish—Comic books, strips,
    etc. | Graphic novels.
Classification: LCC PN6790.B43 M366 2021 (print) | LCC PN6790.B43 (ebook)
    | DDC 741.5/9493—dc23
LC record available at https://lccn.loc.gov/2021014880
LC ebook record available at https://lccn.loc.gov/2021014881

♾ Print editions meet the requirements of ANSI/NISO z39.48-1992 (Permanence of Paper).
Printed in the United States of America.

29 28 27 26 25 24 23 22 21   9 8 7 6 5 4 3 2 1
First printing

Originally written by the author in Dutch.

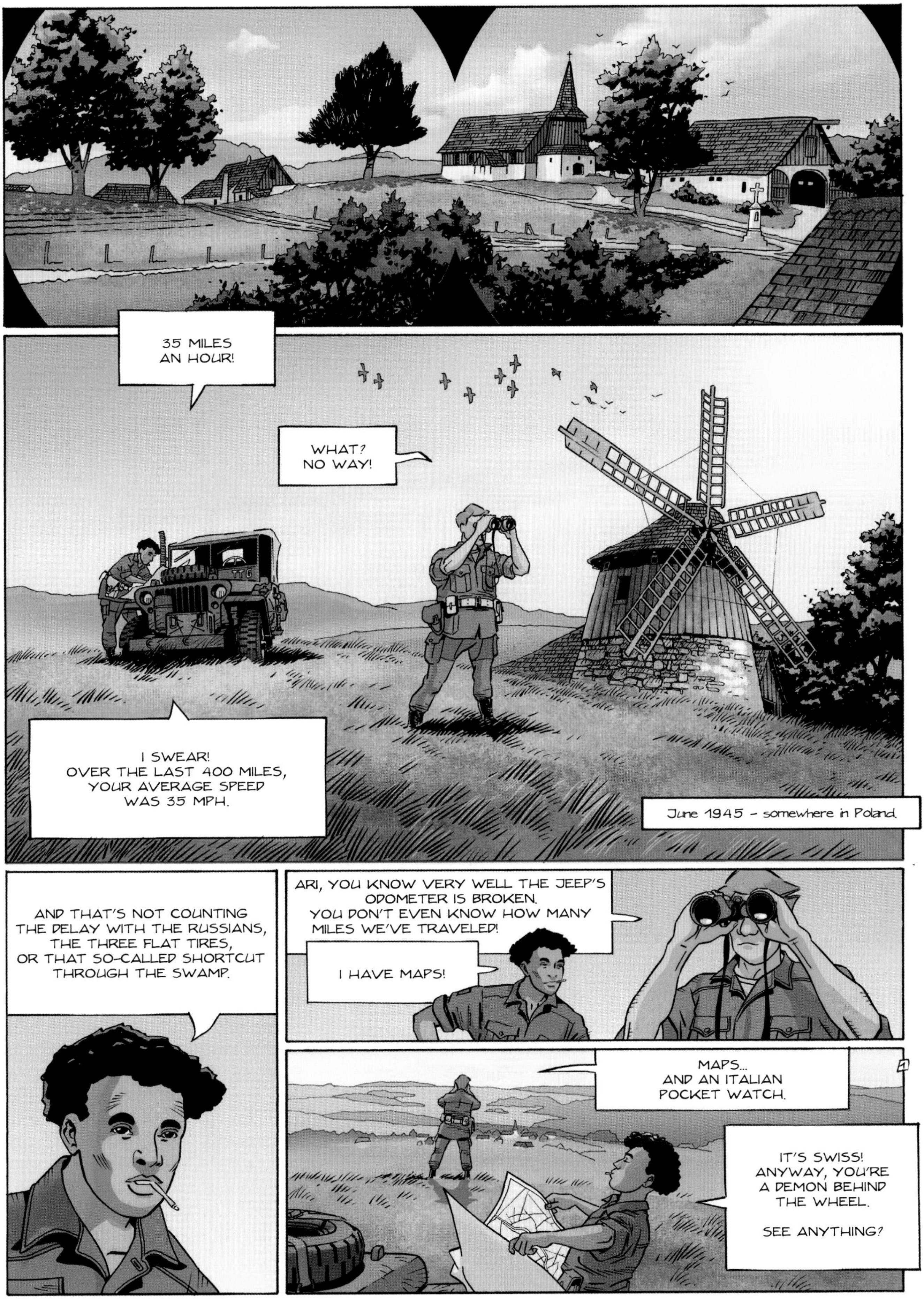
35 MILES AN HOUR!
WHAT? NO WAY!
I SWEAR! OVER THE LAST 400 MILES, YOUR AVERAGE SPEED WAS 35 MPH.
June 1945 - somewhere in Poland.
AND THAT'S NOT COUNTING THE DELAY WITH THE RUSSIANS, THE THREE FLAT TIRES, OR THAT SO-CALLED SHORTCUT THROUGH THE SWAMP.
ARI, YOU KNOW VERY WELL THE JEEP'S ODOMETER IS BROKEN. YOU DON'T EVEN KNOW HOW MANY MILES WE'VE TRAVELED!
I HAVE MAPS!
MAPS... AND AN ITALIAN POCKET WATCH.
IT'S SWISS! ANYWAY, YOU'RE A DEMON BEHIND THE WHEEL.
SEE ANYTHING?

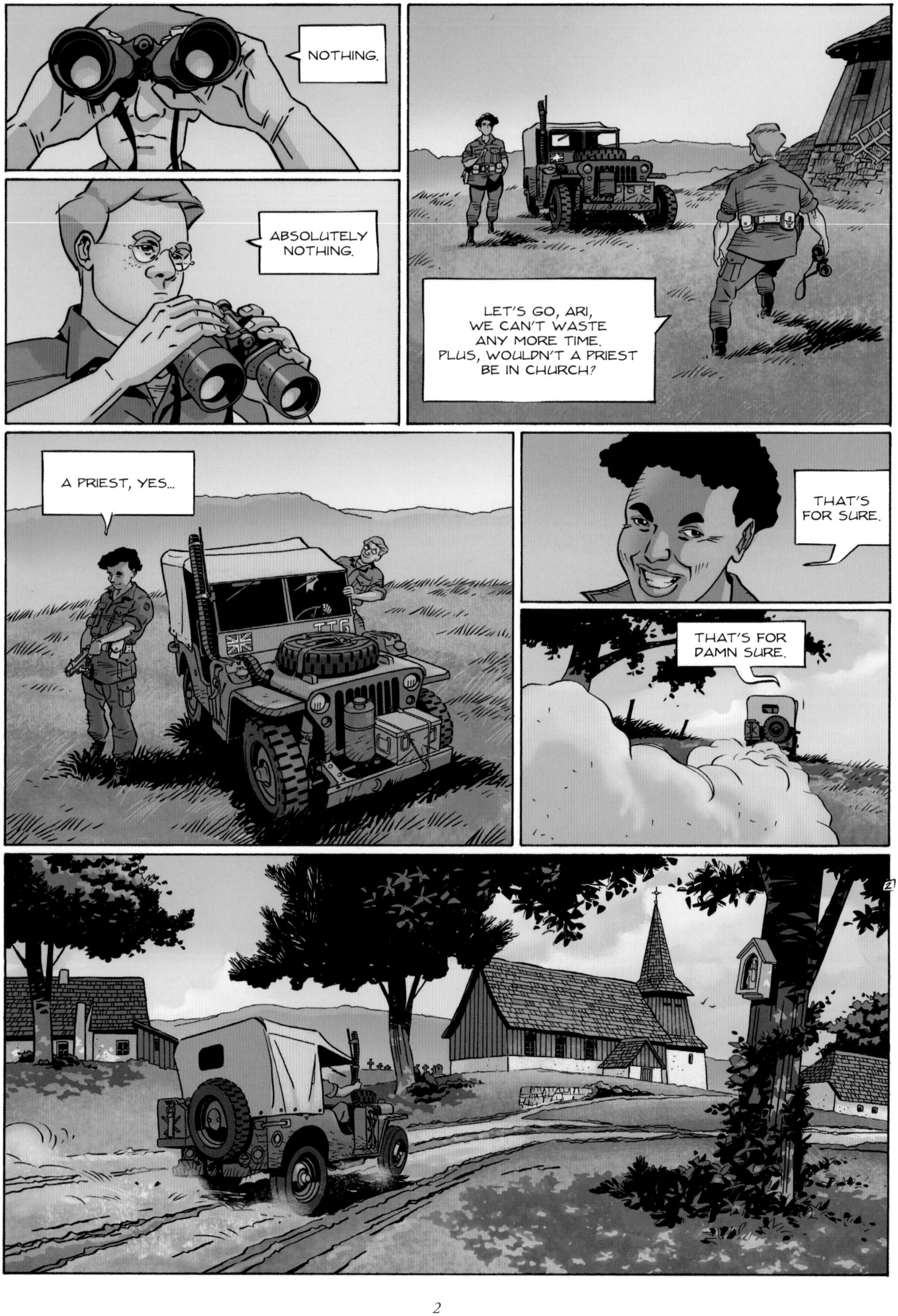
NOTHING.
ABSOLUTELY NOTHING.
LET'S GO, ARI, WE CAN'T WASTE ANY MORE TIME. PLUS, WOULDN'T A PRIEST BE IN CHURCH?
A PRIEST, YES...
THAT'S FOR SURE.
THAT'S FOR DAMN SURE.

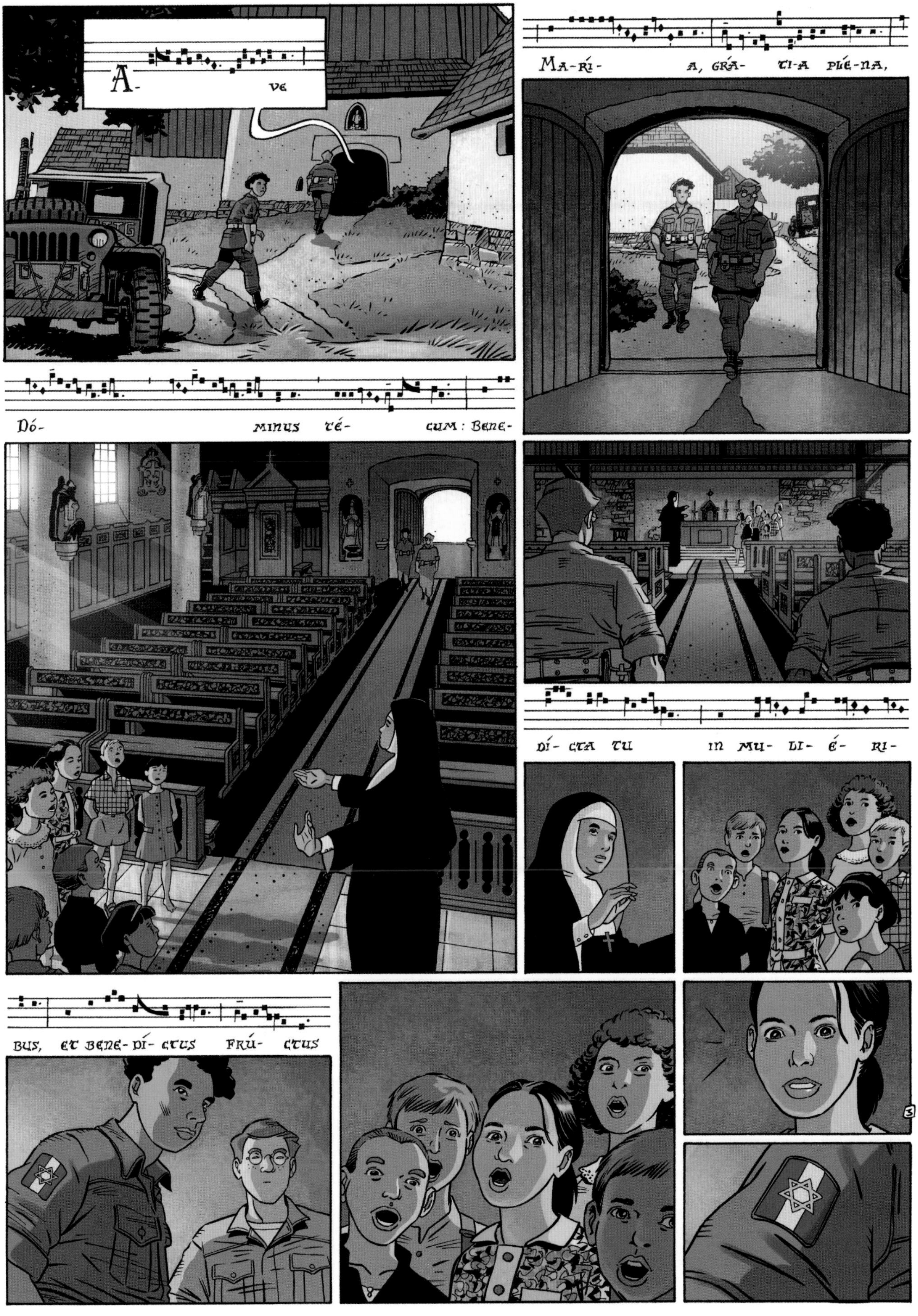
A- ve
Ma-rí- a, grá- ti-a plé-na,
Dó- minus té- cum: Bene-
dí- cta tu in mu- li- é- ri-
bus, et bene- dí- ctus frú- ctus

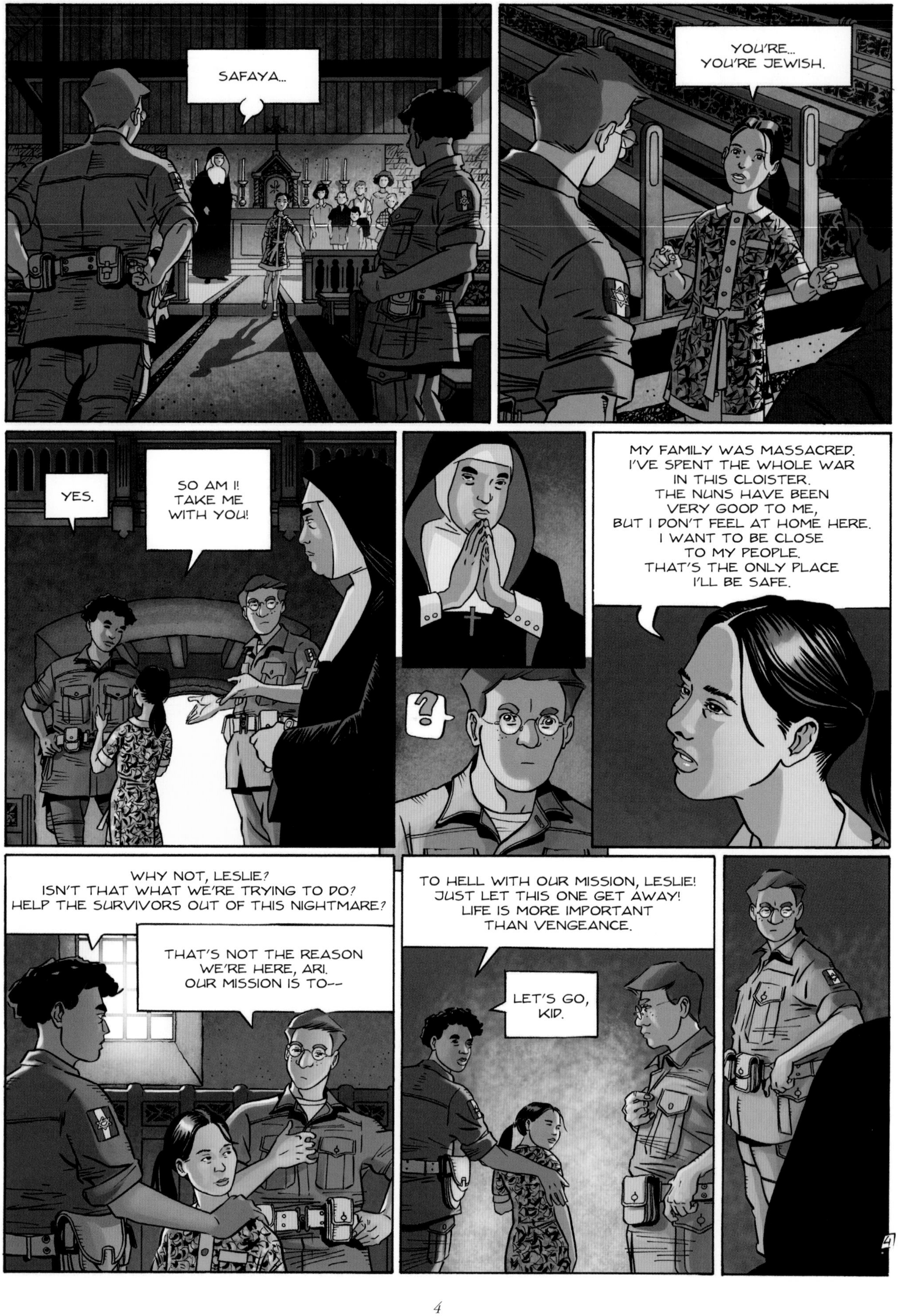

SAFAYA...
YOU'RE... YOU'RE JEWISH.
YES.
SO AM I! TAKE ME WITH YOU!
MY FAMILY WAS MASSACRED. I'VE SPENT THE WHOLE WAR IN THIS CLOISTER. THE NUNS HAVE BEEN VERY GOOD TO ME, BUT I DON'T FEEL AT HOME HERE. I WANT TO BE CLOSE TO MY PEOPLE. THAT'S THE ONLY PLACE I'LL BE SAFE.
?
WHY NOT, LESLIE? ISN'T THAT WHAT WE'RE TRYING TO DO? HELP THE SURVIVORS OUT OF THIS NIGHTMARE?
THAT'S NOT THE REASON WE'RE HERE, ARI. OUR MISSION IS TO--
TO HELL WITH OUR MISSION, LESLIE! JUST LET THIS ONE GET AWAY! LIFE IS MORE IMPORTANT THAN VENGEANCE.
LET'S GO, KID.
4

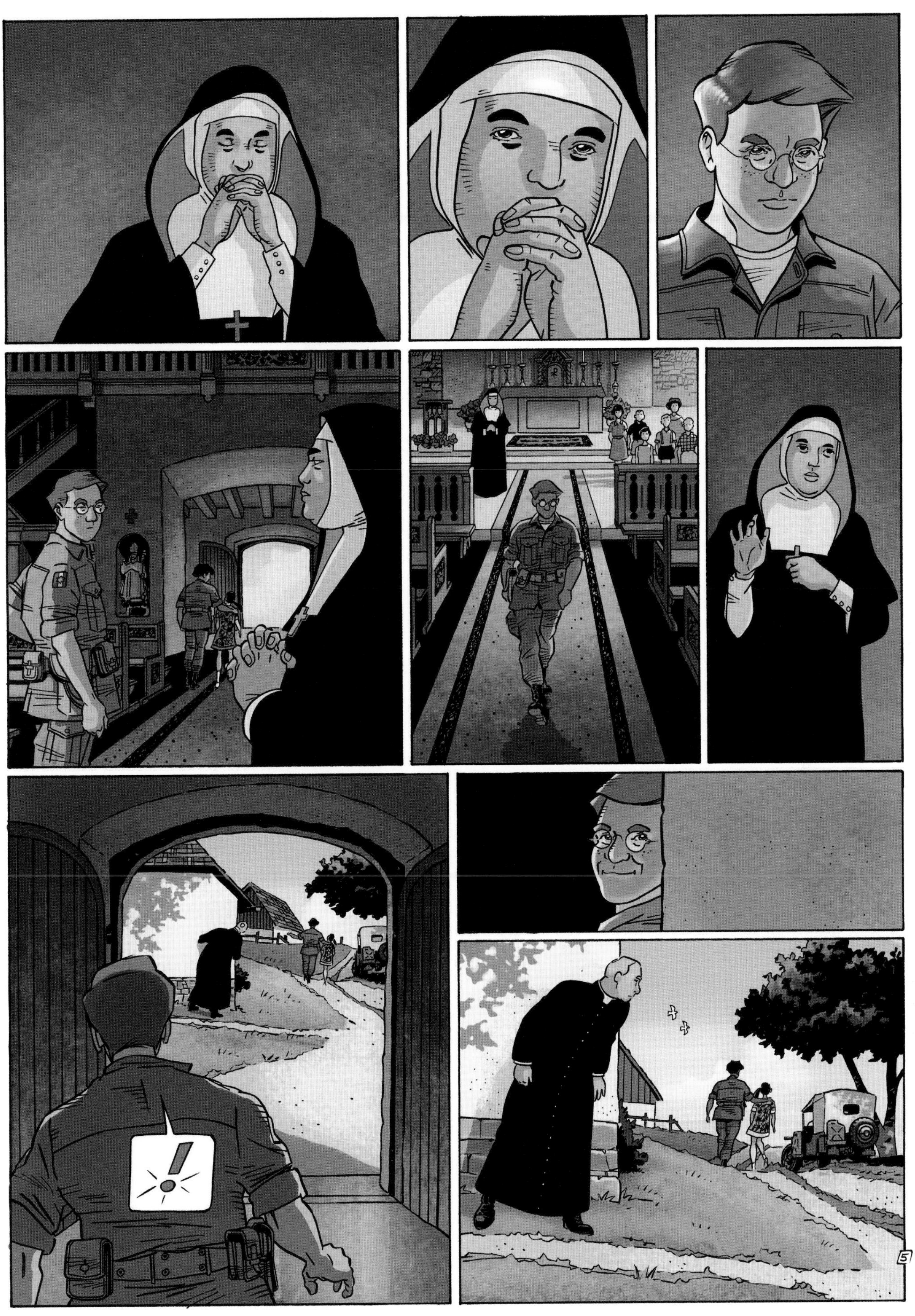
!

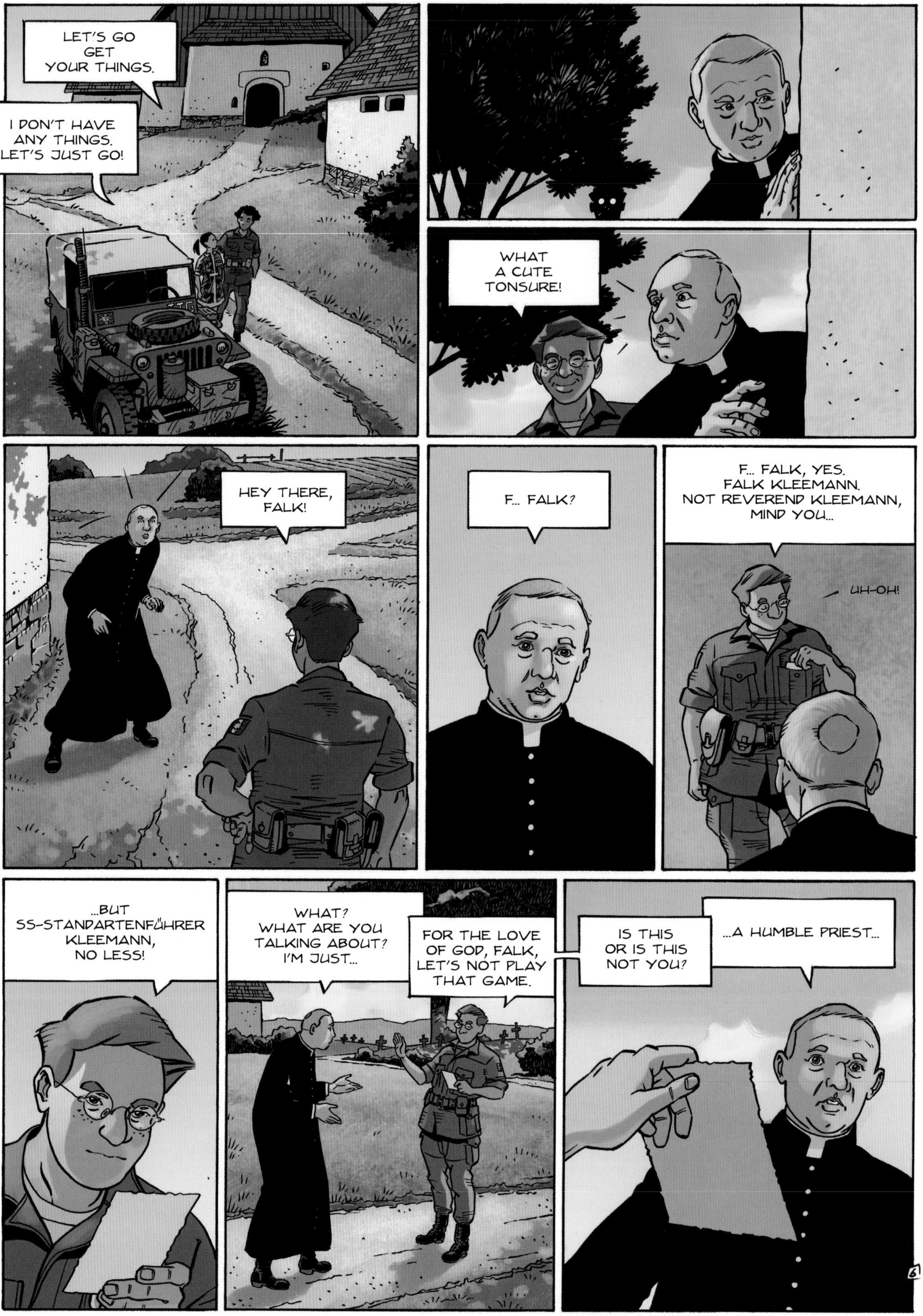
LET'S GO GET YOUR THINGS.
I DON'T HAVE ANY THINGS. LET'S JUST GO!
WHAT A CUTE TONSURE!
HEY THERE, FALK!
F... FALK?
F... FALK, YES. FALK KLEEMANN. NOT REVEREND KLEEMANN, MIND YOU...
UH-OH!
...BUT SS-STANDARTENFÜHRER KLEEMANN, NO LESS!
WHAT? WHAT ARE YOU TALKING ABOUT? I'M JUST...
FOR THE LOVE OF GOD, FALK, LET'S NOT PLAY THAT GAME.
...A HUMBLE PRIEST...
IS THIS OR IS THIS NOT YOU?
6

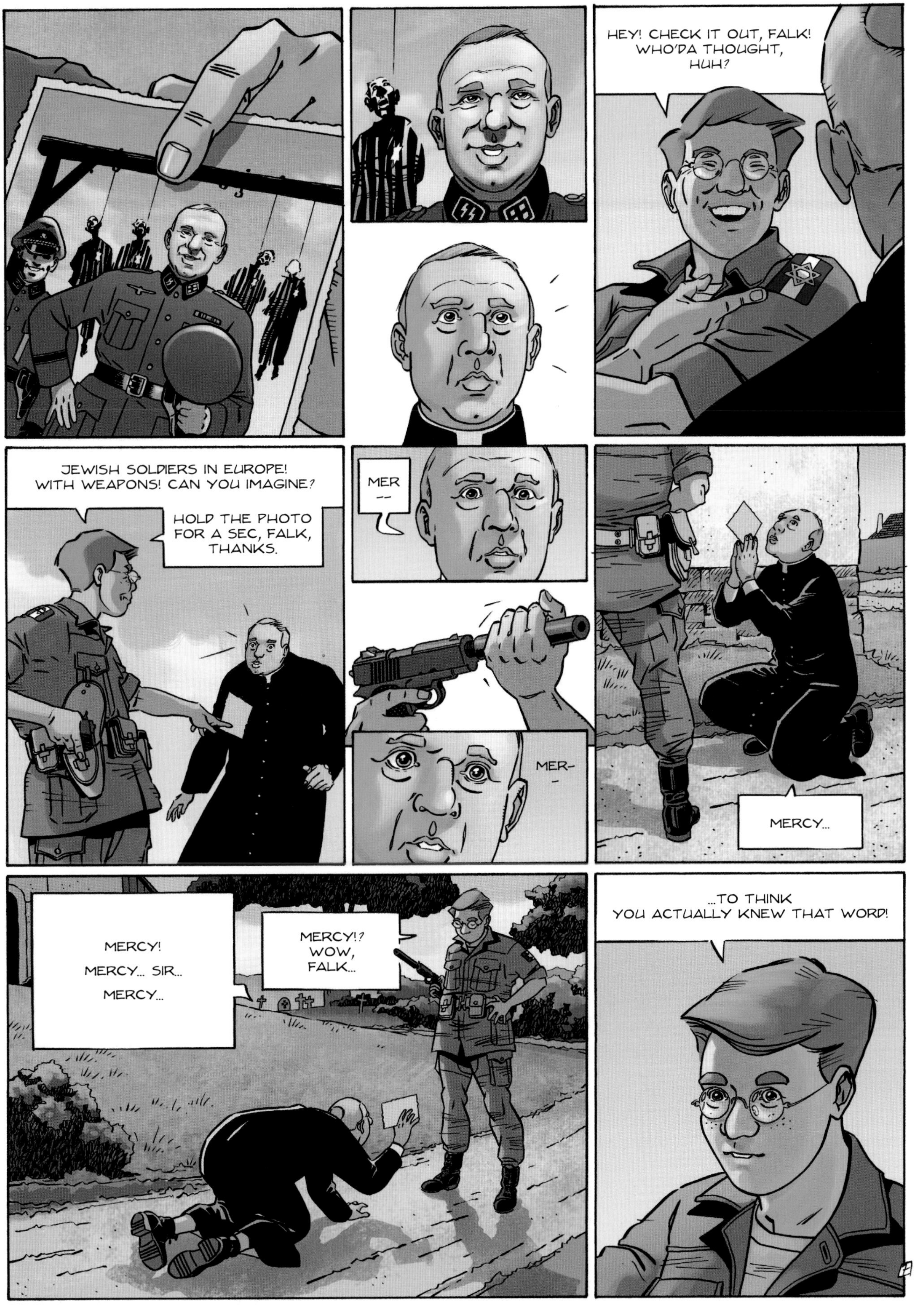

HEY! CHECK IT OUT, FALK! WHO'DA THOUGHT, HUH?
JEWISH SOLDIERS IN EUROPE! WITH WEAPONS! CAN YOU IMAGINE?
HOLD THE PHOTO FOR A SEC, FALK, THANKS.
MER --
MER- -
MERCY...
MERCY! MERCY... SIR... MERCY...
MERCY!? WOW, FALK...
...TO THINK YOU ACTUALLY KNEW THAT WORD!

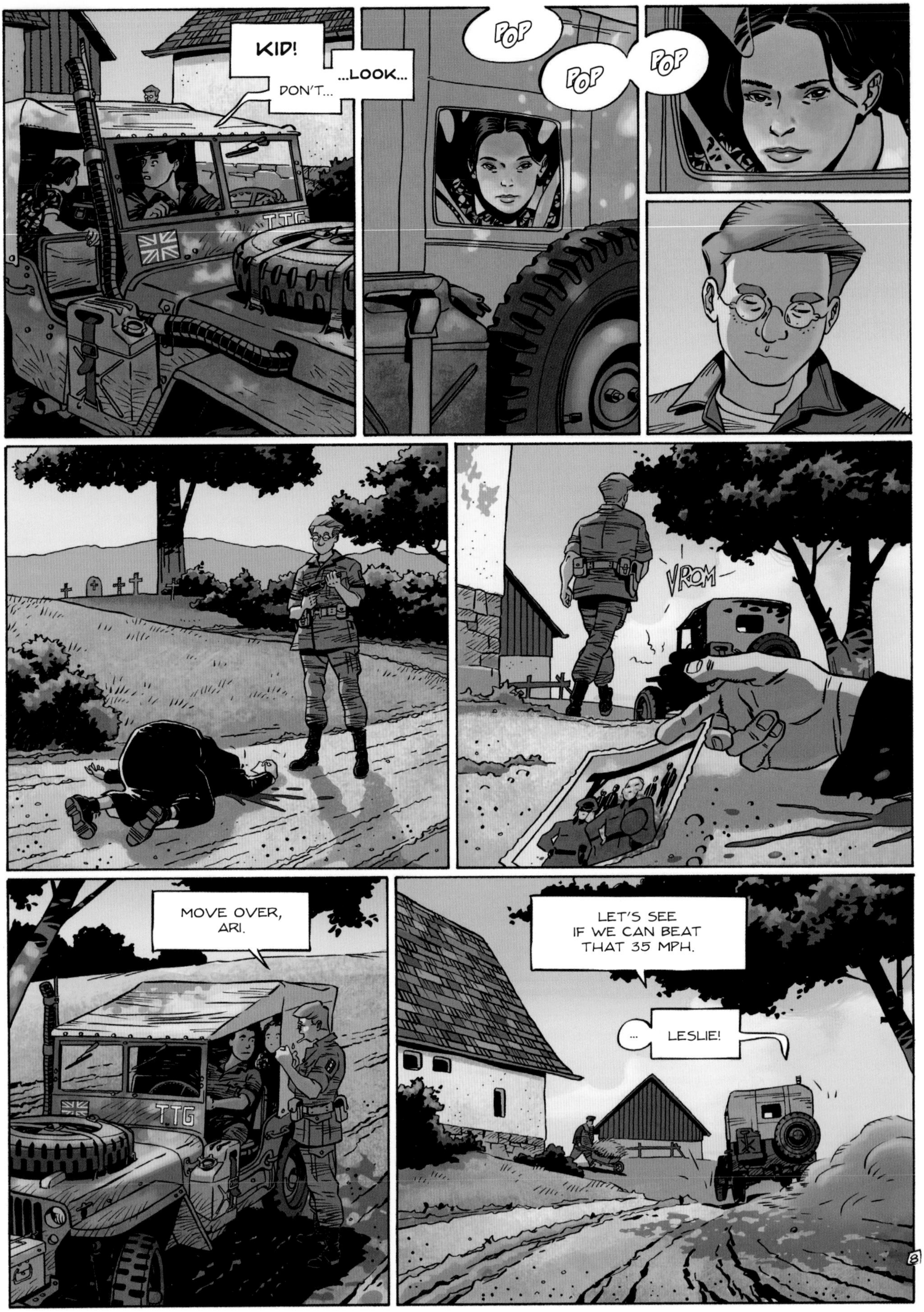
KID!
DON'T...
...LOOK...
POP
POP
POP
VROM
MOVE OVER, ARI.
LET'S SEE IF WE CAN BEAT THAT 35 MPH.
... LESLIE!
8

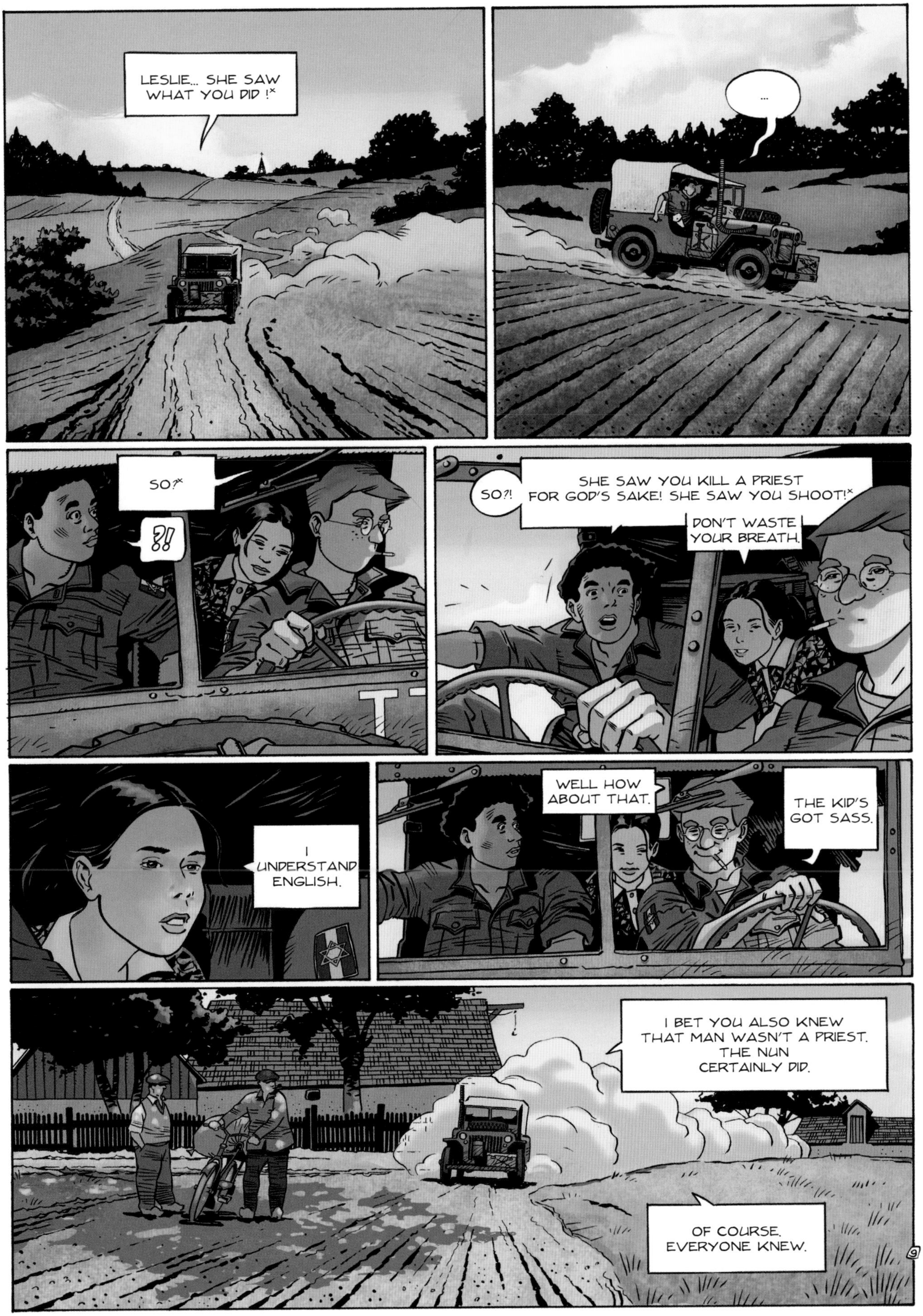
LESLIE... SHE SAW WHAT YOU DID !×
...
SO?×
?!
SO?!
SHE SAW YOU KILL A PRIEST FOR GOD'S SAKE! SHE SAW YOU SHOOT!×
DON'T WASTE YOUR BREATH.
I UNDERSTAND ENGLISH.
WELL HOW ABOUT THAT.
THE KID'S GOT SASS.
I BET YOU ALSO KNEW THAT MAN WASN'T A PRIEST. THE NUN CERTAINLY DID.
OF COURSE. EVERYONE KNEW.
9

×In English in the original version.

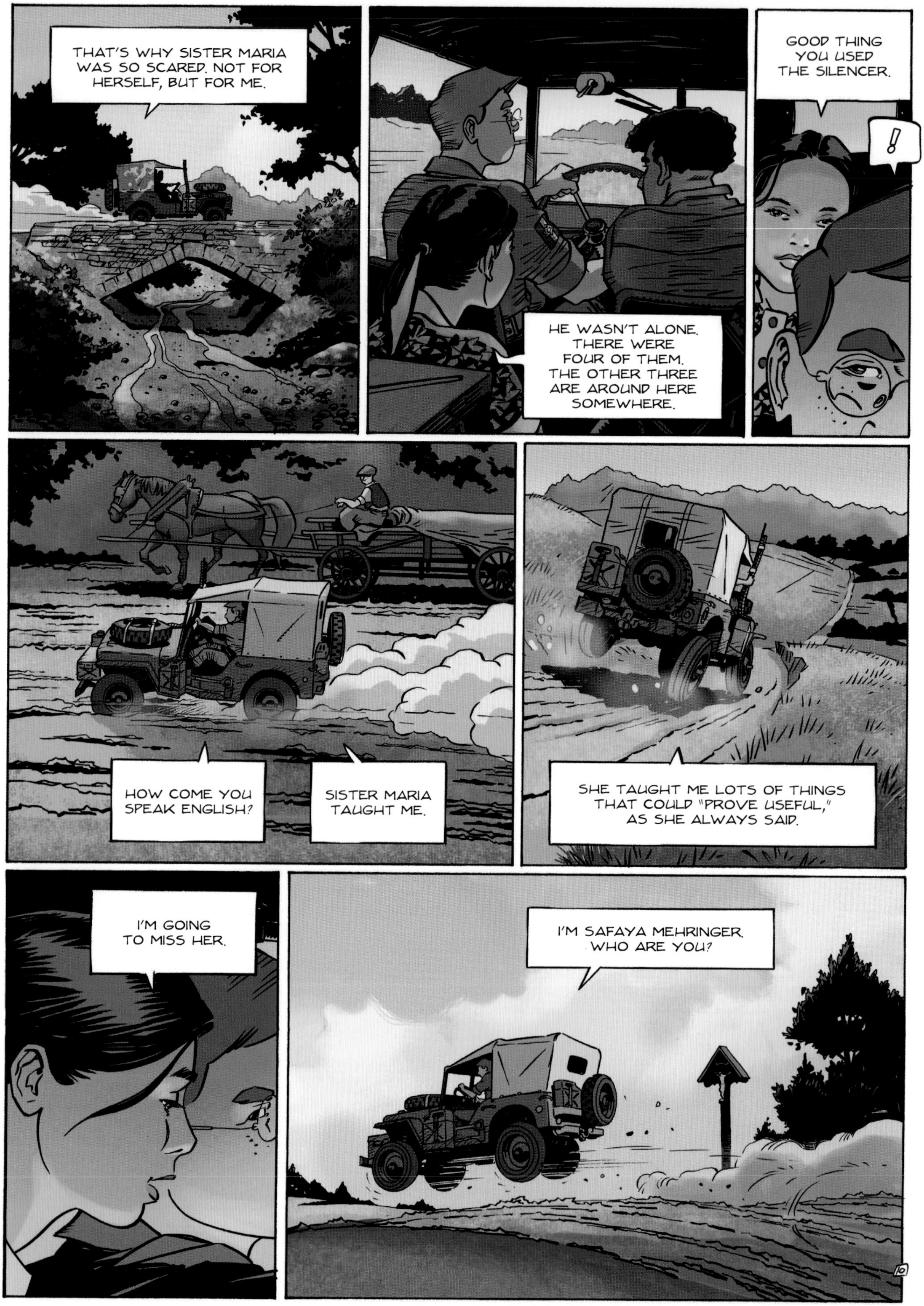
THAT'S WHY SISTER MARIA WAS SO SCARED. NOT FOR HERSELF, BUT FOR ME.
HE WASN'T ALONE. THERE WERE FOUR OF THEM. THE OTHER THREE ARE AROUND HERE SOMEWHERE.
GOOD THING YOU USED THE SILENCER.
!
HOW COME YOU SPEAK ENGLISH?
SISTER MARIA TAUGHT ME.
SHE TAUGHT ME LOTS OF THINGS THAT COULD "PROVE USEFUL," AS SHE ALWAYS SAID.
I'M GOING TO MISS HER.
I'M SAFAYA MEHRINGER. WHO ARE YOU?
10

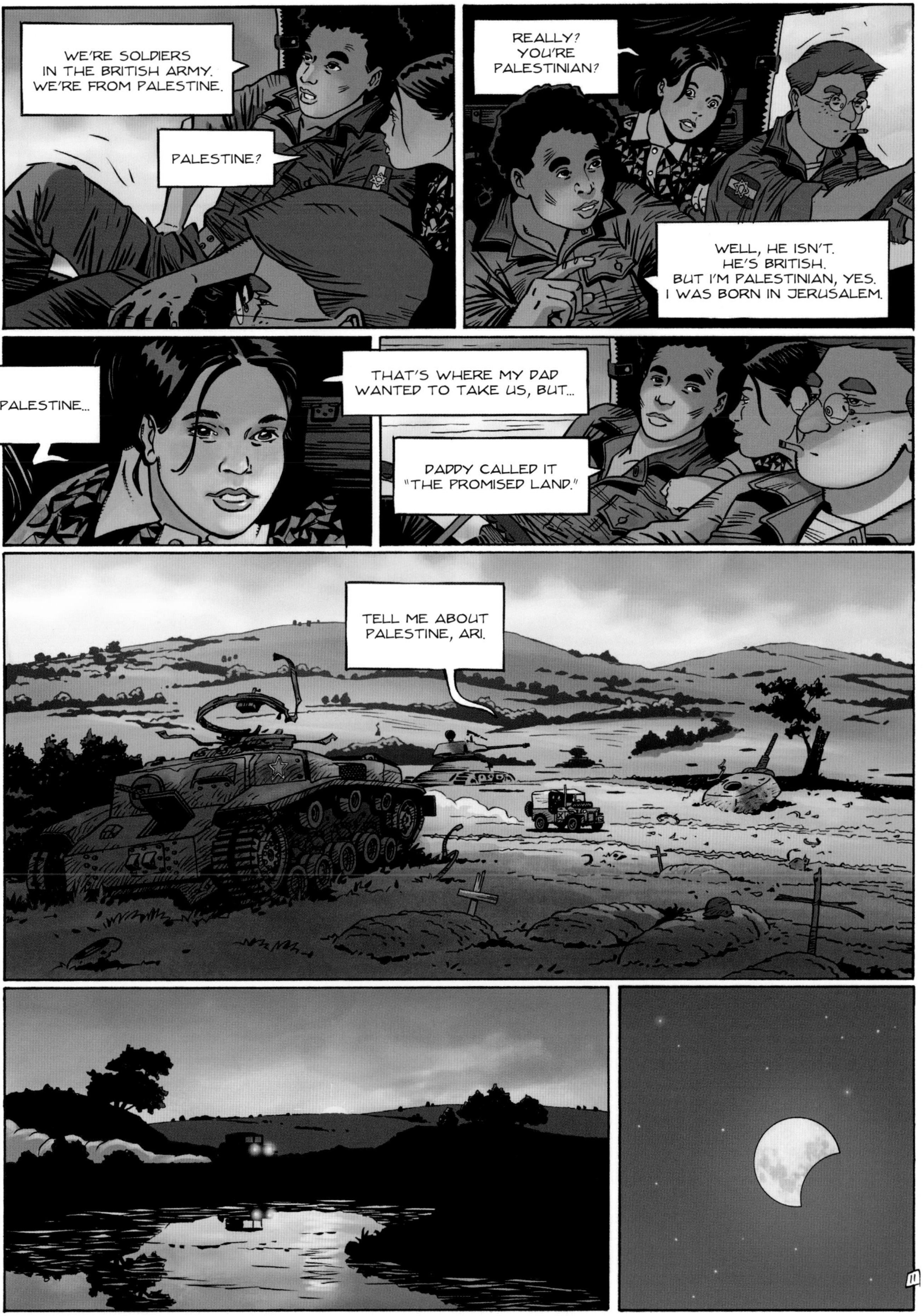
WE'RE SOLDIERS IN THE BRITISH ARMY. WE'RE FROM PALESTINE.
PALESTINE?
REALLY? YOU'RE PALESTINIAN?
WELL, HE ISN'T. HE'S BRITISH. BUT I'M PALESTINIAN, YES. I WAS BORN IN JERUSALEM.
PALESTINE...
THAT'S WHERE MY DAD WANTED TO TAKE US, BUT...
DADDY CALLED IT "THE PROMISED LAND."
TELL ME ABOUT PALESTINE, ARI.
11

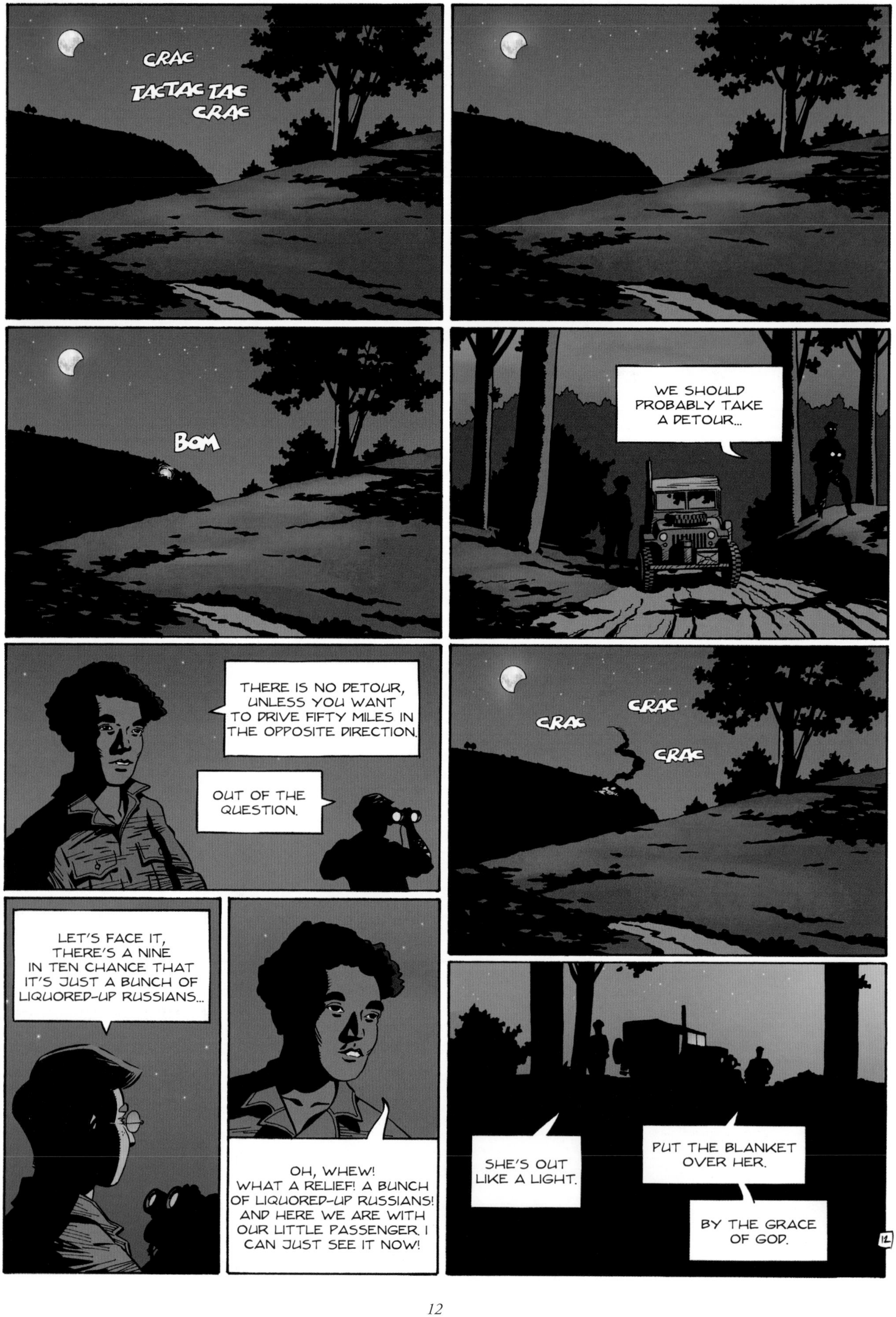
CRAC
TACTAC TAC
CRAC
BOM
WE SHOULD PROBABLY TAKE A DETOUR...
THERE IS NO DETOUR, UNLESS YOU WANT TO DRIVE FIFTY MILES IN THE OPPOSITE DIRECTION.
OUT OF THE QUESTION.
CRAC
CRAC
CRAC
LET'S FACE IT, THERE'S A NINE IN TEN CHANCE THAT IT'S JUST A BUNCH OF LIQUORED-UP RUSSIANS...
OH, WHEW! WHAT A RELIEF! A BUNCH OF LIQUORED-UP RUSSIANS! AND HERE WE ARE WITH OUR LITTLE PASSENGER. I CAN JUST SEE IT NOW!
SHE'S OUT LIKE A LIGHT.
PUT THE BLANKET OVER HER.
BY THE GRACE OF GOD.
12

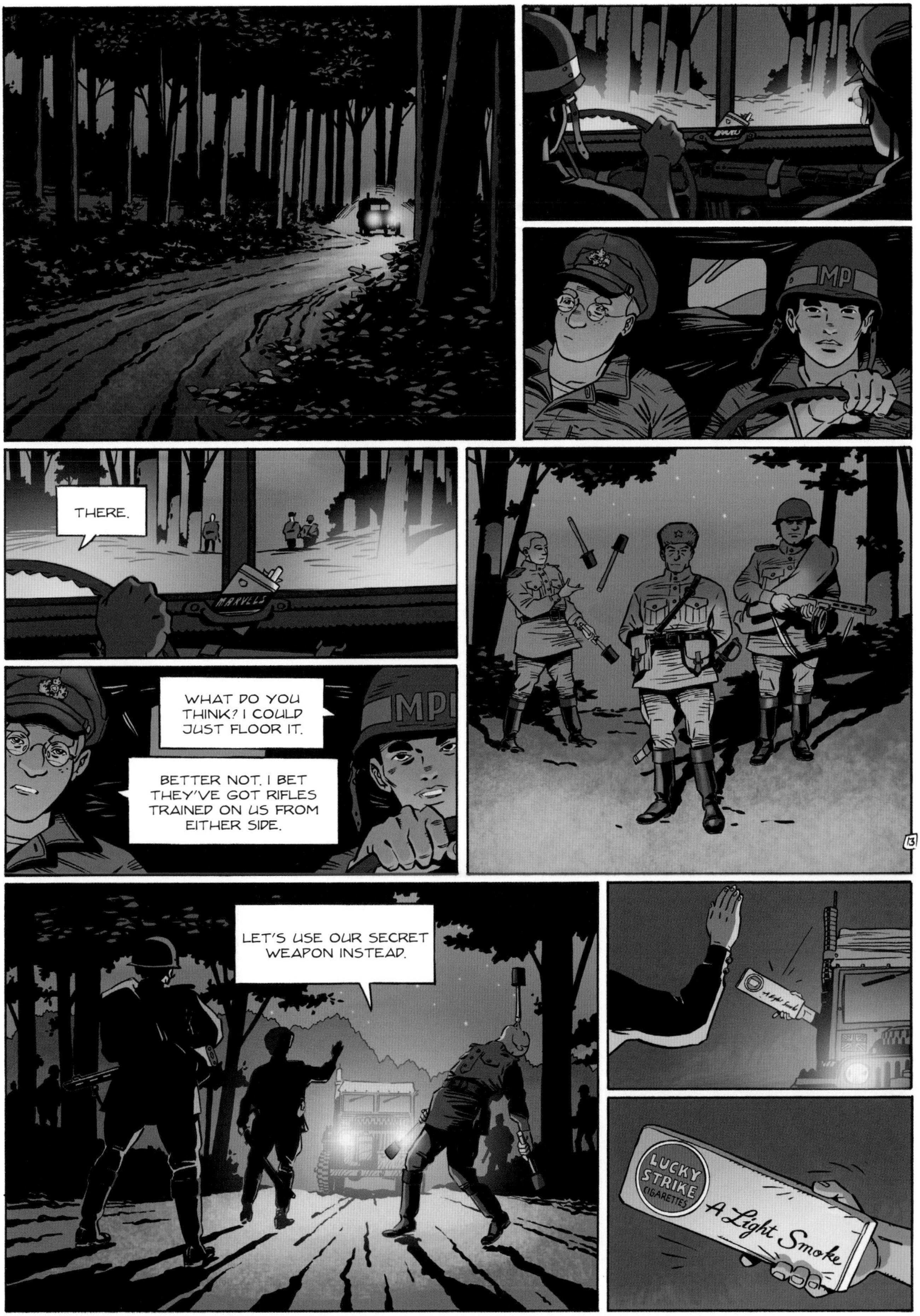
MP
THERE.
MARVELS
WHAT DO YOU THINK? I COULD JUST FLOOR IT.
BETTER NOT. I BET THEY'VE GOT RIFLES TRAINED ON US FROM EITHER SIDE.
LET'S USE OUR SECRET WEAPON INSTEAD.
LUCKY STRIKE CIGARETTES
A Light Smoke

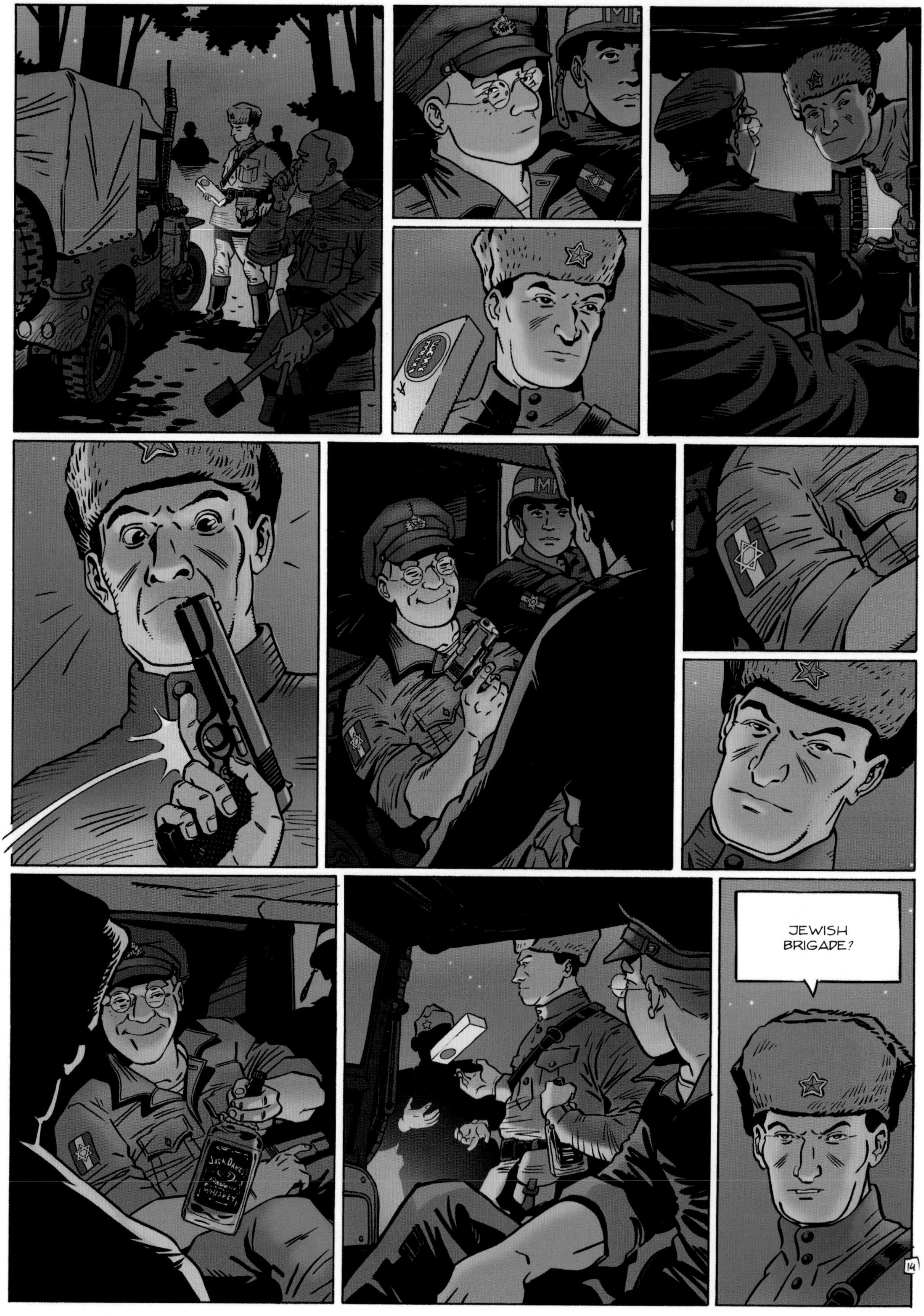
JEWISH BRIGADE?

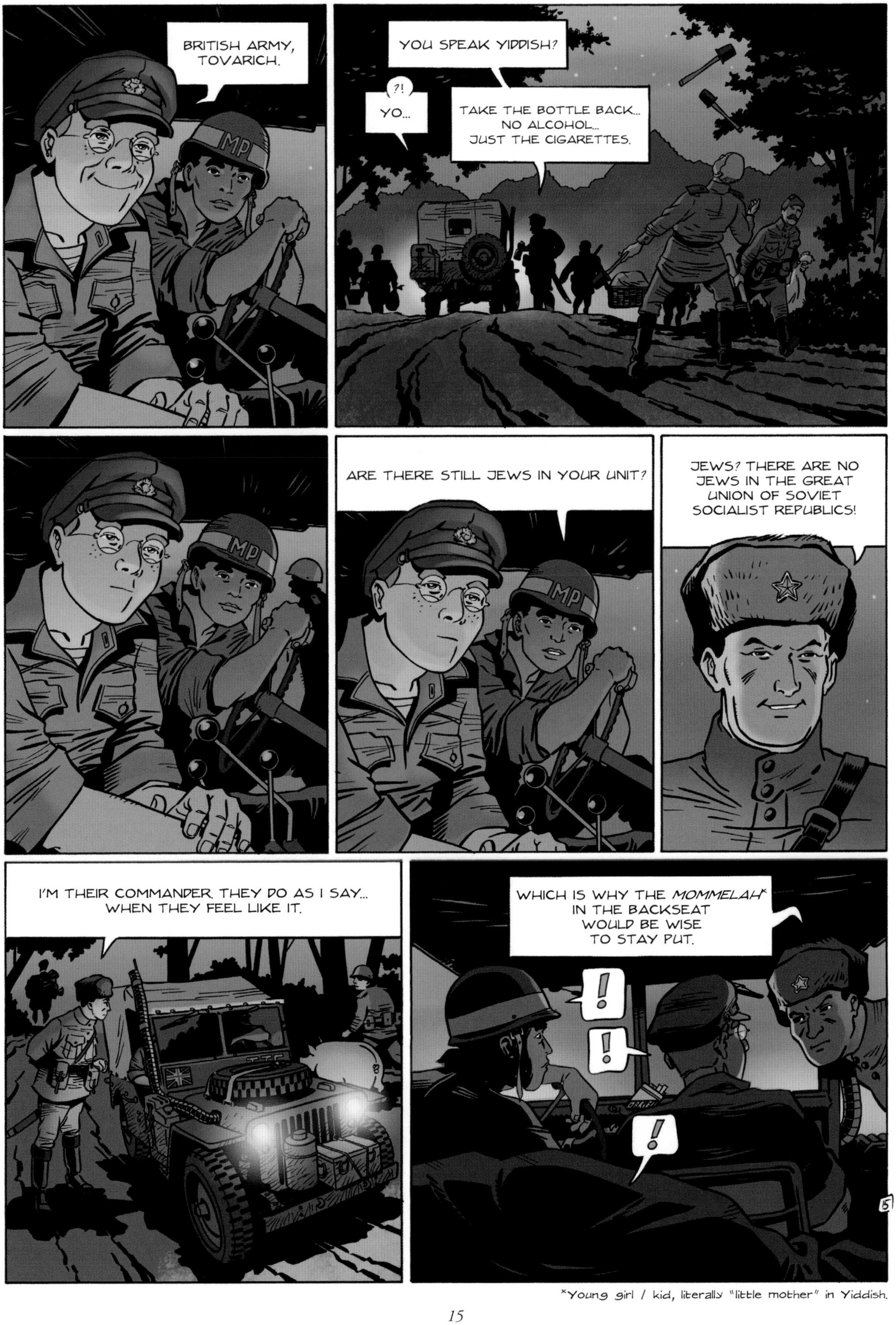
BRITISH ARMY, TOVARICH.
YOU SPEAK YIDDISH?
?!
YO...
TAKE THE BOTTLE BACK... NO ALCOHOL... JUST THE CIGARETTES.
ARE THERE STILL JEWS IN YOUR UNIT?
JEWS? THERE ARE NO JEWS IN THE GREAT UNION OF SOVIET SOCIALIST REPUBLICS!
I'M THEIR COMMANDER. THEY DO AS I SAY... WHEN THEY FEEL LIKE IT.
WHICH IS WHY THE *MOMMELAH*[*] IN THE BACKSEAT WOULD BE WISE TO STAY PUT.
!
!
!

*Young girl / kid, literally "little mother" in Yiddish.

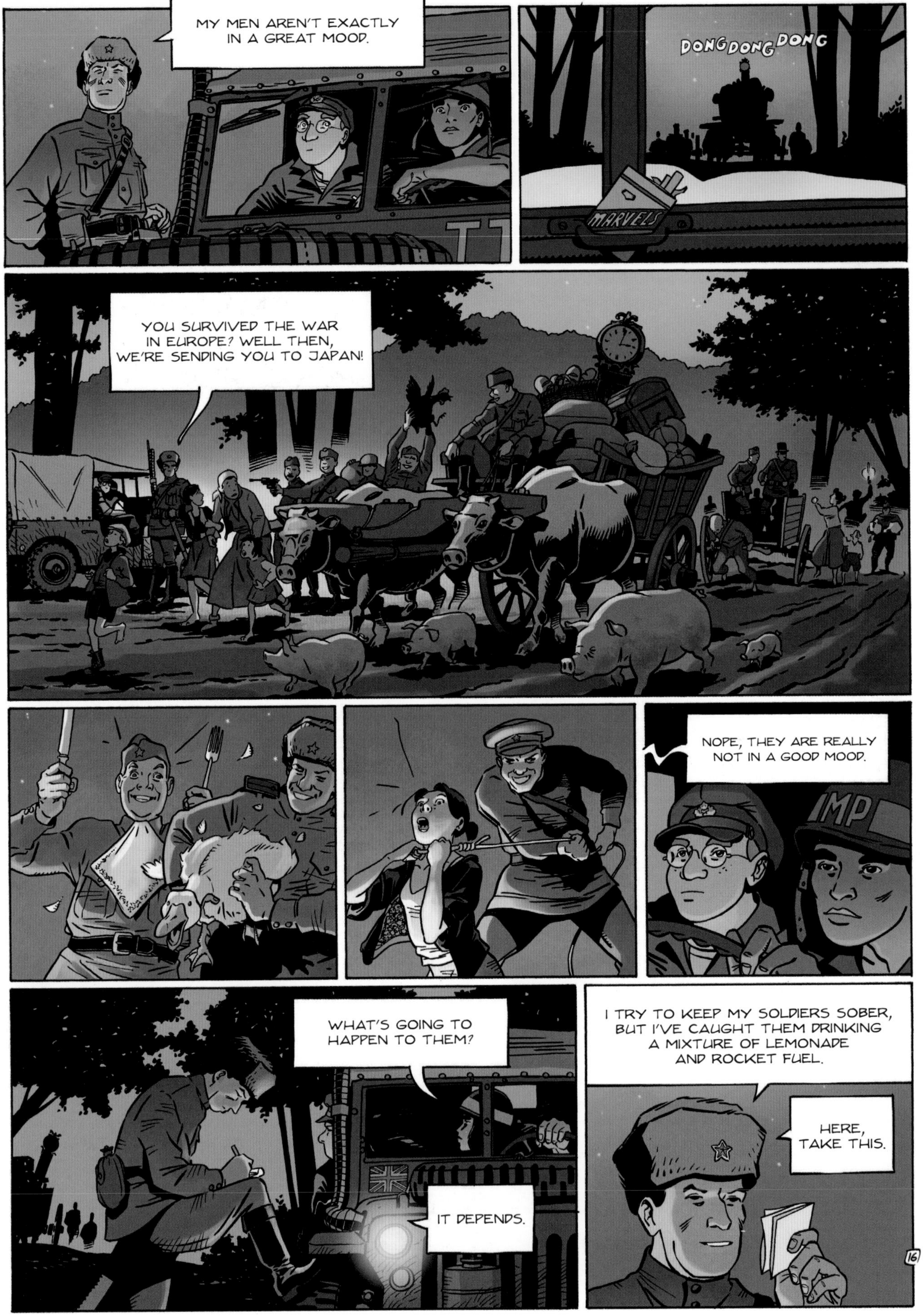
MY MEN AREN'T EXACTLY IN A GREAT MOOD.
DONG DONG DONG
MARVELS
YOU SURVIVED THE WAR IN EUROPE? WELL THEN, WE'RE SENDING YOU TO JAPAN!
NOPE, THEY ARE REALLY NOT IN A GOOD MOOD.
MP
WHAT'S GOING TO HAPPEN TO THEM?
IT DEPENDS.
I TRY TO KEEP MY SOLDIERS SOBER, BUT I'VE CAUGHT THEM DRINKING A MIXTURE OF LEMONADE AND ROCKET FUEL.
HERE, TAKE THIS.
16

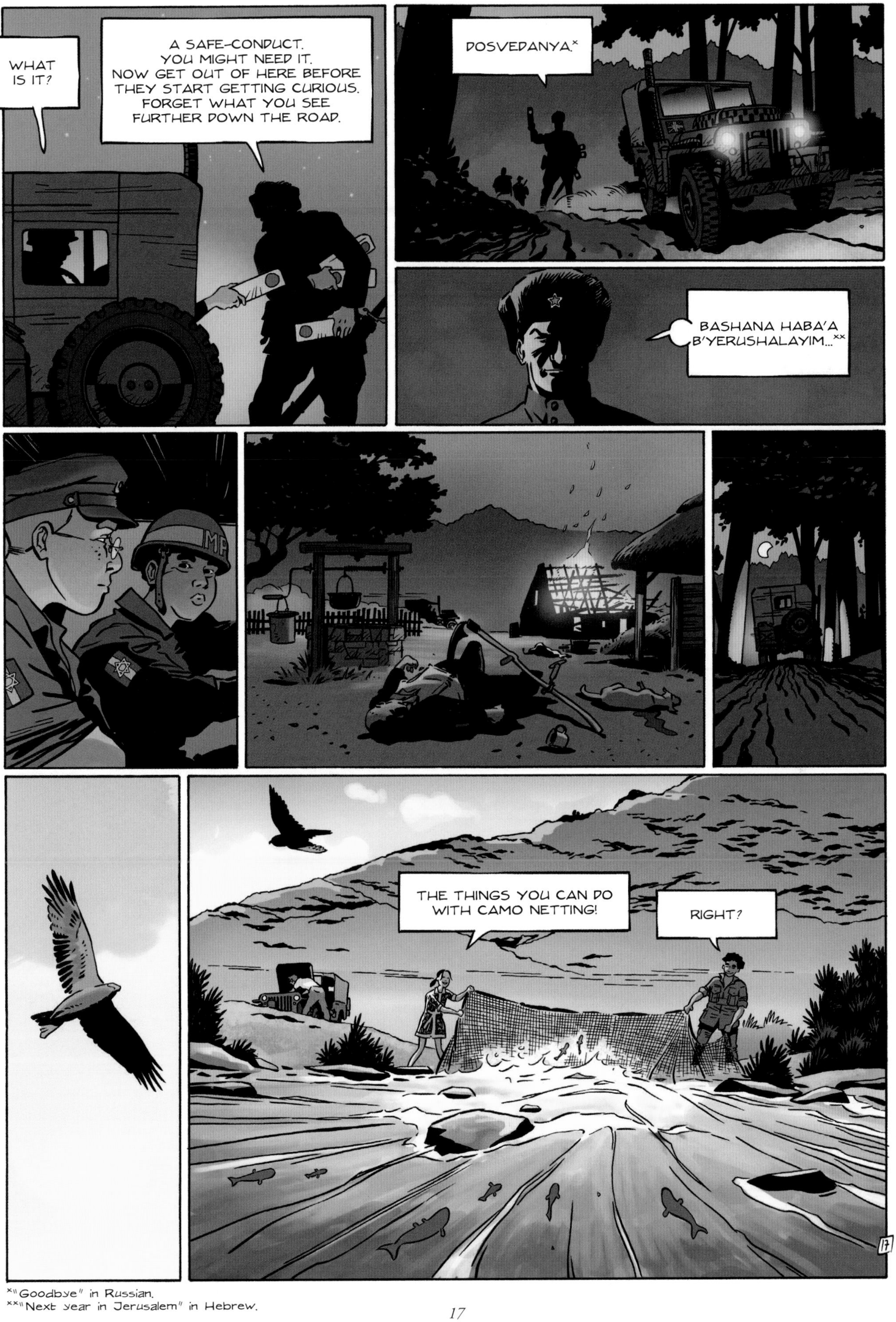
WHAT IS IT?
A SAFE-CONDUCT. YOU MIGHT NEED IT. NOW GET OUT OF HERE BEFORE THEY START GETTING CURIOUS. FORGET WHAT YOU SEE FURTHER DOWN THE ROAD.
DOSVEDANYA.x
BASHANA HABA'A B'YERUSHALAYIM...xx
MP
THE THINGS YOU CAN DO WITH CAMO NETTING!
RIGHT?
17

x"Goodbye" in Russian.
xx"Next year in Jerusalem" in Hebrew.

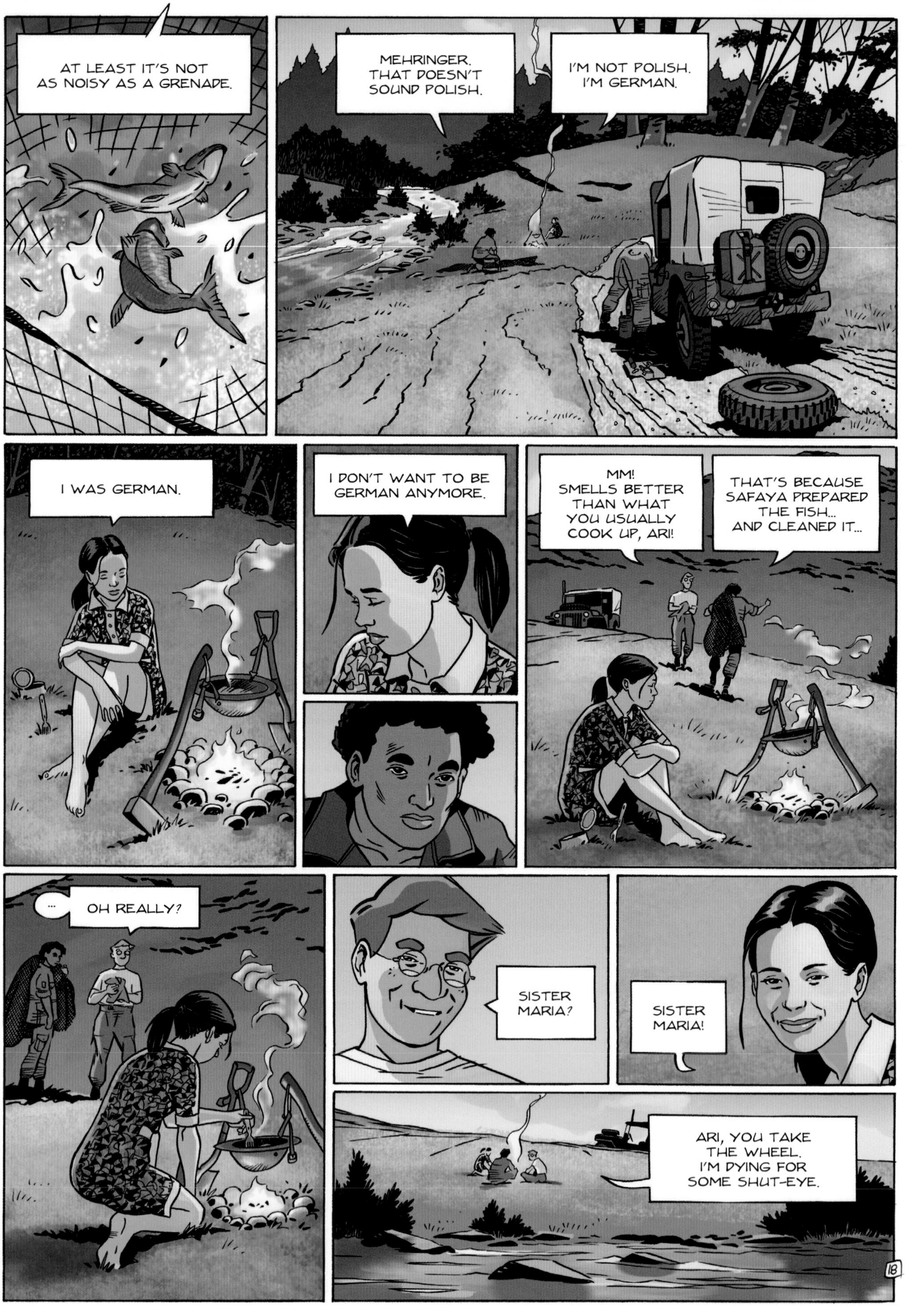
AT LEAST IT'S NOT AS NOISY AS A GRENADE.
MEHRINGER. THAT DOESN'T SOUND POLISH.
I'M NOT POLISH. I'M GERMAN.
I WAS GERMAN.
I DON'T WANT TO BE GERMAN ANYMORE.
MM! SMELLS BETTER THAN WHAT YOU USUALLY COOK UP, ARI!
THAT'S BECAUSE SAFAYA PREPARED THE FISH... AND CLEANED IT...
...
OH REALLY?
SISTER MARIA?
SISTER MARIA!
ARI, YOU TAKE THE WHEEL. I'M DYING FOR SOME SHUT-EYE.
18

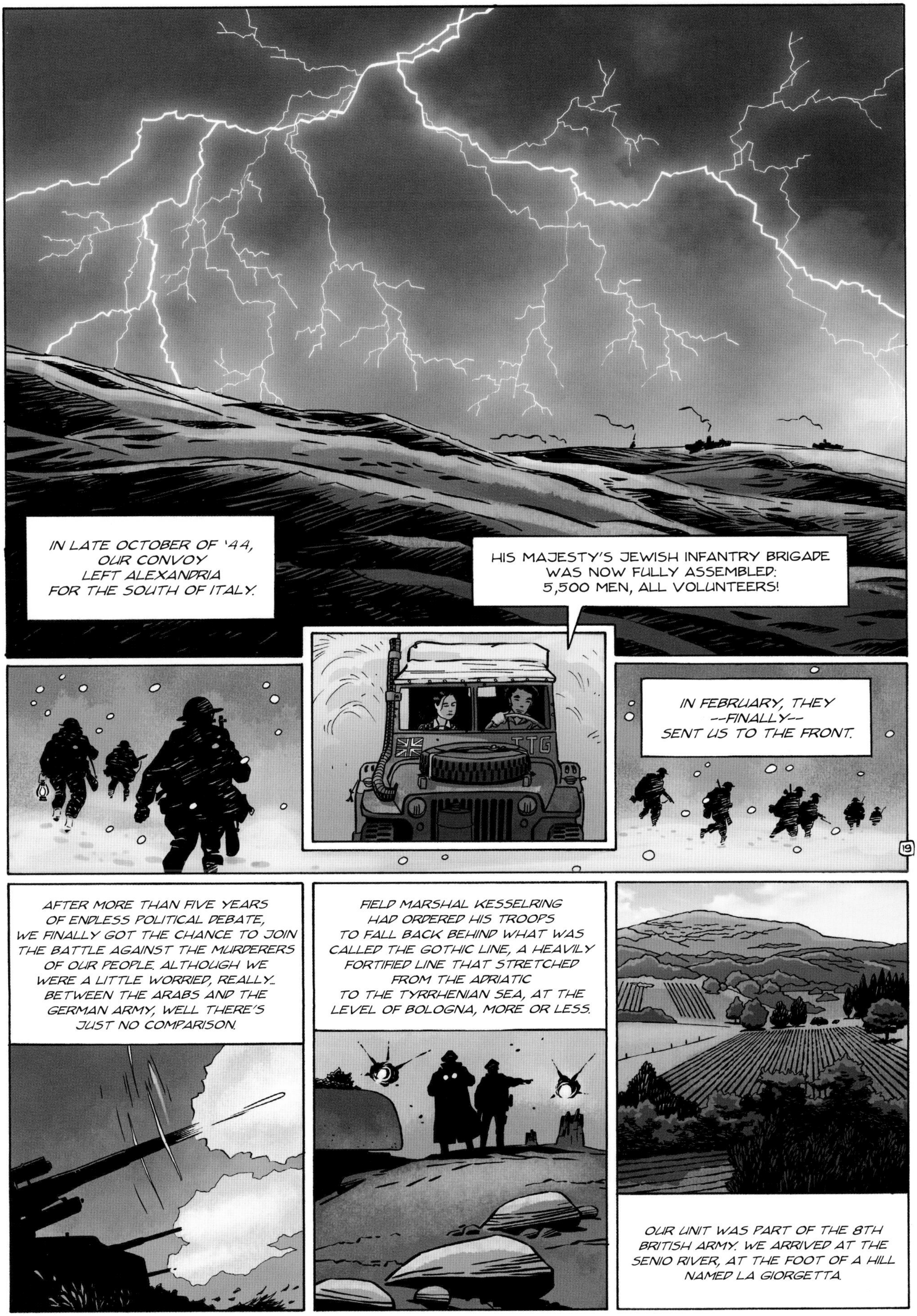
IN LATE OCTOBER OF '44, OUR CONVOY LEFT ALEXANDRIA FOR THE SOUTH OF ITALY.
HIS MAJESTY'S JEWISH INFANTRY BRIGADE WAS NOW FULLY ASSEMBLED: 5,500 MEN, ALL VOLUNTEERS!
TTG
IN FEBRUARY, THEY --FINALLY-- SENT US TO THE FRONT.
AFTER MORE THAN FIVE YEARS OF ENDLESS POLITICAL DEBATE, WE FINALLY GOT THE CHANCE TO JOIN THE BATTLE AGAINST THE MURDERERS OF OUR PEOPLE. ALTHOUGH WE WERE A LITTLE WORRIED, REALLY... BETWEEN THE ARABS AND THE GERMAN ARMY, WELL THERE'S JUST NO COMPARISON.
FIELD MARSHAL KESSELRING HAD ORDERED HIS TROOPS TO FALL BACK BEHIND WHAT WAS CALLED THE GOTHIC LINE, A HEAVILY FORTIFIED LINE THAT STRETCHED FROM THE ADRIATIC TO THE TYRRHENIAN SEA, AT THE LEVEL OF BOLOGNA, MORE OR LESS.
OUR UNIT WAS PART OF THE 8TH BRITISH ARMY. WE ARRIVED AT THE SENIO RIVER, AT THE FOOT OF A HILL NAMED LA GIORGETTA.

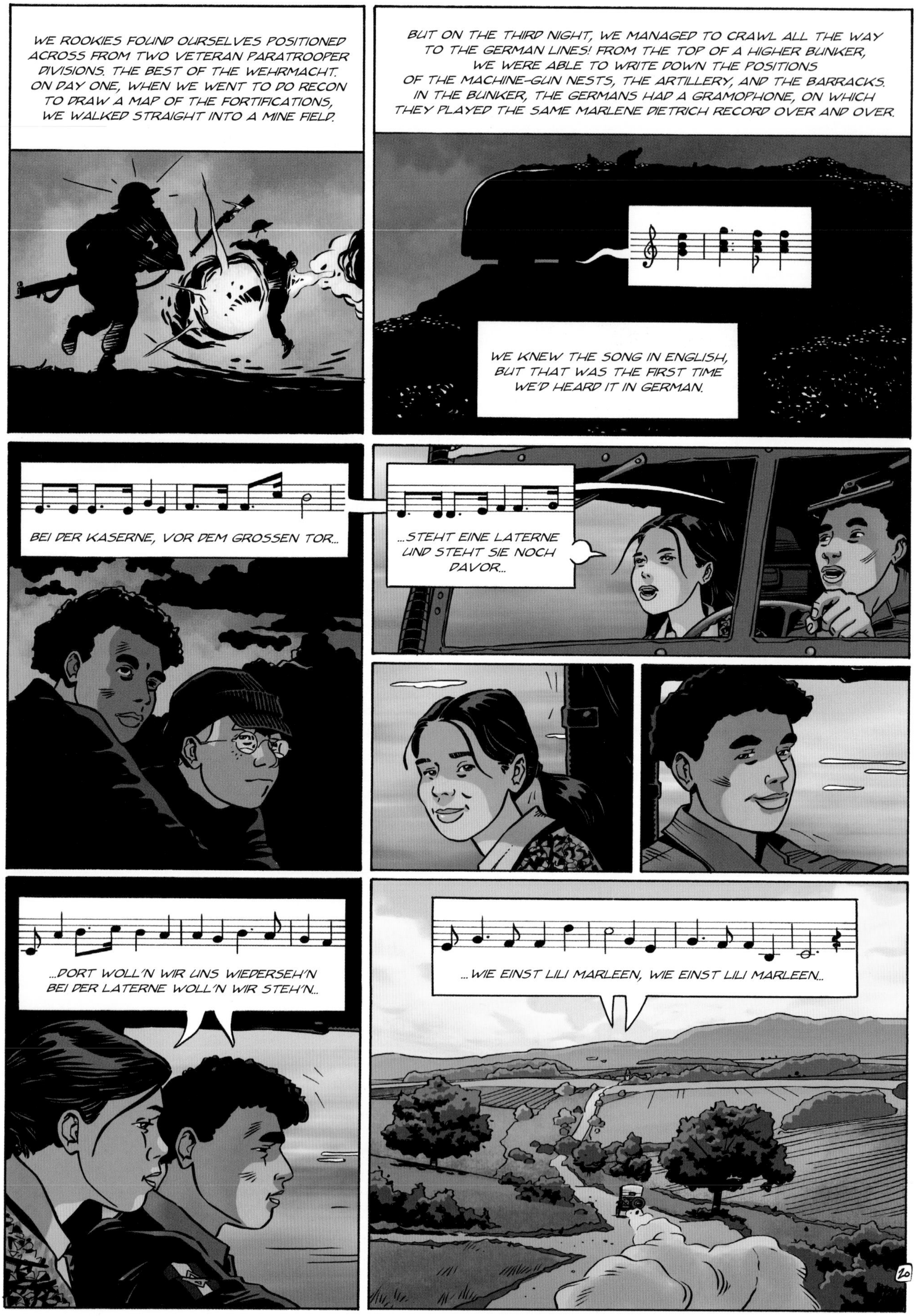
WE ROOKIES FOUND OURSELVES POSITIONED ACROSS FROM TWO VETERAN PARATROOPER DIVISIONS. THE BEST OF THE WEHRMACHT. ON DAY ONE, WHEN WE WENT TO DO RECON TO DRAW A MAP OF THE FORTIFICATIONS, WE WALKED STRAIGHT INTO A MINE FIELD.
BUT ON THE THIRD NIGHT, WE MANAGED TO CRAWL ALL THE WAY TO THE GERMAN LINES! FROM THE TOP OF A HIGHER BUNKER, WE WERE ABLE TO WRITE DOWN THE POSITIONS OF THE MACHINE-GUN NESTS, THE ARTILLERY, AND THE BARRACKS. IN THE BUNKER, THE GERMANS HAD A GRAMOPHONE, ON WHICH THEY PLAYED THE SAME MARLENE DIETRICH RECORD OVER AND OVER.
WE KNEW THE SONG IN ENGLISH, BUT THAT WAS THE FIRST TIME WE'D HEARD IT IN GERMAN.
BEI DER KASERNE, VOR DEM GROSSEN TOR...
...STEHT EINE LATERNE UND STEHT SIE NOCH DAVOR...
...DORT WOLL'N WIR UNS WIEDERSEH'N BEI DER LATERNE WOLL'N WIR STEH'N...
...WIE EINST LILI MARLEEN, WIE EINST LILI MARLEEN...
20

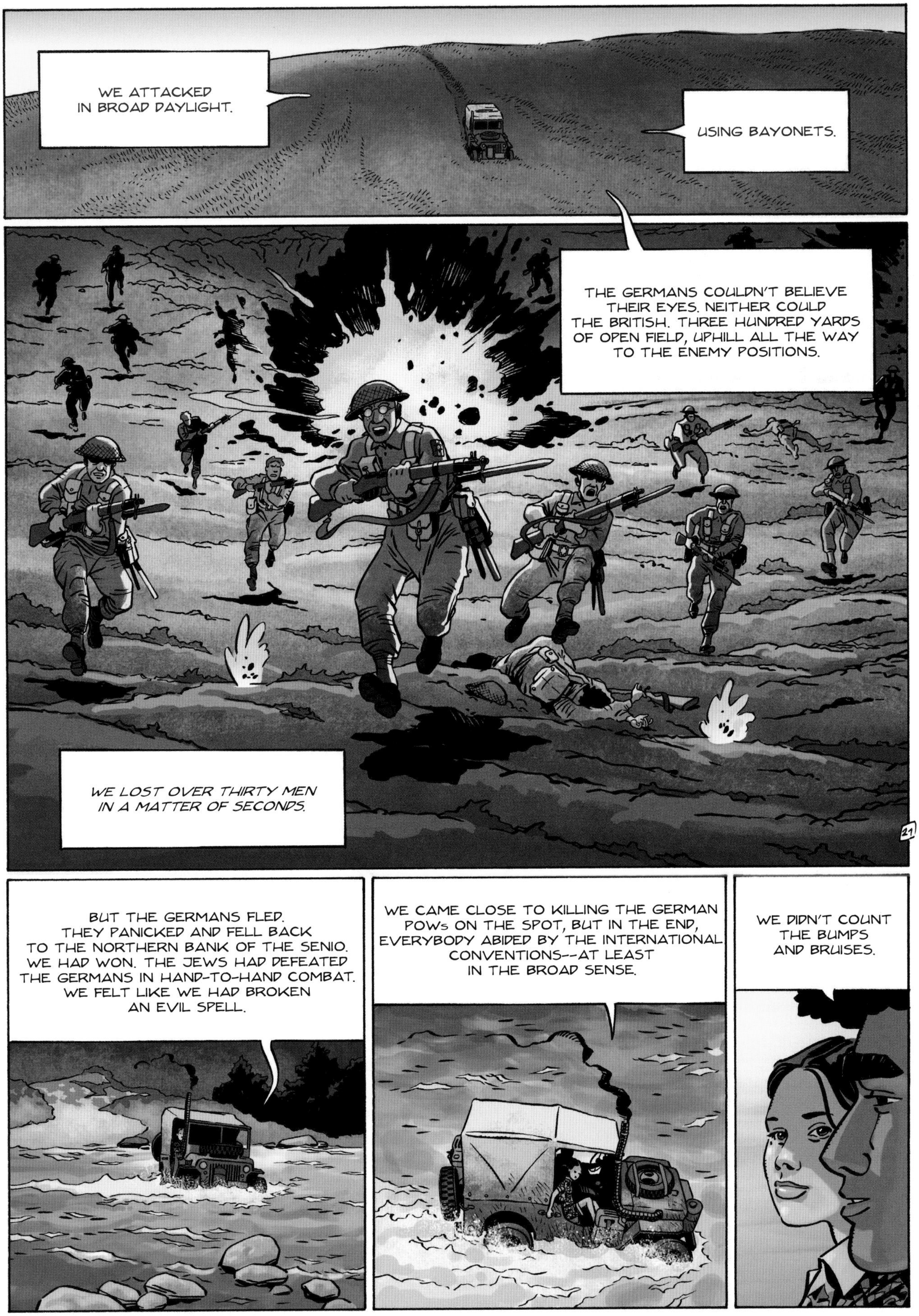
WE ATTACKED IN BROAD DAYLIGHT.
USING BAYONETS.
THE GERMANS COULDN'T BELIEVE THEIR EYES. NEITHER COULD THE BRITISH. THREE HUNDRED YARDS OF OPEN FIELD, UPHILL ALL THE WAY TO THE ENEMY POSITIONS.
WE LOST OVER THIRTY MEN IN A MATTER OF SECONDS.
BUT THE GERMANS FLED. THEY PANICKED AND FELL BACK TO THE NORTHERN BANK OF THE SENIO. WE HAD WON. THE JEWS HAD DEFEATED THE GERMANS IN HAND-TO-HAND COMBAT. WE FELT LIKE WE HAD BROKEN AN EVIL SPELL.
WE CAME CLOSE TO KILLING THE GERMAN POWs ON THE SPOT, BUT IN THE END, EVERYBODY ABIDED BY THE INTERNATIONAL CONVENTIONS--AT LEAST IN THE BROAD SENSE.
WE DIDN'T COUNT THE BUMPS AND BRUISES.

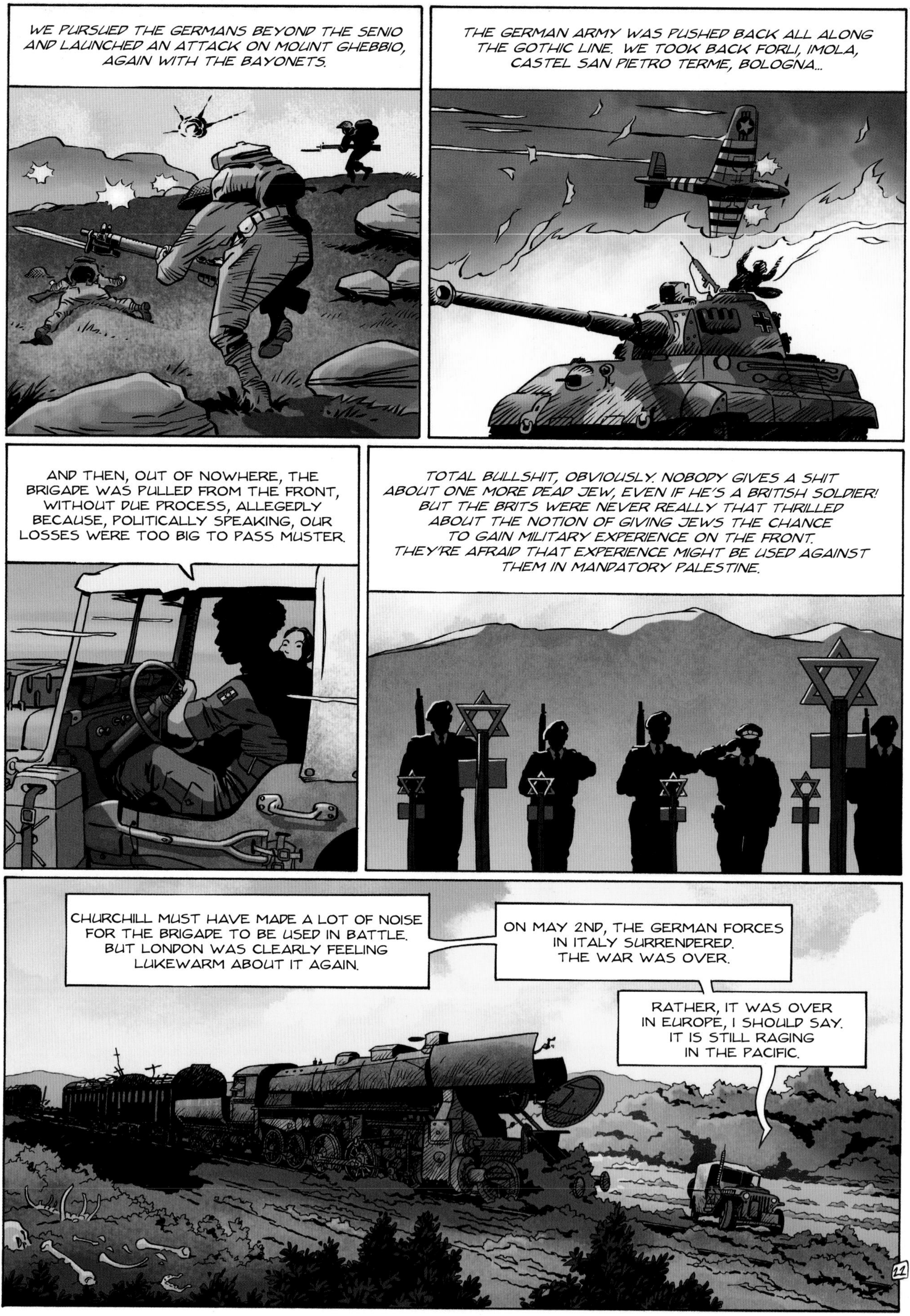
WE PURSUED THE GERMANS BEYOND THE SENIO AND LAUNCHED AN ATTACK ON MOUNT GHEBBIO, AGAIN WITH THE BAYONETS.
THE GERMAN ARMY WAS PUSHED BACK ALL ALONG THE GOTHIC LINE. WE TOOK BACK FORLI, IMOLA, CASTEL SAN PIETRO TERME, BOLOGNA...
AND THEN, OUT OF NOWHERE, THE BRIGADE WAS PULLED FROM THE FRONT, WITHOUT DUE PROCESS, ALLEGEDLY BECAUSE, POLITICALLY SPEAKING, OUR LOSSES WERE TOO BIG TO PASS MUSTER.
TOTAL BULLSHIT, OBVIOUSLY. NOBODY GIVES A SHIT ABOUT ONE MORE DEAD JEW, EVEN IF HE'S A BRITISH SOLDIER! BUT THE BRITS WERE NEVER REALLY THAT THRILLED ABOUT THE NOTION OF GIVING JEWS THE CHANCE TO GAIN MILITARY EXPERIENCE ON THE FRONT. THEY'RE AFRAID THAT EXPERIENCE MIGHT BE USED AGAINST THEM IN MANDATORY PALESTINE.
CHURCHILL MUST HAVE MADE A LOT OF NOISE FOR THE BRIGADE TO BE USED IN BATTLE. BUT LONDON WAS CLEARLY FEELING LUKEWARM ABOUT IT AGAIN.
ON MAY 2ND, THE GERMAN FORCES IN ITALY SURRENDERED. THE WAR WAS OVER.
RATHER, IT WAS OVER IN EUROPE, I SHOULD SAY. IT IS STILL RAGING IN THE PACIFIC.

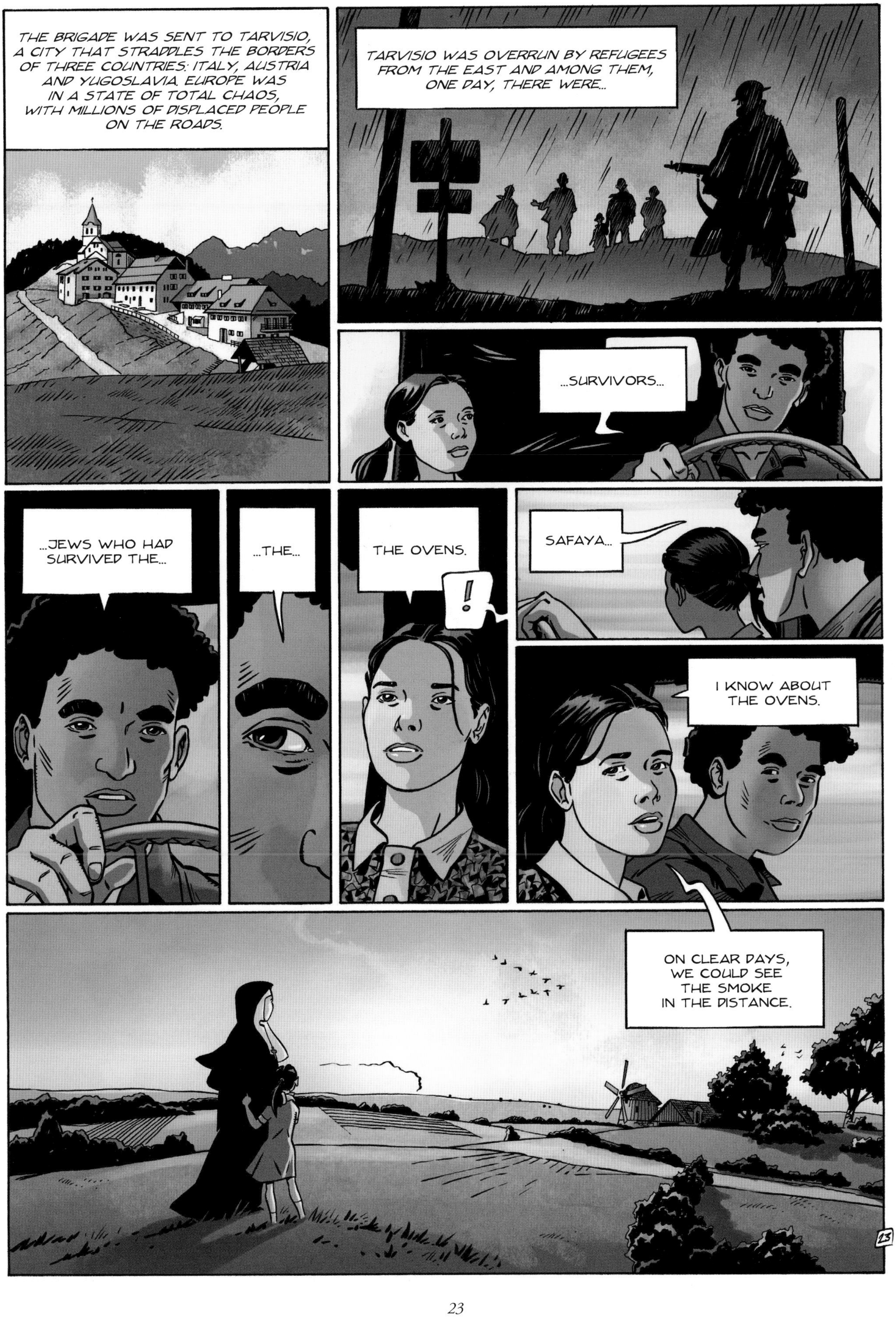
THE BRIGADE WAS SENT TO TARVISIO, A CITY THAT STRADDLES THE BORDERS OF THREE COUNTRIES: ITALY, AUSTRIA AND YUGOSLAVIA. EUROPE WAS IN A STATE OF TOTAL CHAOS, WITH MILLIONS OF DISPLACED PEOPLE ON THE ROADS.
TARVISIO WAS OVERRUN BY REFUGEES FROM THE EAST AND AMONG THEM, ONE DAY, THERE WERE...
...SURVIVORS...
...JEWS WHO HAD SURVIVED THE...
...THE...
THE OVENS.
!
SAFAYA...
I KNOW ABOUT THE OVENS.
ON CLEAR DAYS, WE COULD SEE THE SMOKE IN THE DISTANCE.
23

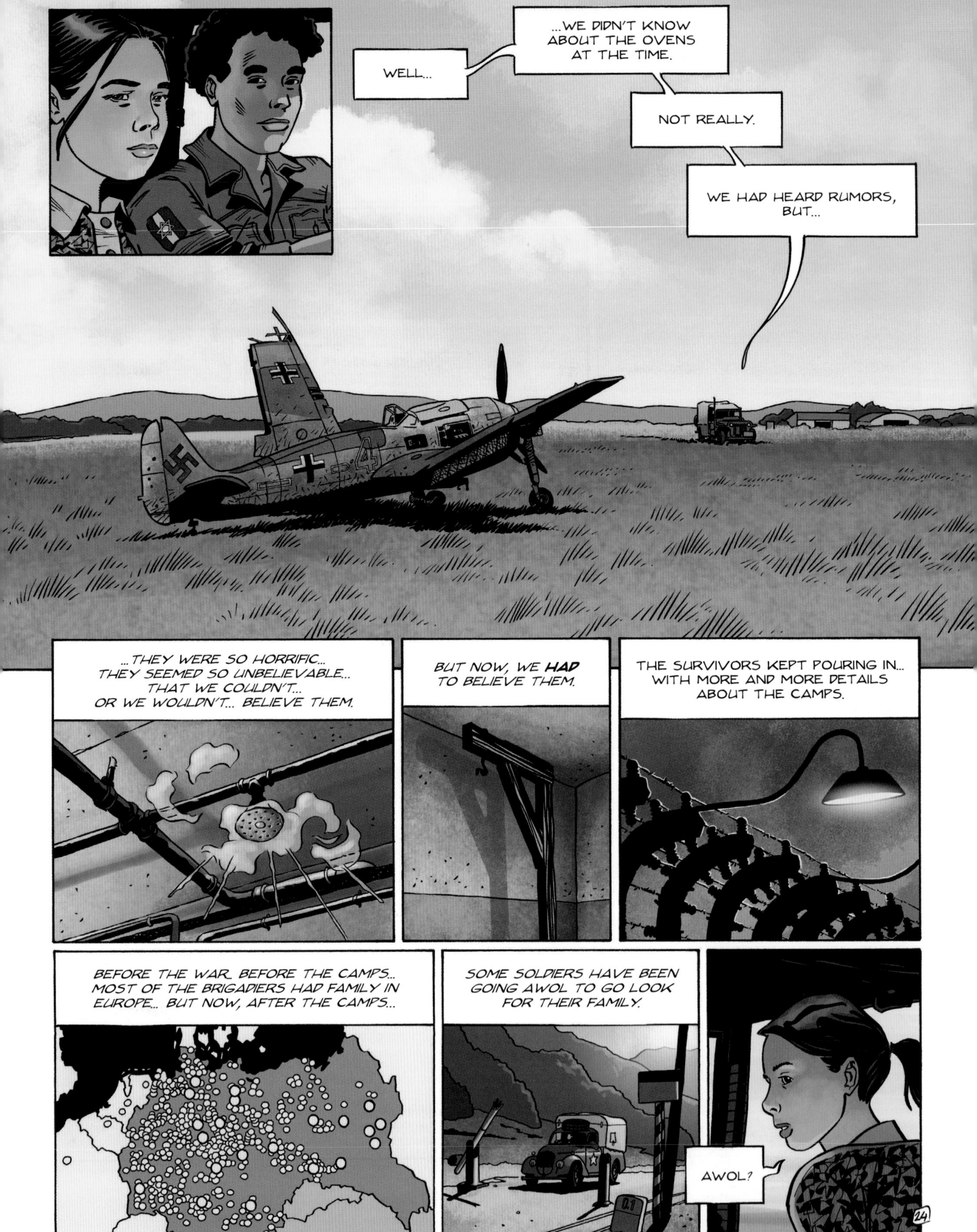
WELL...
...WE DIDN'T KNOW ABOUT THE OVENS AT THE TIME.
NOT REALLY.
WE HAD HEARD RUMORS, BUT...
...THEY WERE SO HORRIFIC... THEY SEEMED SO UNBELIEVABLE... THAT WE COULDN'T... OR WE WOULDN'T... BELIEVE THEM.
BUT NOW, WE HAD TO BELIEVE THEM.
THE SURVIVORS KEPT POURING IN... WITH MORE AND MORE DETAILS ABOUT THE CAMPS.
BEFORE THE WAR.. BEFORE THE CAMPS... MOST OF THE BRIGADIERS HAD FAMILY IN EUROPE... BUT NOW, AFTER THE CAMPS...
SOME SOLDIERS HAVE BEEN GOING AWOL TO GO LOOK FOR THEIR FAMILY.
AWOL?
24

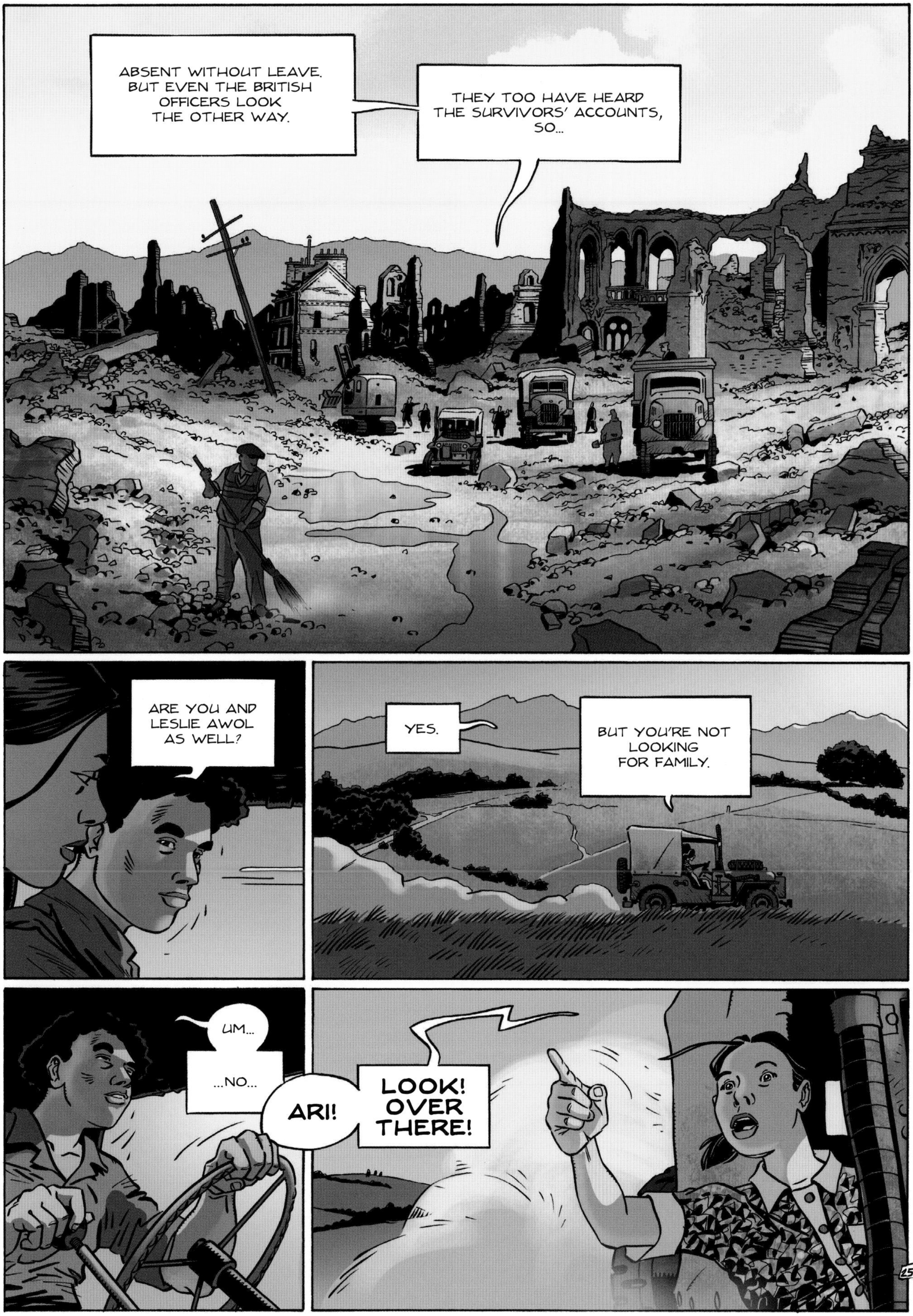
ABSENT WITHOUT LEAVE. BUT EVEN THE BRITISH OFFICERS LOOK THE OTHER WAY.
THEY TOO HAVE HEARD THE SURVIVORS' ACCOUNTS, SO...
ARE YOU AND LESLIE AWOL AS WELL?
YES.
BUT YOU'RE NOT LOOKING FOR FAMILY.
UM...
...NO...
ARI!
LOOK! OVER THERE!
25

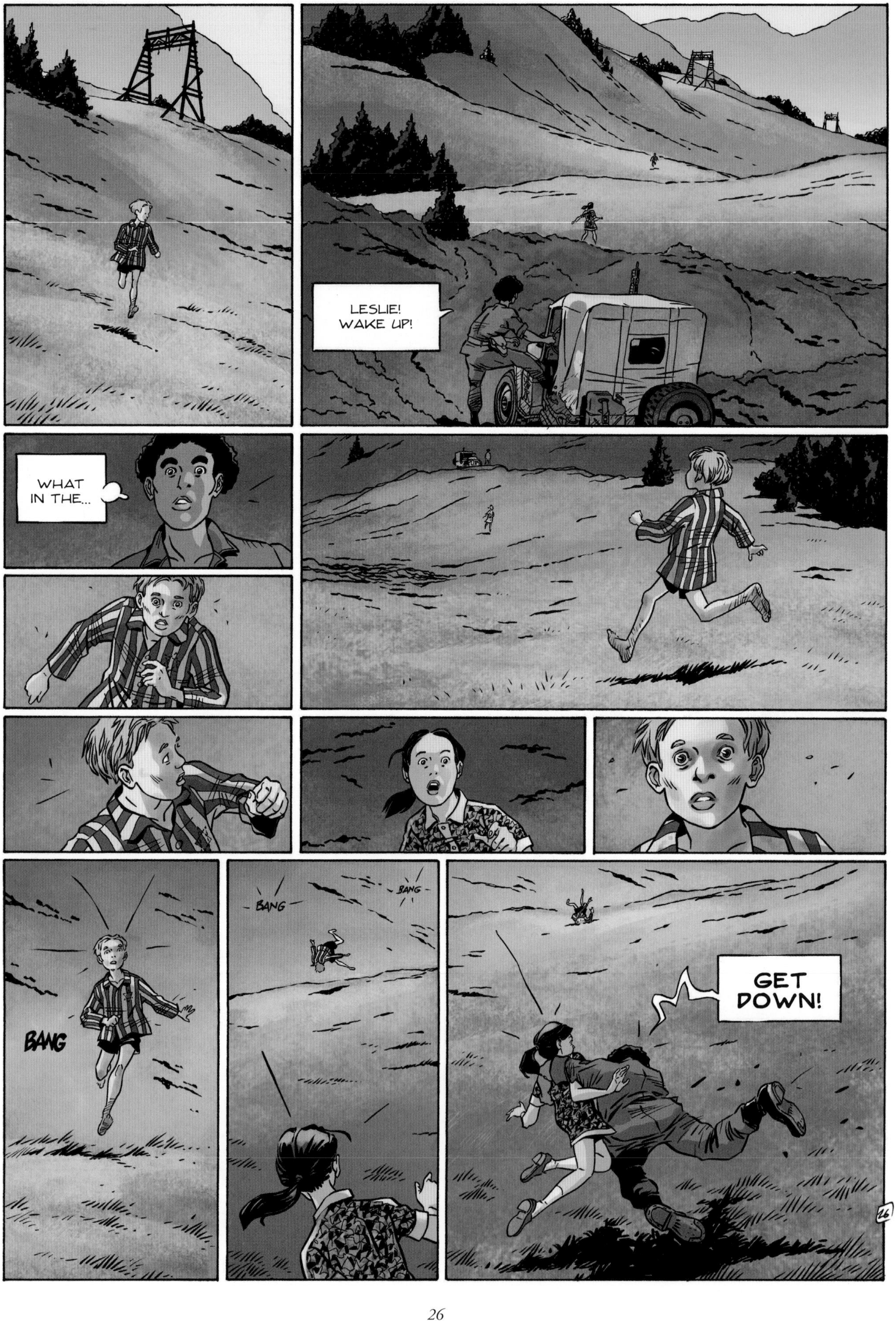
LESLIE! WAKE UP!
WHAT IN THE...
BANG
BANG
BANG
GET DOWN!
26

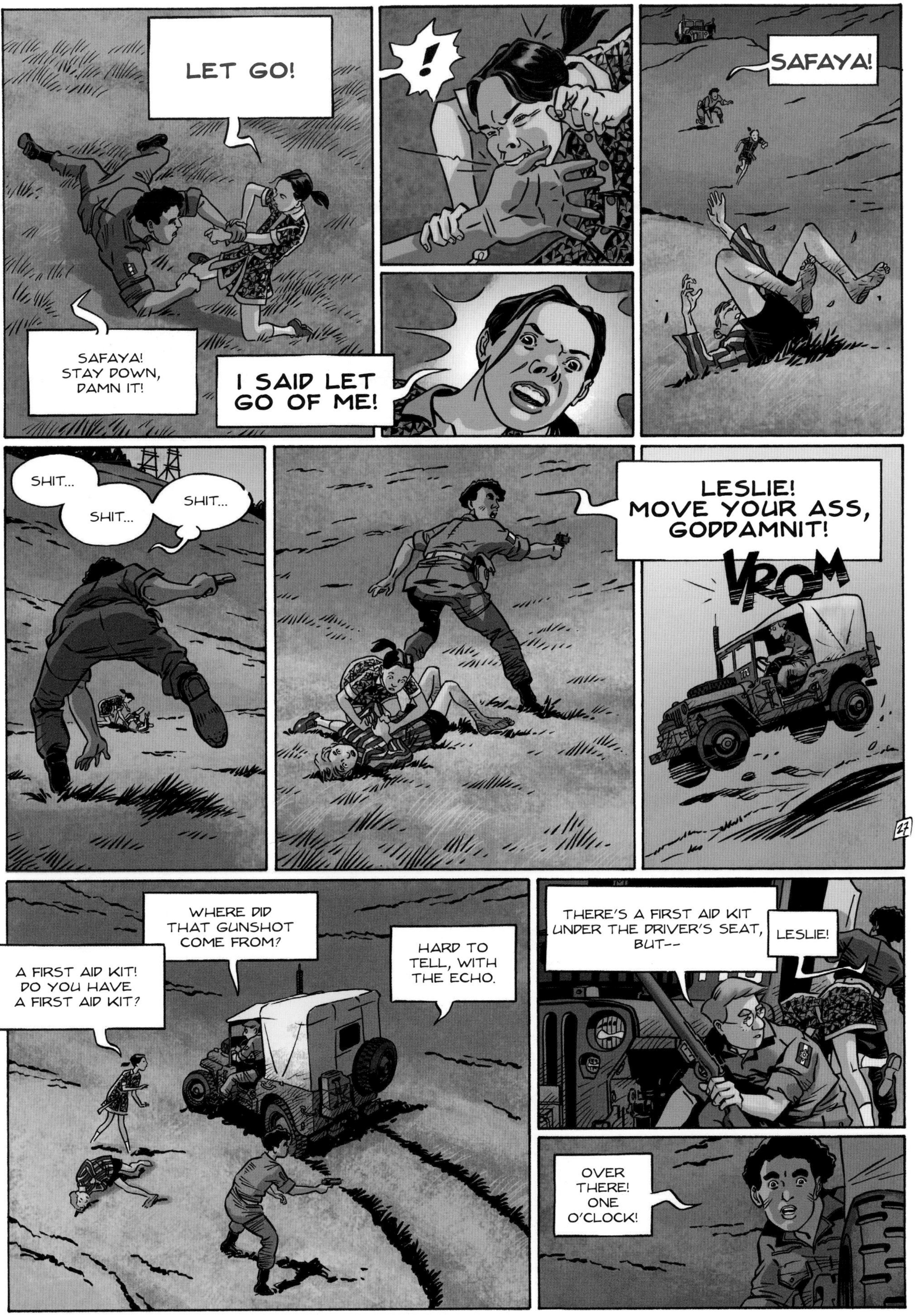

SAFAYA! STAY DOWN, DAMN IT!
LET GO!
!
I SAID LET GO OF ME!
SAFAYA!
SHIT...
SHIT...
SHIT...
LESLIE! MOVE YOUR ASS, GODDAMNIT!
VROM
A FIRST AID KIT! DO YOU HAVE A FIRST AID KIT?
WHERE DID THAT GUNSHOT COME FROM?
HARD TO TELL, WITH THE ECHO.
THERE'S A FIRST AID KIT UNDER THE DRIVER'S SEAT, BUT--
LESLIE!
OVER THERE! ONE O'CLOCK!

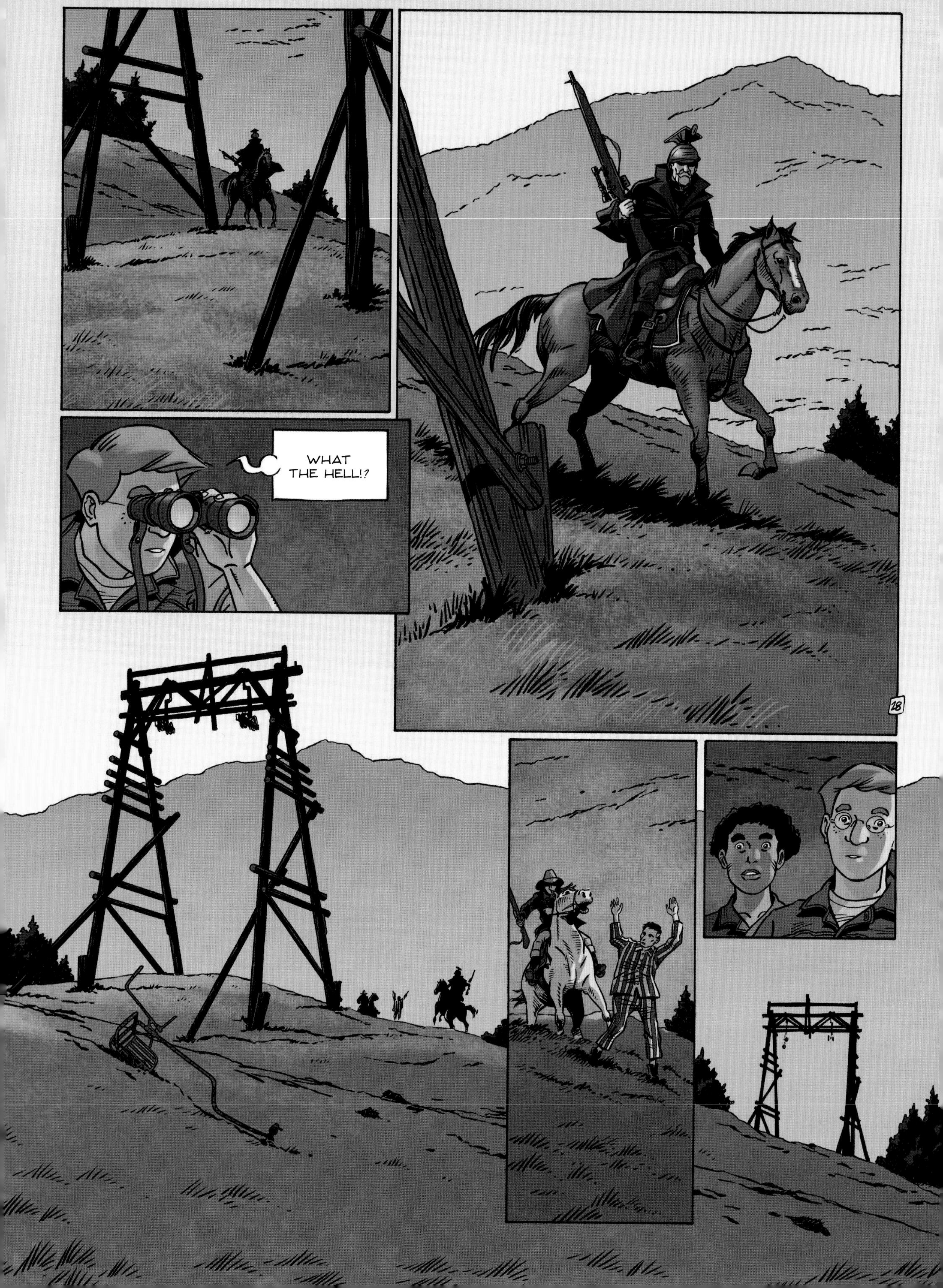
WHAT THE HELL!?
28

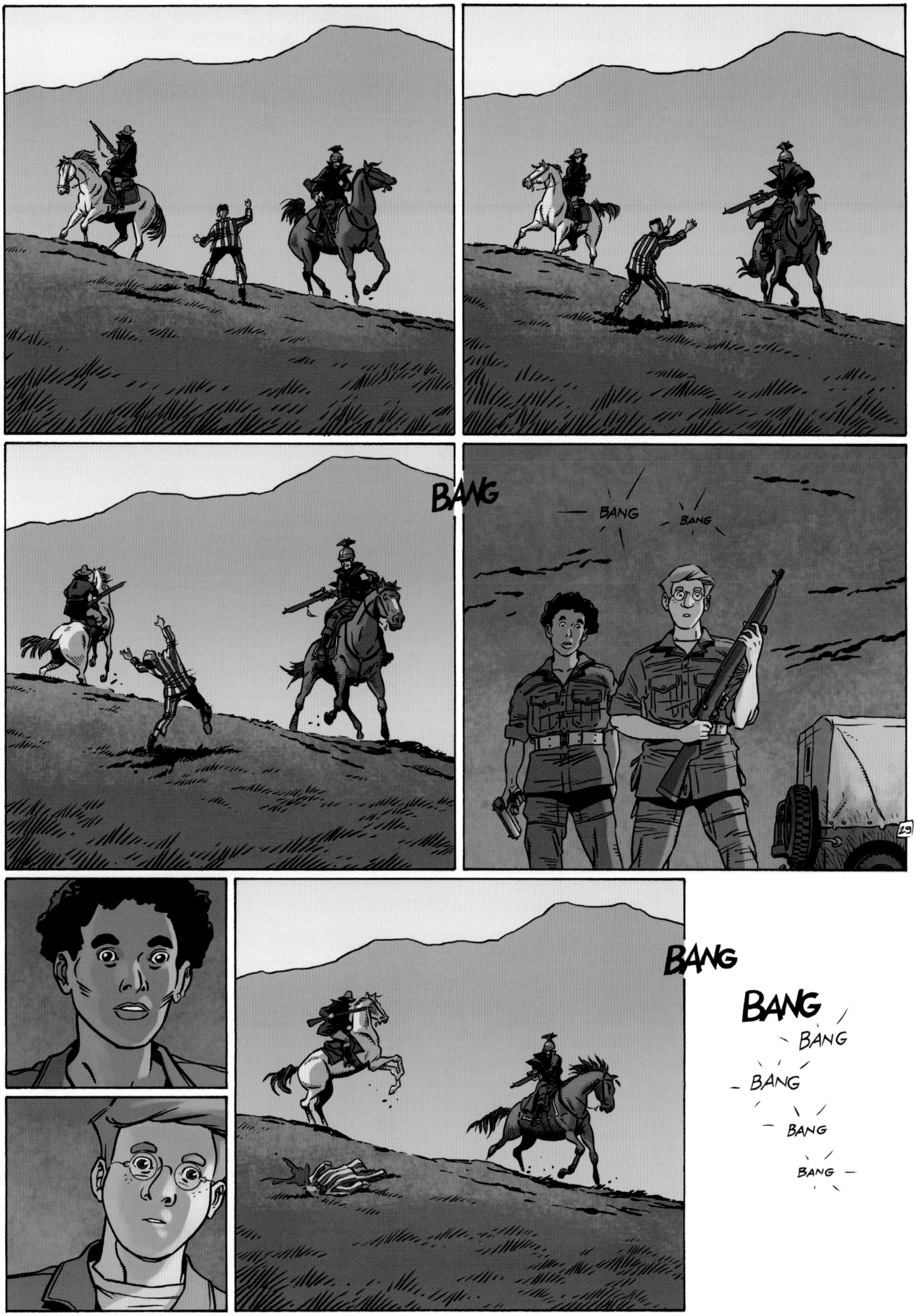
BANG
BANG
BANG
29
BANG
BANG
BANG
BANG
BANG
BANG

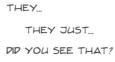

THEY...

THEY JUST...

DID YOU SEE THAT?

THEY...

THEY JUST...

ALL THE DEVILS IN HELL! ARI, STAY WITH SAFAYA AND THE BOY.

!

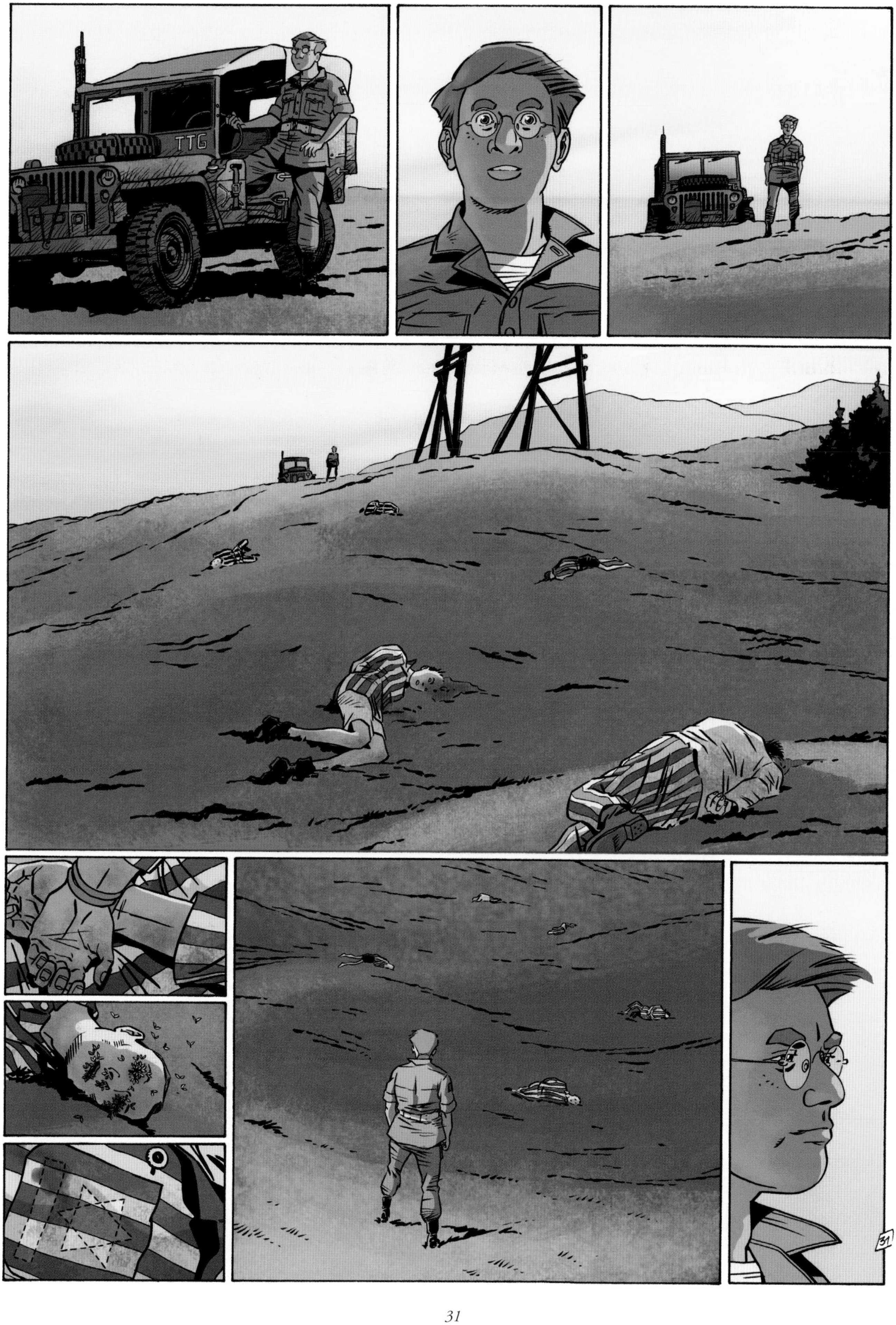
TTG

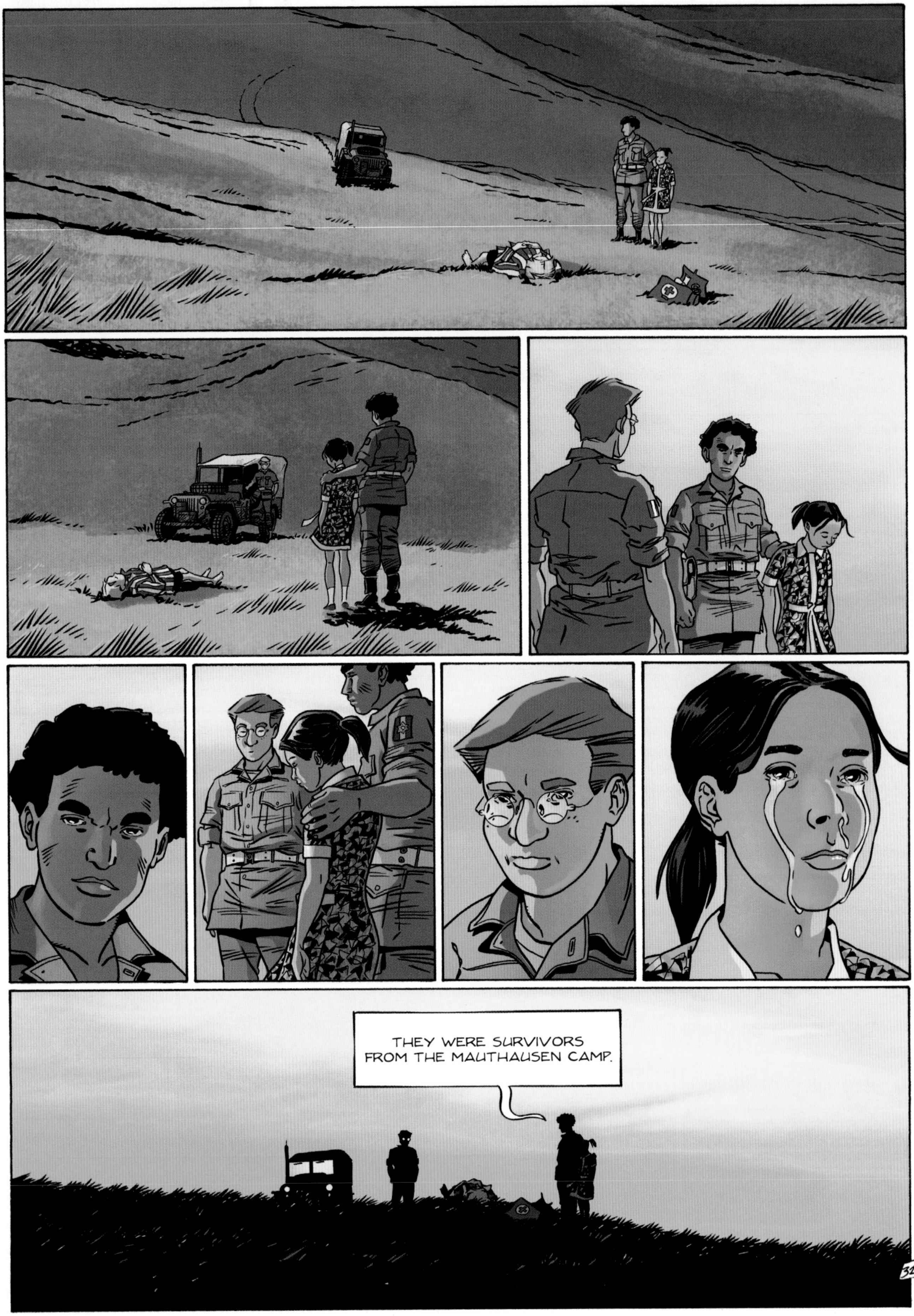
THEY WERE SURVIVORS FROM THE MAUTHAUSEN CAMP.
32

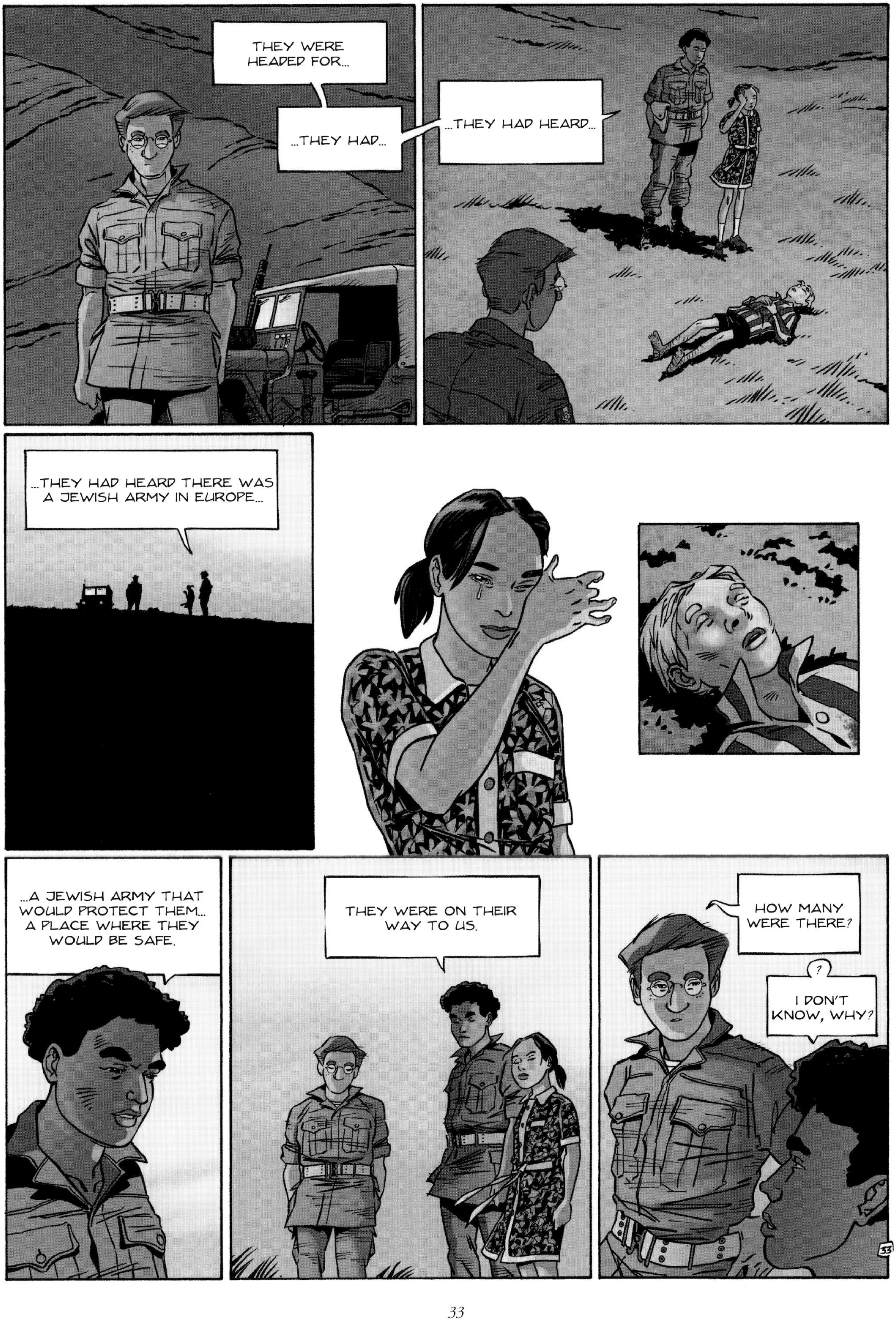
THEY WERE HEADED FOR...
...THEY HAD...
...THEY HAD HEARD...
...THEY HAD HEARD THERE WAS A JEWISH ARMY IN EUROPE...
...A JEWISH ARMY THAT WOULD PROTECT THEM... A PLACE WHERE THEY WOULD BE SAFE.
THEY WERE ON THEIR WAY TO US.
HOW MANY WERE THERE?
?
I DON'T KNOW, WHY?
33

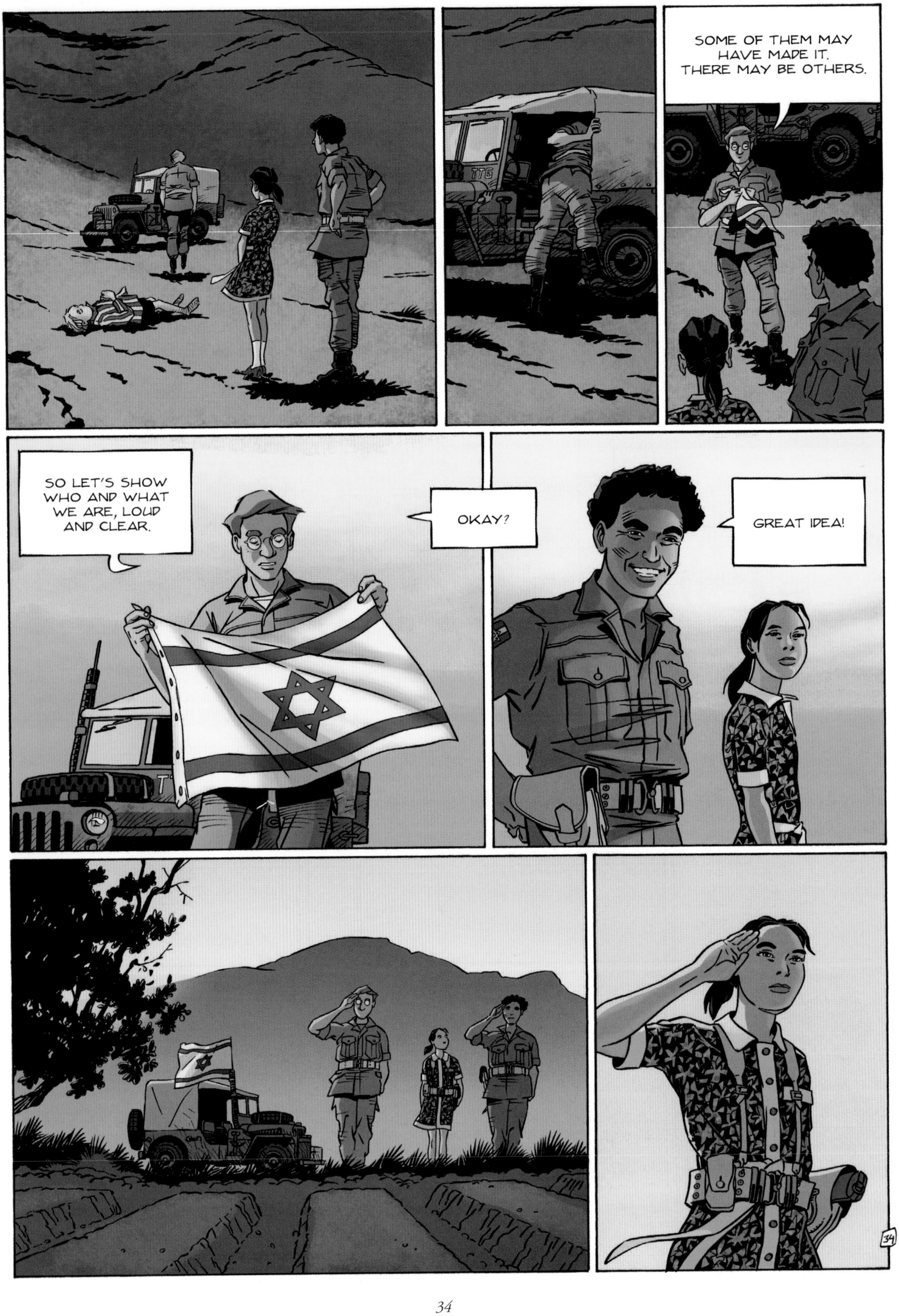
SOME OF THEM MAY HAVE MADE IT. THERE MAY BE OTHERS.
SO LET'S SHOW WHO AND WHAT WE ARE, LOUD AND CLEAR.
OKAY?
GREAT IDEA!
34

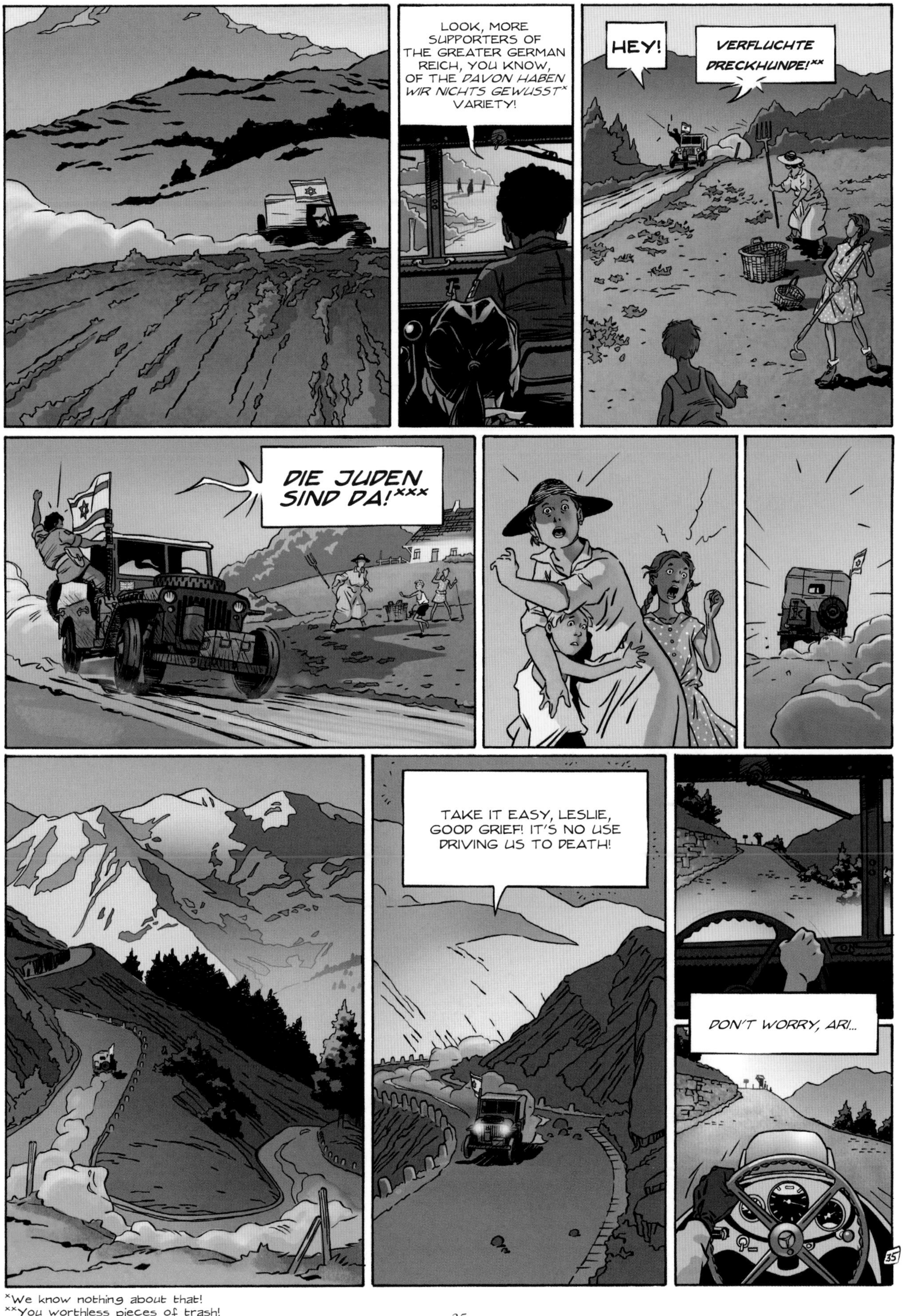
LOOK, MORE SUPPORTERS OF THE GREATER GERMAN REICH, YOU KNOW, OF THE *DAVON HABEN WIR NICHTS GEWUSST*ˣ VARIETY!
HEY!
VERFLUCHTE DRECKHUNDE!ˣˣ
DIE JUDEN SIND DA!ˣˣˣ
TAKE IT EASY, LESLIE, GOOD GRIEF! IT'S NO USE DRIVING US TO DEATH!
DON'T WORRY, ARI...
35

ˣWe know nothing about that!
ˣˣYou worthless pieces of trash!
ˣˣˣThe Jews are here!

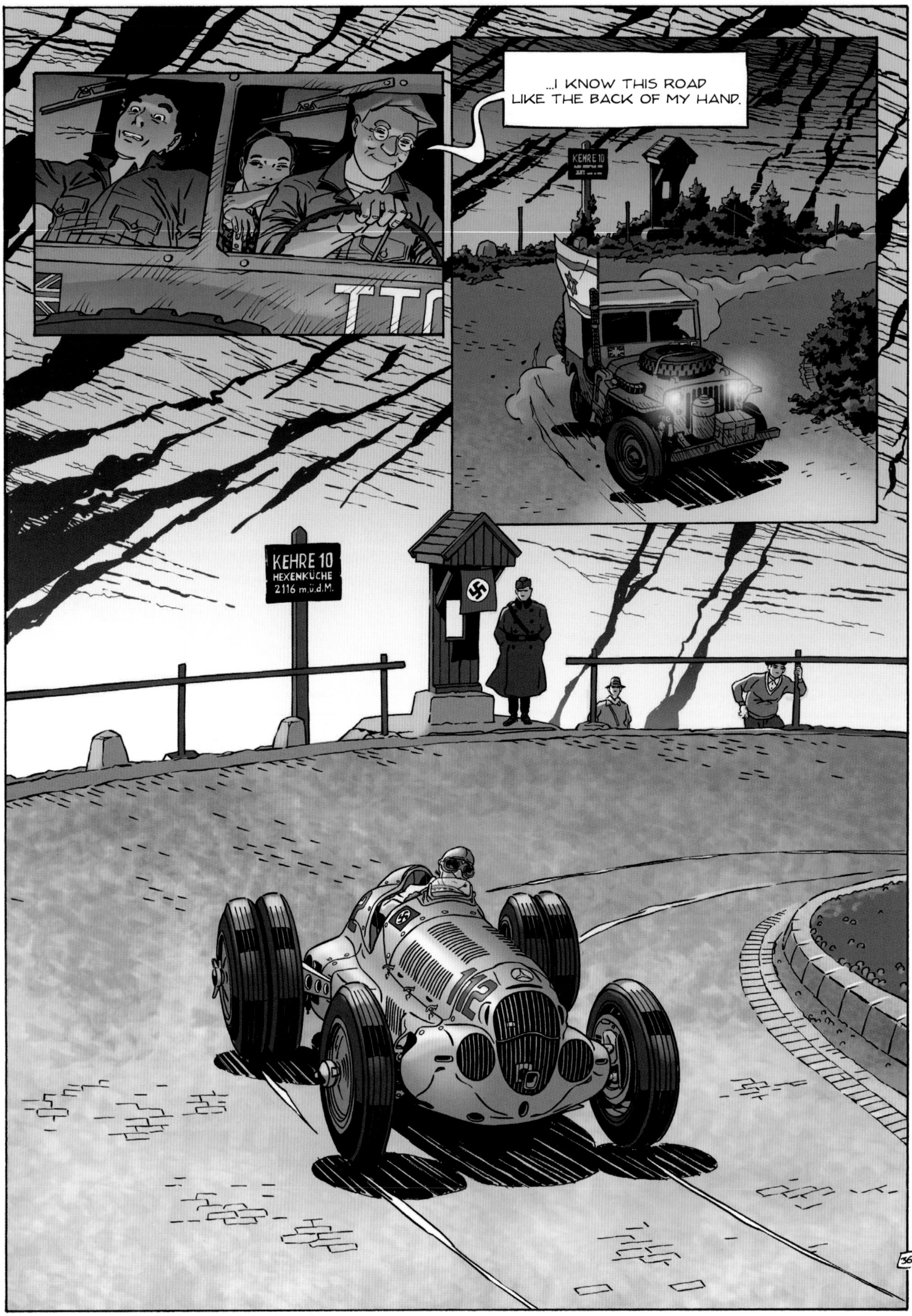
...I KNOW THIS ROAD LIKE THE BACK OF MY HAND.
KEHRE 10
KEHRE 10
HEXENKÜCHE
2116 m.ü.d.M.

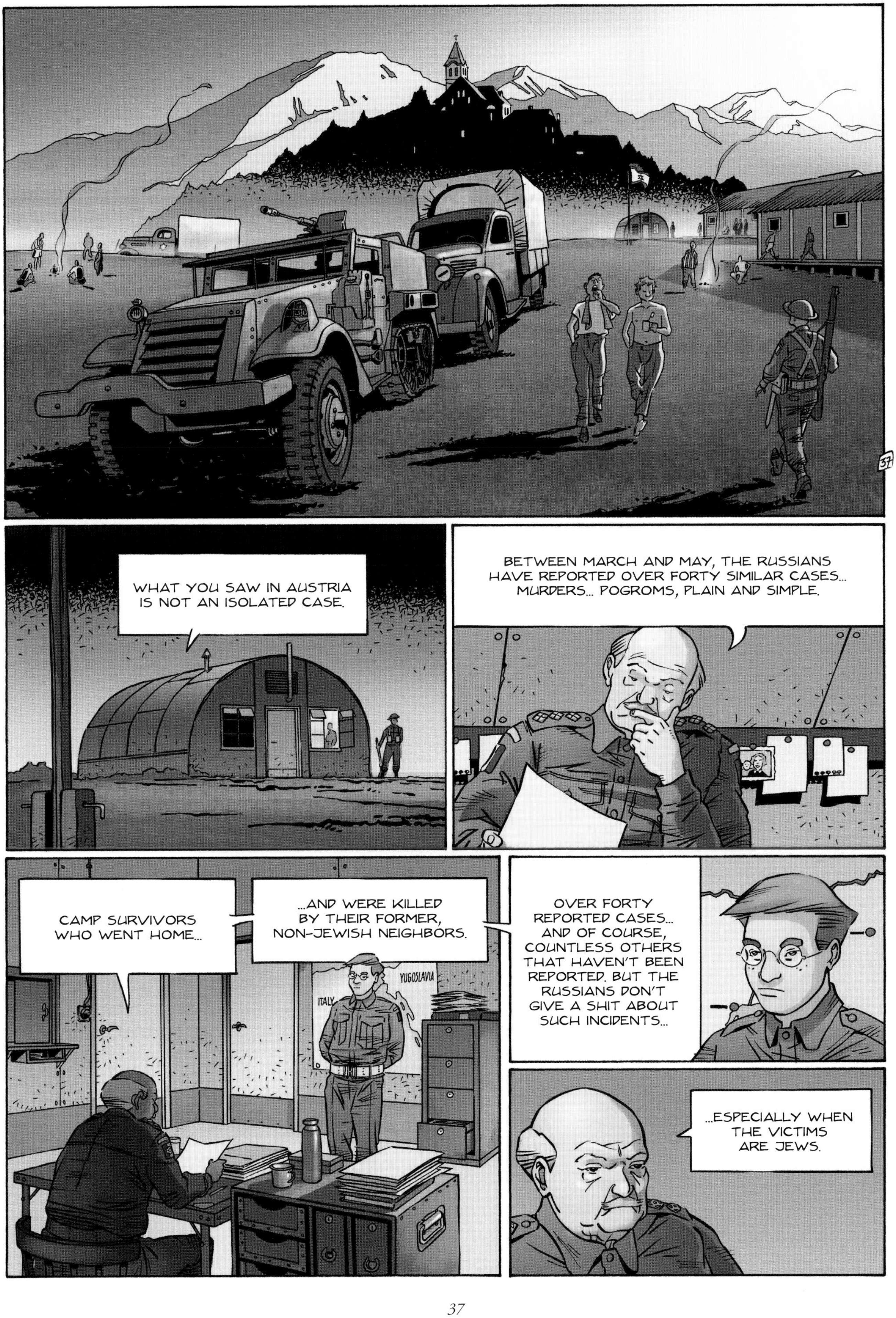
WHAT YOU SAW IN AUSTRIA IS NOT AN ISOLATED CASE.
BETWEEN MARCH AND MAY, THE RUSSIANS HAVE REPORTED OVER FORTY SIMILAR CASES... MURDERS... POGROMS, PLAIN AND SIMPLE.
CAMP SURVIVORS WHO WENT HOME...
...AND WERE KILLED BY THEIR FORMER, NON-JEWISH NEIGHBORS.
ITALY
YUGOSLAVIA
OVER FORTY REPORTED CASES... AND OF COURSE, COUNTLESS OTHERS THAT HAVEN'T BEEN REPORTED. BUT THE RUSSIANS DON'T GIVE A SHIT ABOUT SUCH INCIDENTS...
...ESPECIALLY WHEN THE VICTIMS ARE JEWS.

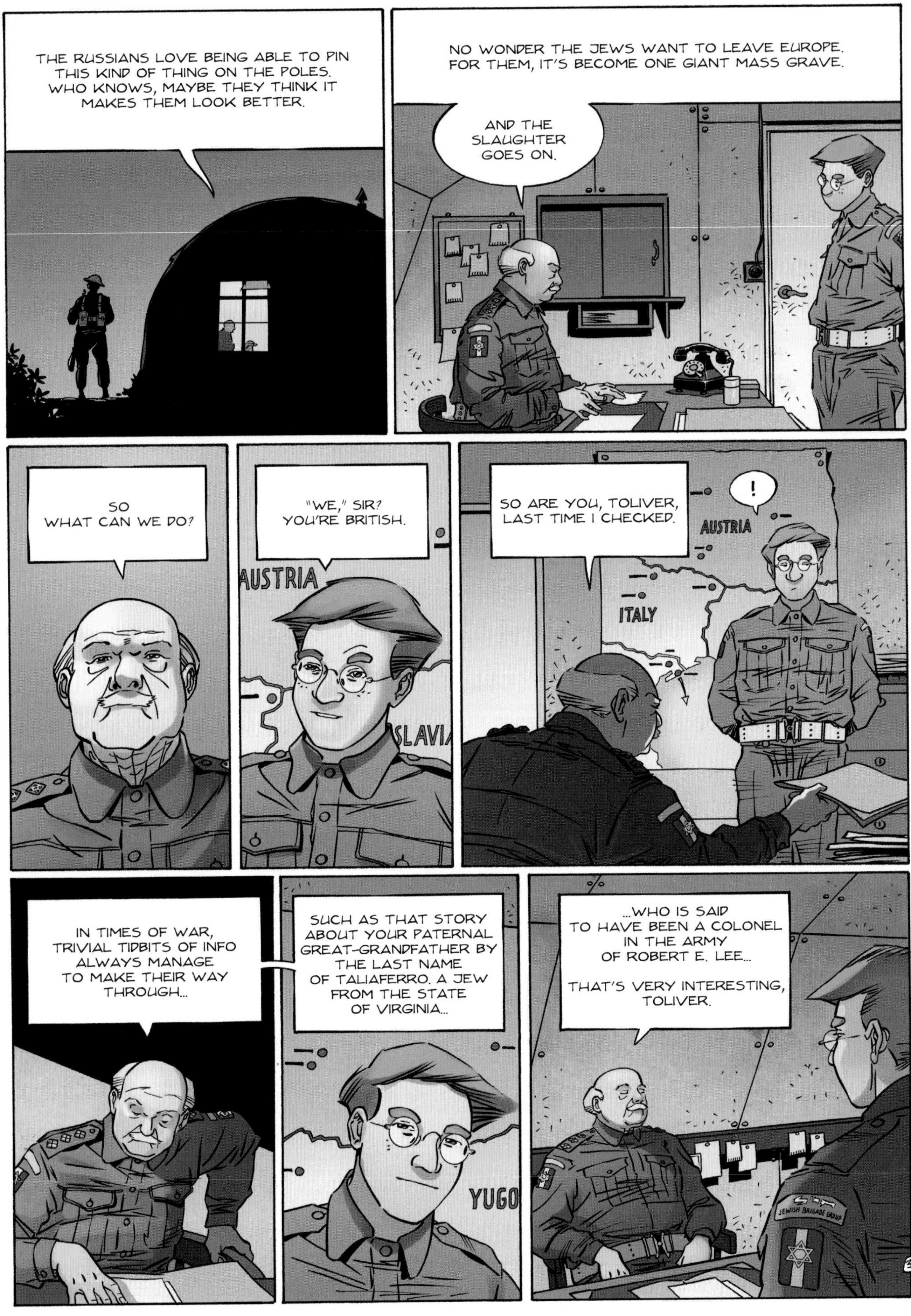
THE RUSSIANS LOVE BEING ABLE TO PIN THIS KIND OF THING ON THE POLES. WHO KNOWS, MAYBE THEY THINK IT MAKES THEM LOOK BETTER.
NO WONDER THE JEWS WANT TO LEAVE EUROPE. FOR THEM, IT'S BECOME ONE GIANT MASS GRAVE.
AND THE SLAUGHTER GOES ON.
SO WHAT CAN WE DO?
"WE," SIR? YOU'RE BRITISH.
AUSTRIA
SLAVIA
SO ARE YOU, TOLIVER, LAST TIME I CHECKED.
!
AUSTRIA
ITALY
IN TIMES OF WAR, TRIVIAL TIDBITS OF INFO ALWAYS MANAGE TO MAKE THEIR WAY THROUGH...
SUCH AS THAT STORY ABOUT YOUR PATERNAL GREAT-GRANDFATHER BY THE LAST NAME OF TALIAFERRO. A JEW FROM THE STATE OF VIRGINIA...
YUGO
...WHO IS SAID TO HAVE BEEN A COLONEL IN THE ARMY OF ROBERT E. LEE...
THAT'S VERY INTERESTING, TOLIVER.
JEWISH BRIGADE GROUP
38

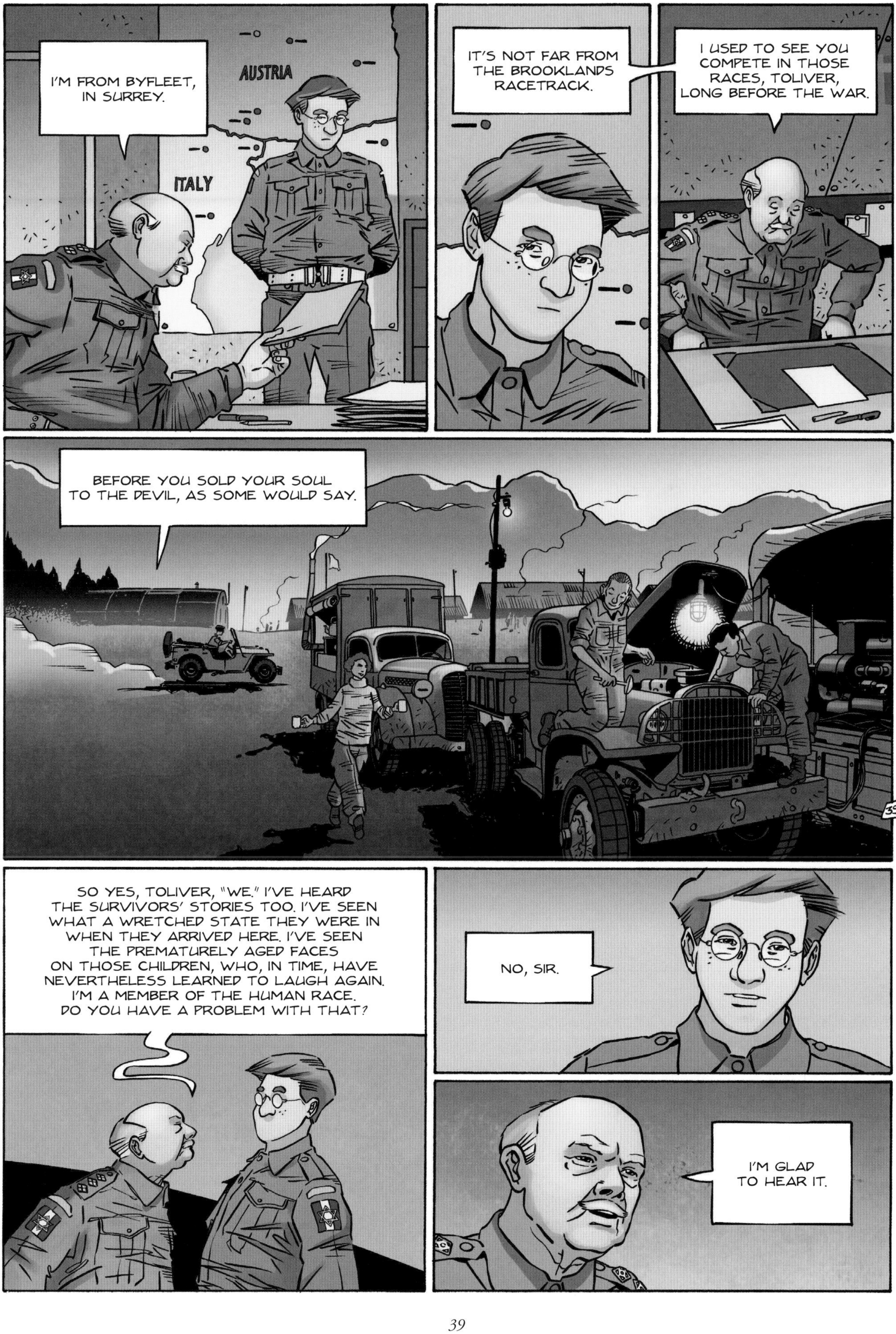
AUSTRIA
ITALY
I'M FROM BYFLEET, IN SURREY.
IT'S NOT FAR FROM THE BROOKLANDS RACETRACK.
I USED TO SEE YOU COMPETE IN THOSE RACES, TOLIVER, LONG BEFORE THE WAR.
BEFORE YOU SOLD YOUR SOUL TO THE DEVIL, AS SOME WOULD SAY.
SO YES, TOLIVER, "WE." I'VE HEARD THE SURVIVORS' STORIES TOO. I'VE SEEN WHAT A WRETCHED STATE THEY WERE IN WHEN THEY ARRIVED HERE. I'VE SEEN THE PREMATURELY AGED FACES ON THOSE CHILDREN, WHO, IN TIME, HAVE NEVERTHELESS LEARNED TO LAUGH AGAIN. I'M A MEMBER OF THE HUMAN RACE. DO YOU HAVE A PROBLEM WITH THAT?
NO, SIR.
I'M GLAD TO HEAR IT.

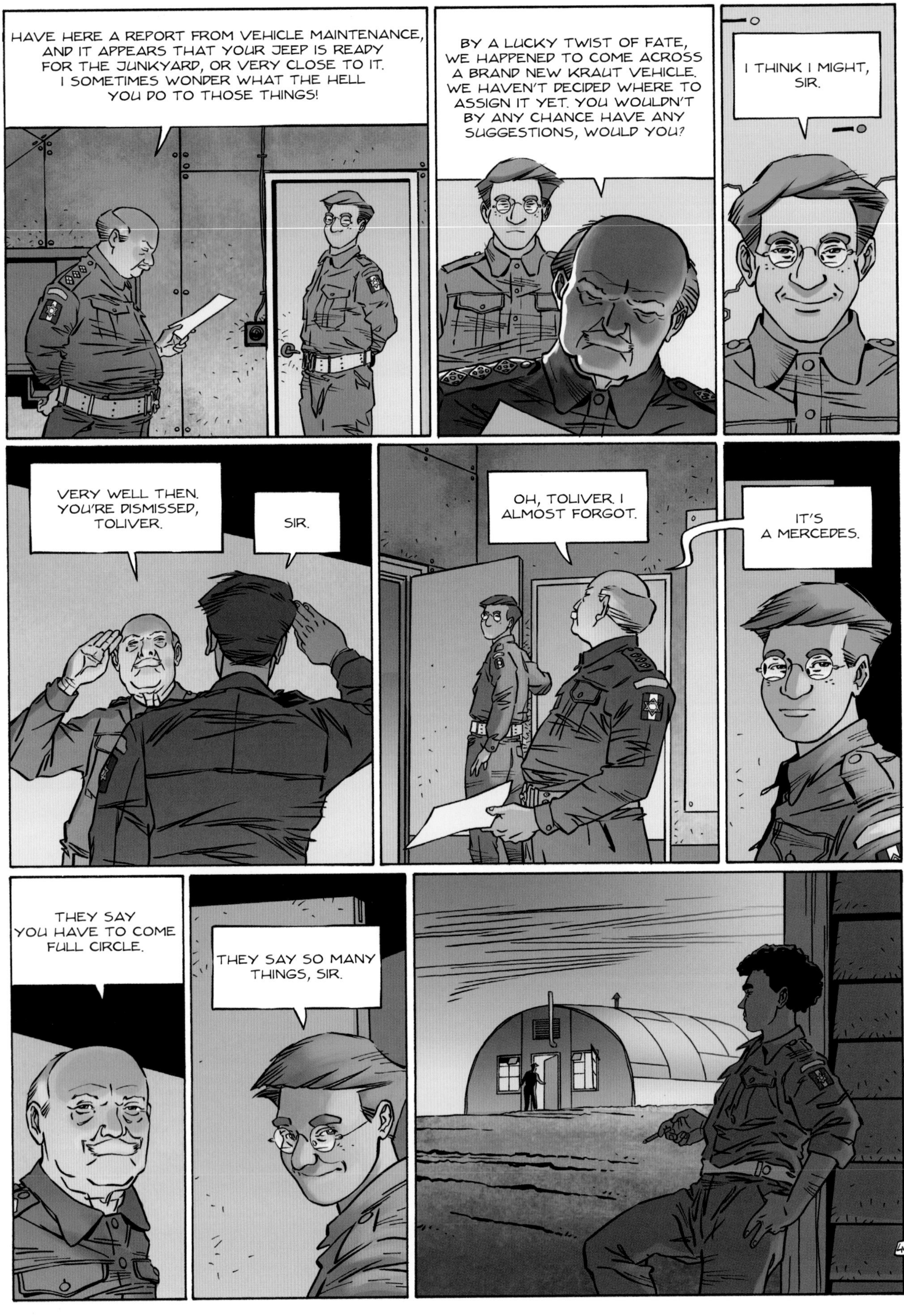
HAVE HERE A REPORT FROM VEHICLE MAINTENANCE, AND IT APPEARS THAT YOUR JEEP IS READY FOR THE JUNKYARD, OR VERY CLOSE TO IT. I SOMETIMES WONDER WHAT THE HELL YOU DO TO THOSE THINGS!
BY A LUCKY TWIST OF FATE, WE HAPPENED TO COME ACROSS A BRAND NEW KRAUT VEHICLE. WE HAVEN'T DECIDED WHERE TO ASSIGN IT YET. YOU WOULDN'T BY ANY CHANCE HAVE ANY SUGGESTIONS, WOULD YOU?
I THINK I MIGHT, SIR.
VERY WELL THEN. YOU'RE DISMISSED, TOLIVER.
SIR.
OH, TOLIVER. I ALMOST FORGOT.
IT'S A MERCEDES.
THEY SAY YOU HAVE TO COME FULL CIRCLE.
THEY SAY SO MANY THINGS, SIR.
40

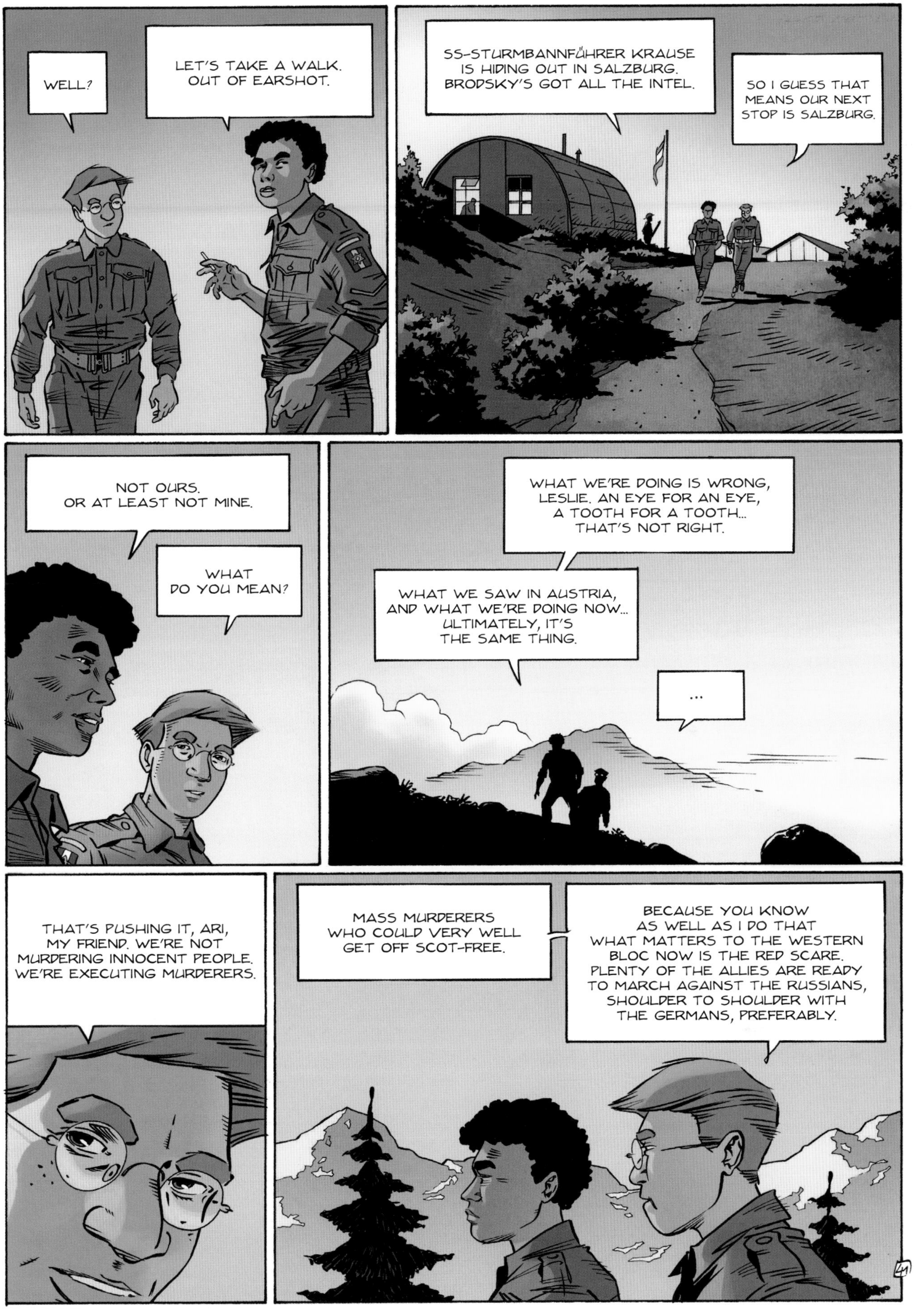
WELL?
LET'S TAKE A WALK. OUT OF EARSHOT.
SS-STURMBANNFÜHRER KRAUSE IS HIDING OUT IN SALZBURG. BRODSKY'S GOT ALL THE INTEL.
SO I GUESS THAT MEANS OUR NEXT STOP IS SALZBURG.
NOT OURS. OR AT LEAST NOT MINE.
WHAT DO YOU MEAN?
WHAT WE'RE DOING IS WRONG, LESLIE. AN EYE FOR AN EYE, A TOOTH FOR A TOOTH... THAT'S NOT RIGHT.
WHAT WE SAW IN AUSTRIA, AND WHAT WE'RE DOING NOW... ULTIMATELY, IT'S THE SAME THING.
...
THAT'S PUSHING IT, ARI, MY FRIEND. WE'RE NOT MURDERING INNOCENT PEOPLE. WE'RE EXECUTING MURDERERS.
MASS MURDERERS WHO COULD VERY WELL GET OFF SCOT-FREE.
BECAUSE YOU KNOW AS WELL AS I DO THAT WHAT MATTERS TO THE WESTERN BLOC NOW IS THE RED SCARE. PLENTY OF THE ALLIES ARE READY TO MARCH AGAINST THE RUSSIANS, SHOULDER TO SHOULDER WITH THE GERMANS, PREFERABLY.

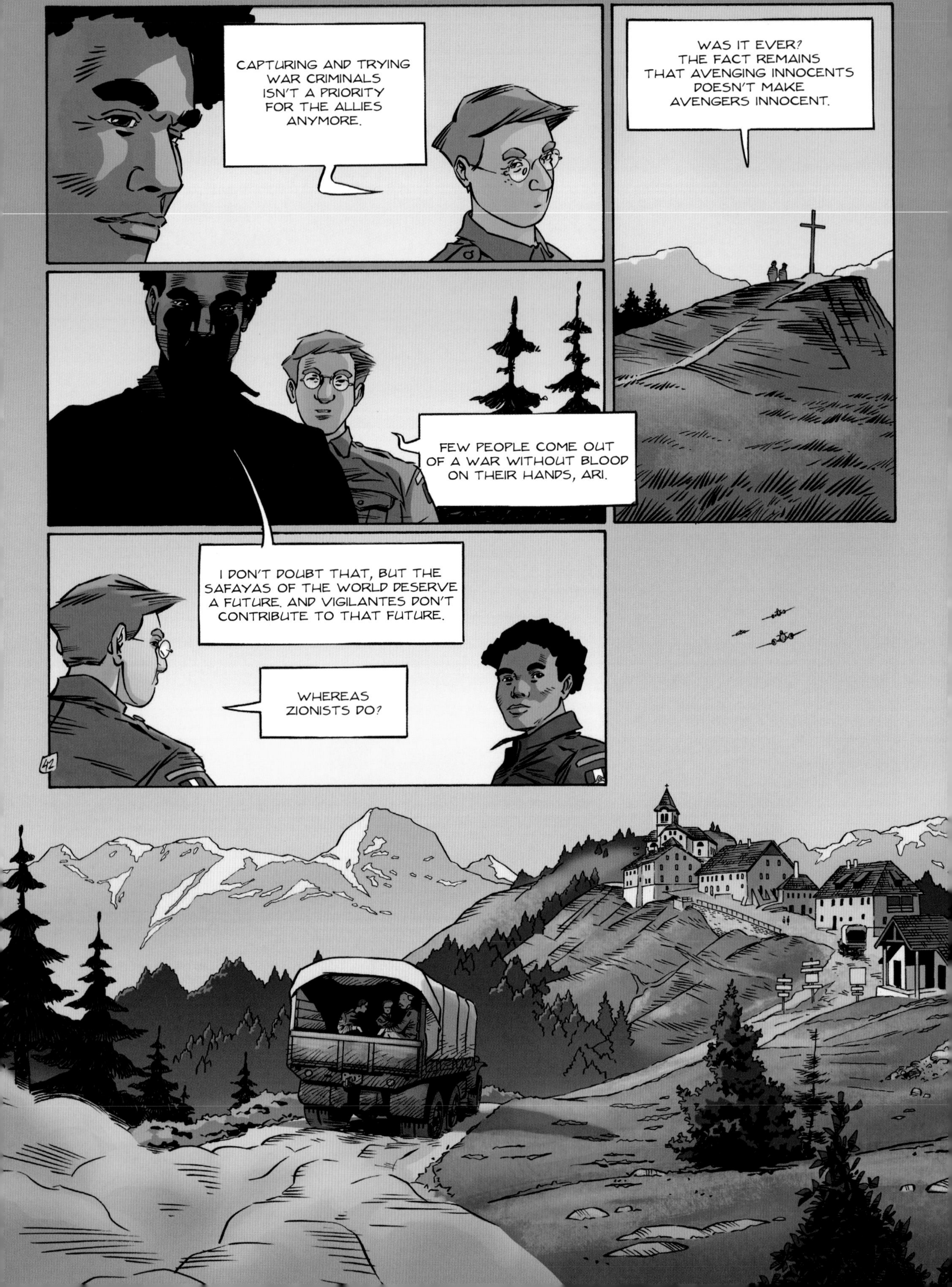
CAPTURING AND TRYING WAR CRIMINALS ISN'T A PRIORITY FOR THE ALLIES ANYMORE.
WAS IT EVER? THE FACT REMAINS THAT AVENGING INNOCENTS DOESN'T MAKE AVENGERS INNOCENT.
FEW PEOPLE COME OUT OF A WAR WITHOUT BLOOD ON THEIR HANDS, ARI.
I DON'T DOUBT THAT, BUT THE SAFAYAS OF THE WORLD DESERVE A FUTURE. AND VIGILANTES DON'T CONTRIBUTE TO THAT FUTURE.
WHEREAS ZIONISTS DO?
42

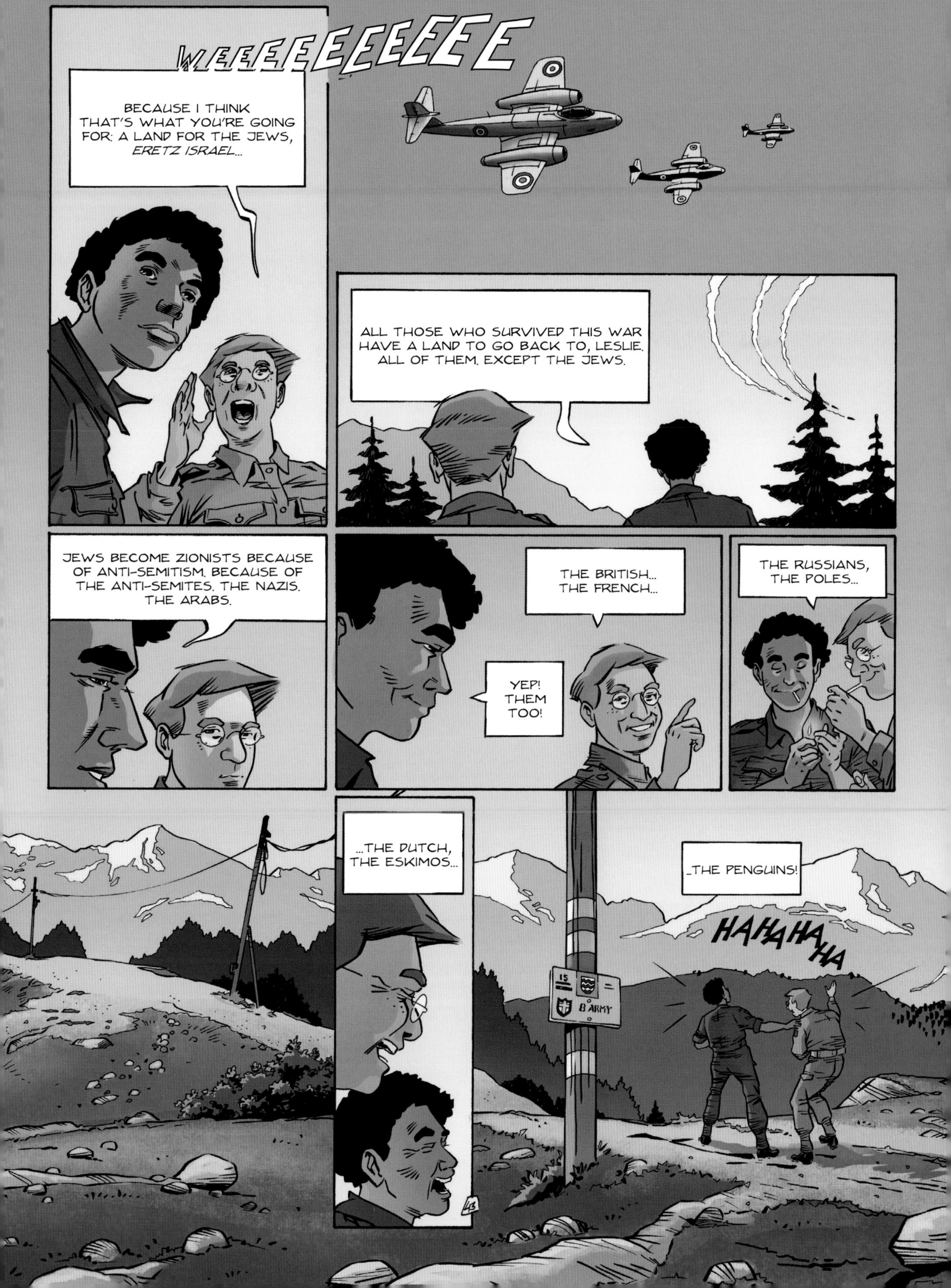
WEEEEEEEEEEE
BECAUSE I THINK THAT'S WHAT YOU'RE GOING FOR: A LAND FOR THE JEWS, *ERETZ ISRAEL*...
ALL THOSE WHO SURVIVED THIS WAR HAVE A LAND TO GO BACK TO, LESLIE. ALL OF THEM. EXCEPT THE JEWS.
JEWS BECOME ZIONISTS BECAUSE OF ANTI-SEMITISM. BECAUSE OF THE ANTI-SEMITES. THE NAZIS. THE ARABS.
THE BRITISH... THE FRENCH...
YEP! THEM TOO!
THE RUSSIANS, THE POLES...
...THE DUTCH, THE ESKIMOS...
...THE PENGUINS!
HAHAHAHAHA
8 ARMY

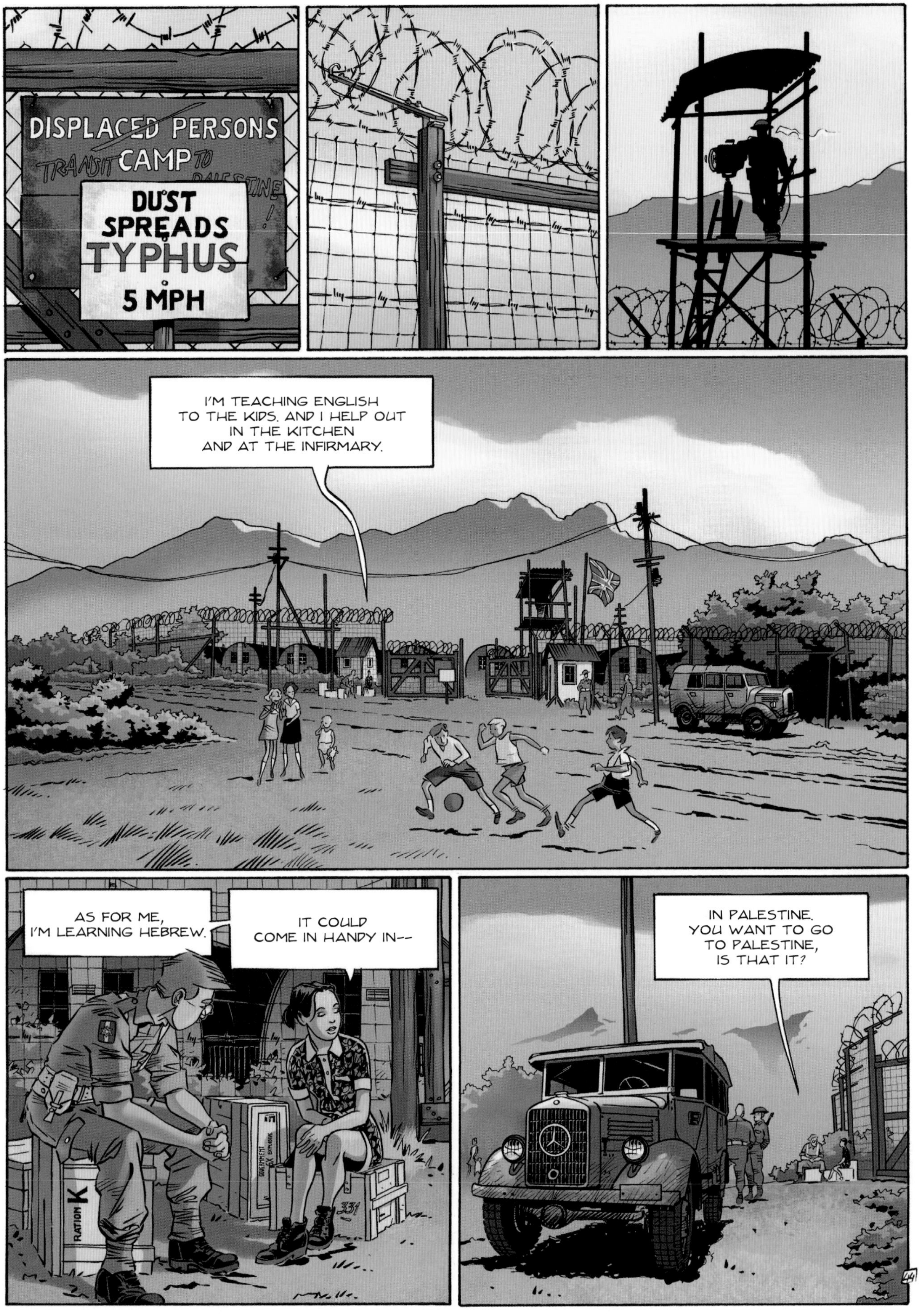
DISPLACED PERSONS TRANSIT CAMP TO PALESTINE!
DUST SPREADS TYPHUS
5 MPH
I'M TEACHING ENGLISH TO THE KIDS. AND I HELP OUT IN THE KITCHEN AND AT THE INFIRMARY.
AS FOR ME, I'M LEARNING HEBREW.
IT COULD COME IN HANDY IN--
RATION K
331
IN PALESTINE. YOU WANT TO GO TO PALESTINE, IS THAT IT?

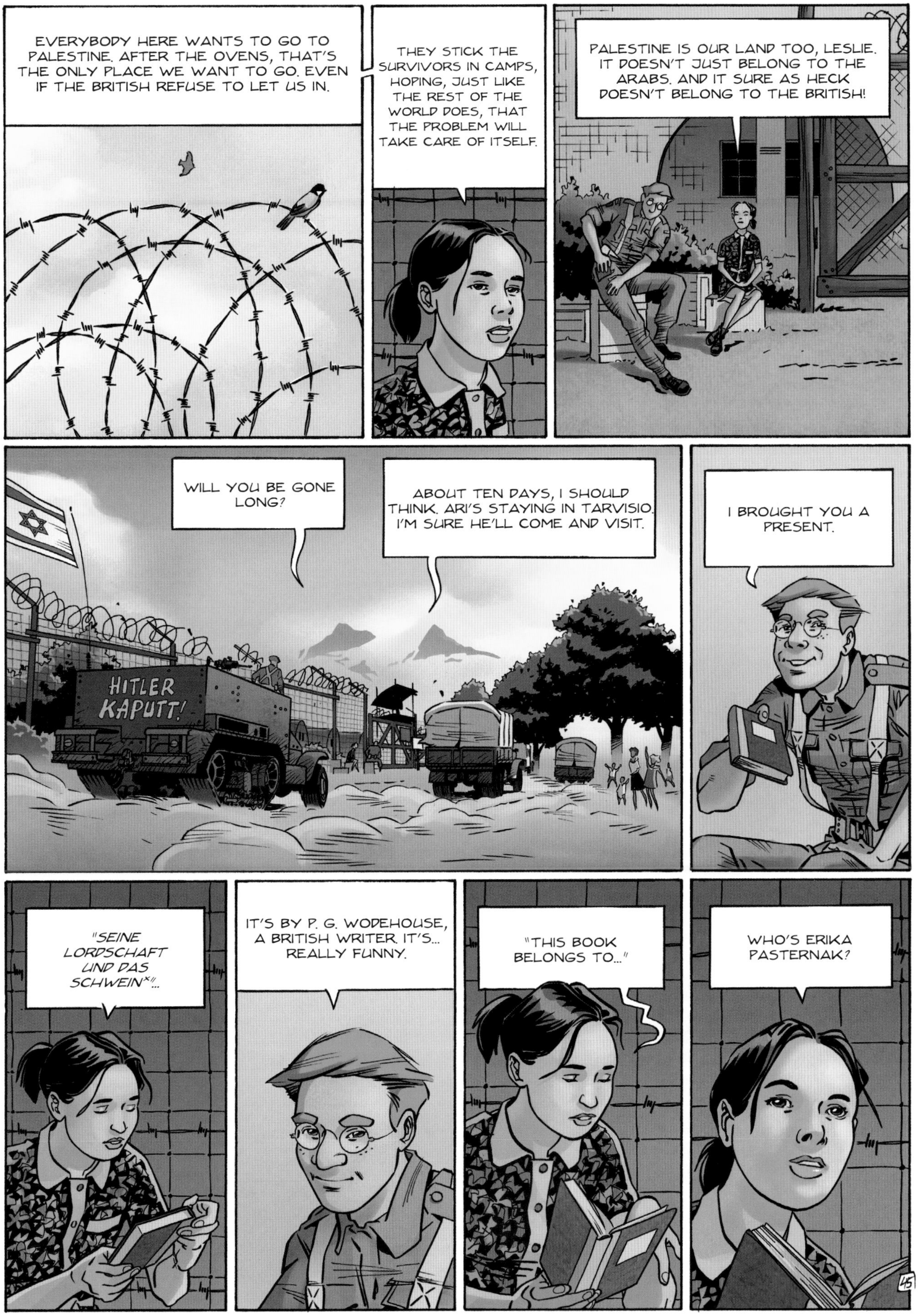
EVERYBODY HERE WANTS TO GO TO PALESTINE. AFTER THE OVENS, THAT'S THE ONLY PLACE WE WANT TO GO. EVEN IF THE BRITISH REFUSE TO LET US IN.
THEY STICK THE SURVIVORS IN CAMPS, HOPING, JUST LIKE THE REST OF THE WORLD DOES, THAT THE PROBLEM WILL TAKE CARE OF ITSELF.
PALESTINE IS OUR LAND TOO, LESLIE. IT DOESN'T JUST BELONG TO THE ARABS. AND IT SURE AS HECK DOESN'T BELONG TO THE BRITISH!
WILL YOU BE GONE LONG?
ABOUT TEN DAYS, I SHOULD THINK. ARI'S STAYING IN TARVISIO. I'M SURE HE'LL COME AND VISIT.
HITLER KAPUTT!
I BROUGHT YOU A PRESENT.
"SEINE LORDSCHAFT UND DAS SCHWEIN*"...
IT'S BY P. G. WODEHOUSE, A BRITISH WRITER. IT'S... REALLY FUNNY.
"THIS BOOK BELONGS TO..."
WHO'S ERIKA PASTERNAK?
45

*"His Lordship and the pig..." (from *Heavy Weather* by P. G. Wodehouse).

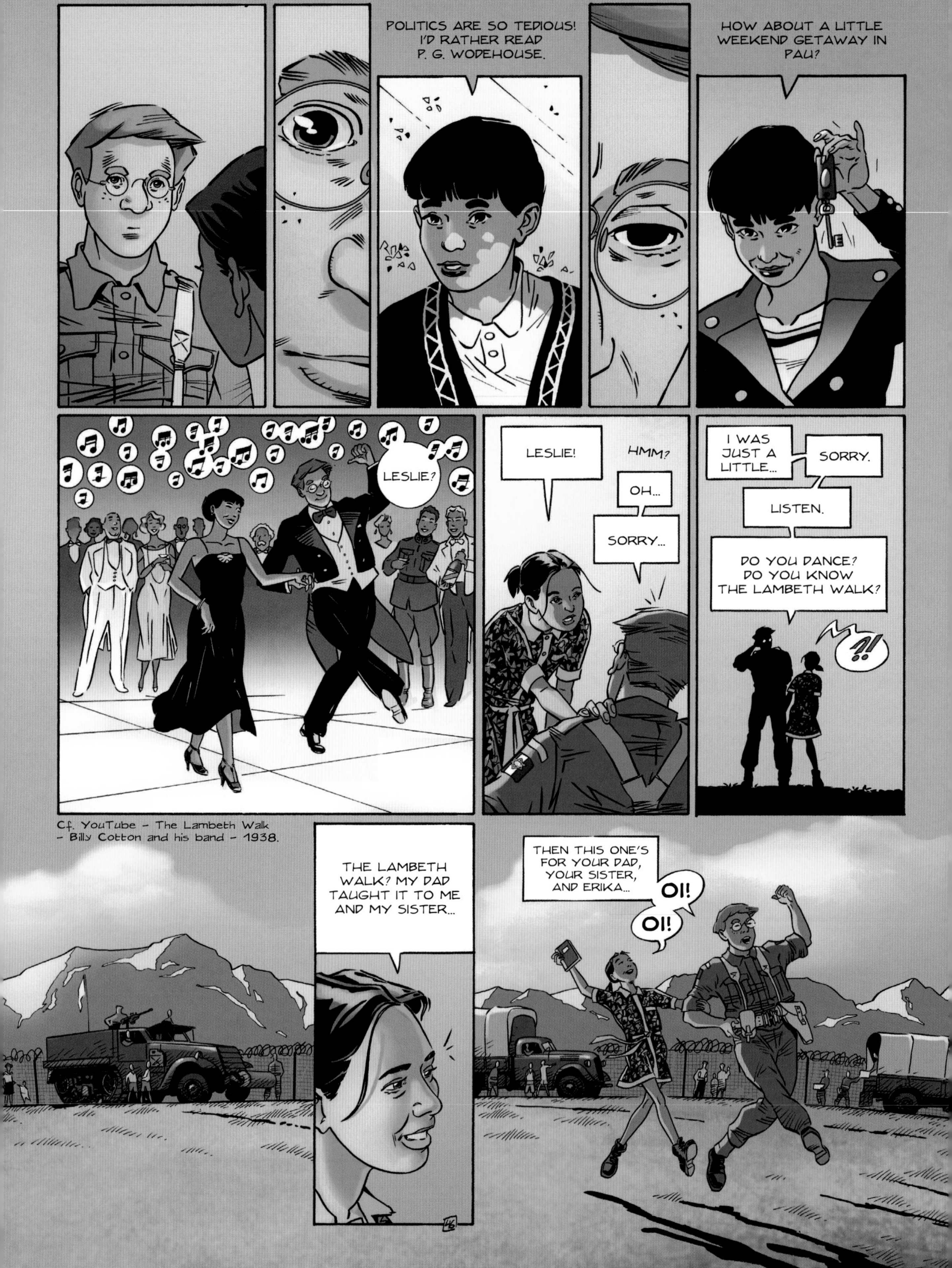
POLITICS ARE SO TEDIOUS! I'D RATHER READ P. G. WODEHOUSE.
HOW ABOUT A LITTLE WEEKEND GETAWAY IN PAU?
LESLIE?
LESLIE!
HMM?
OH...
SORRY...
I WAS JUST A LITTLE...
SORRY.
LISTEN.
DO YOU DANCE? DO YOU KNOW THE LAMBETH WALK?
?!!
THE LAMBETH WALK? MY DAD TAUGHT IT TO ME AND MY SISTER...
THEN THIS ONE'S FOR YOUR DAD, YOUR SISTER, AND ERIKA...
OI!
OI!

Cf. YouTube – The Lambeth Walk – Billy Cotton and his band – 1938.

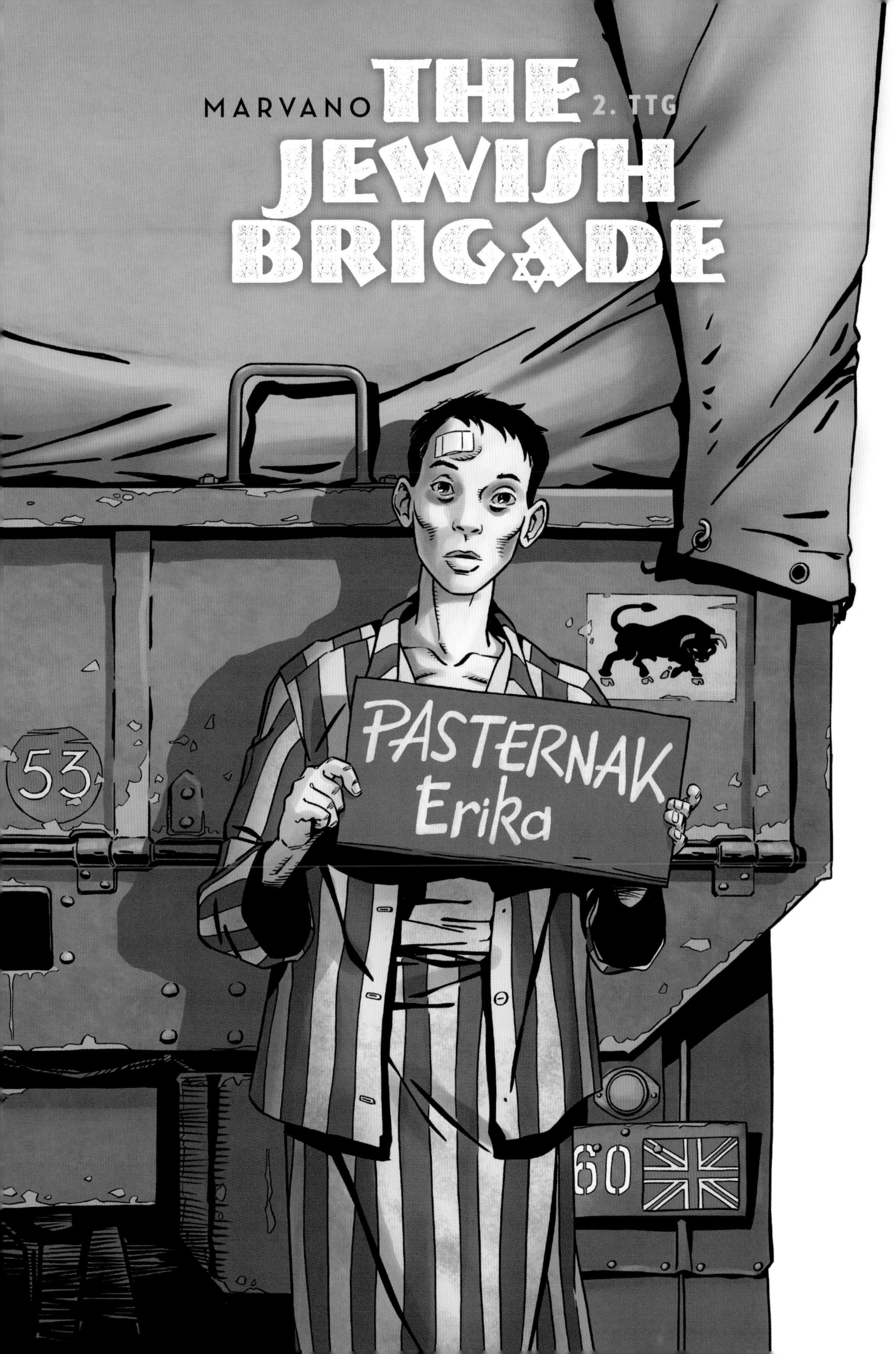
MARVANO
THE JEWISH BRIGADE
2. TTG
PASTERNAK
Erika
53
60

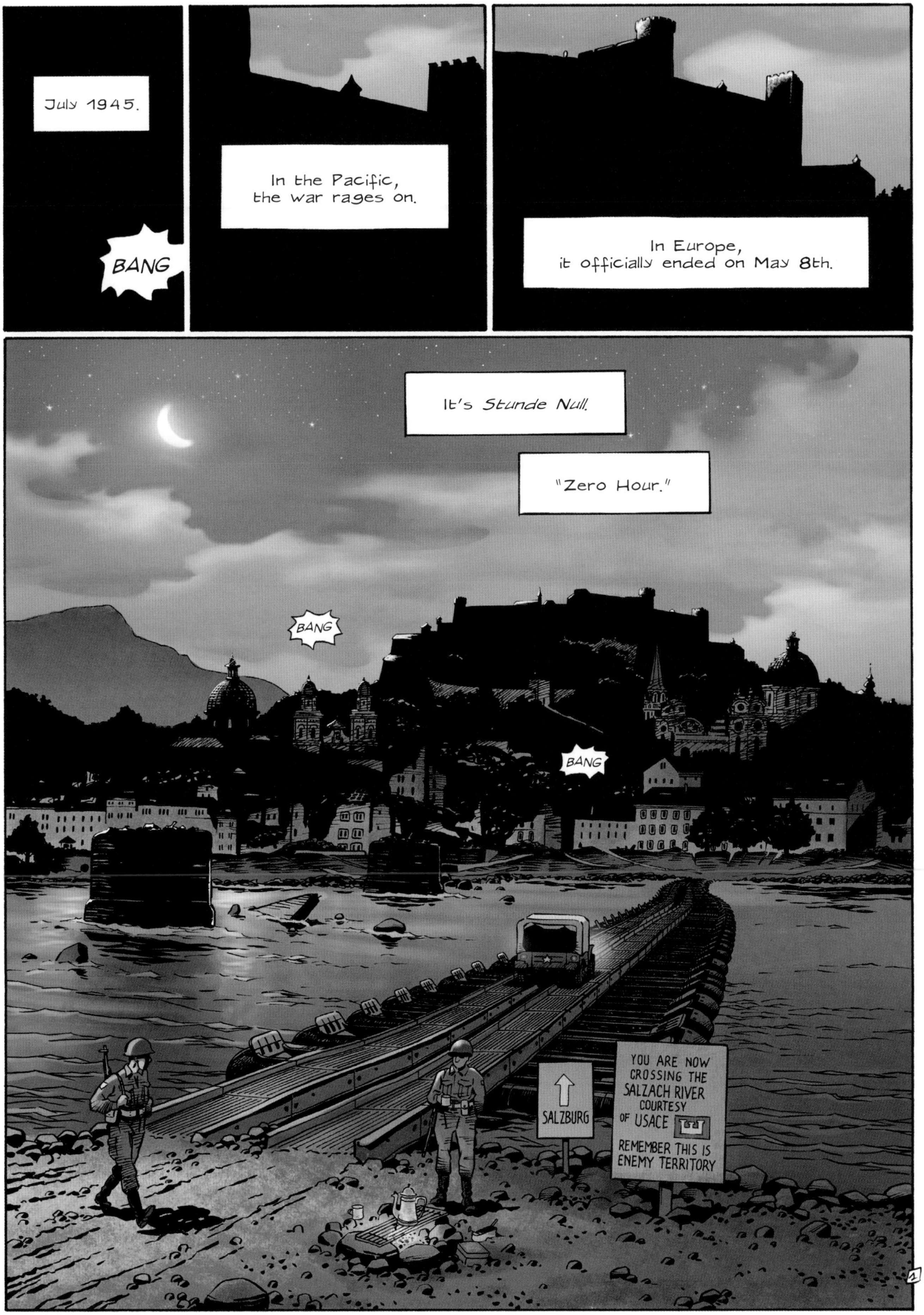
July 1945.
BANG
In the Pacific, the war rages on.
In Europe, it officially ended on May 8th.
It's *Stunde Null*.
"Zero Hour."
BANG
BANG
SALZBURG
YOU ARE NOW CROSSING THE SALZACH RIVER COURTESY OF USACE
REMEMBER THIS IS ENEMY TERRITORY
1

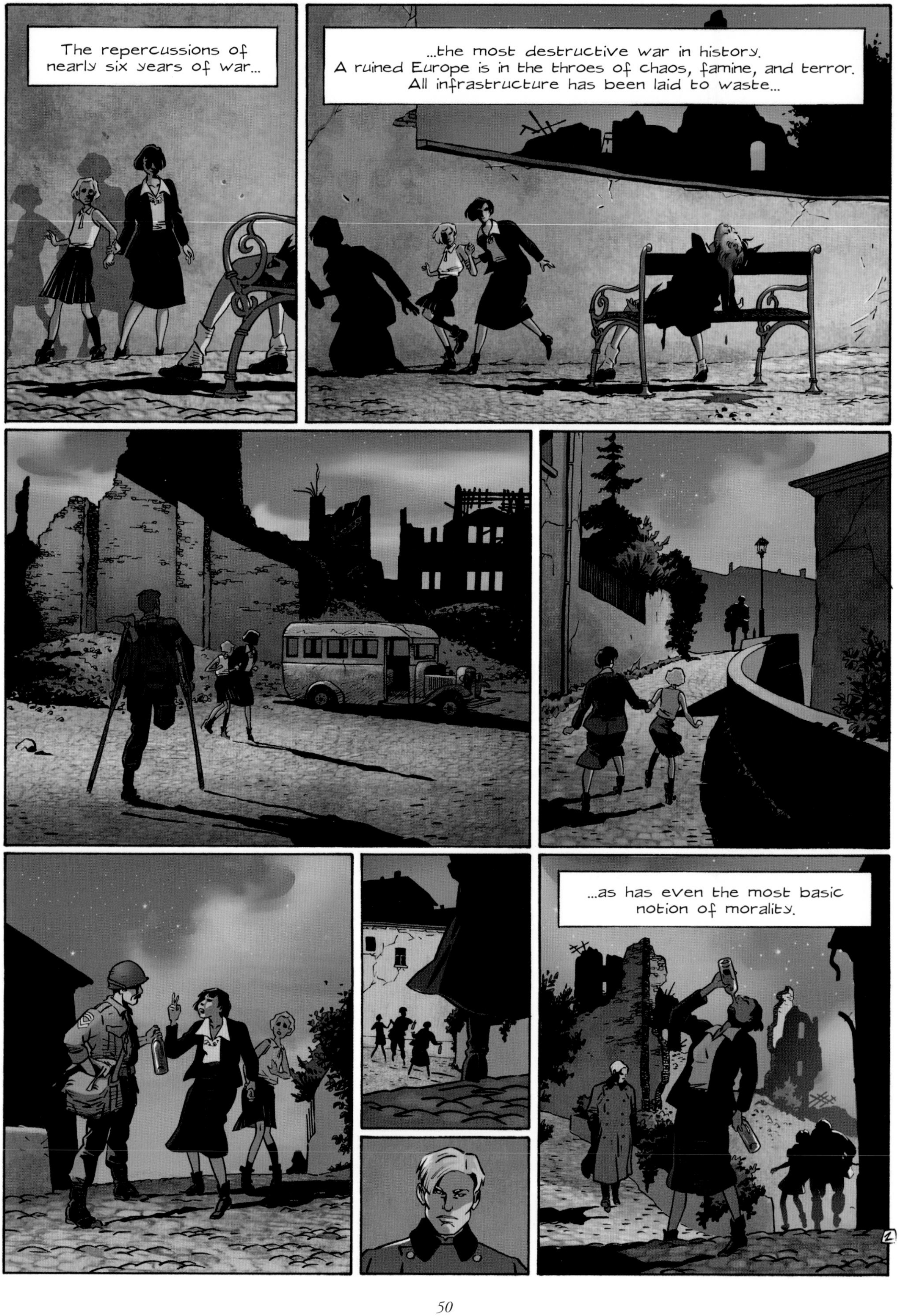

The repercussions of nearly six years of war...
...the most destructive war in history.
A ruined Europe is in the throes of chaos, famine, and terror.
All infrastructure has been laid to waste...
...as has even the most basic notion of morality.

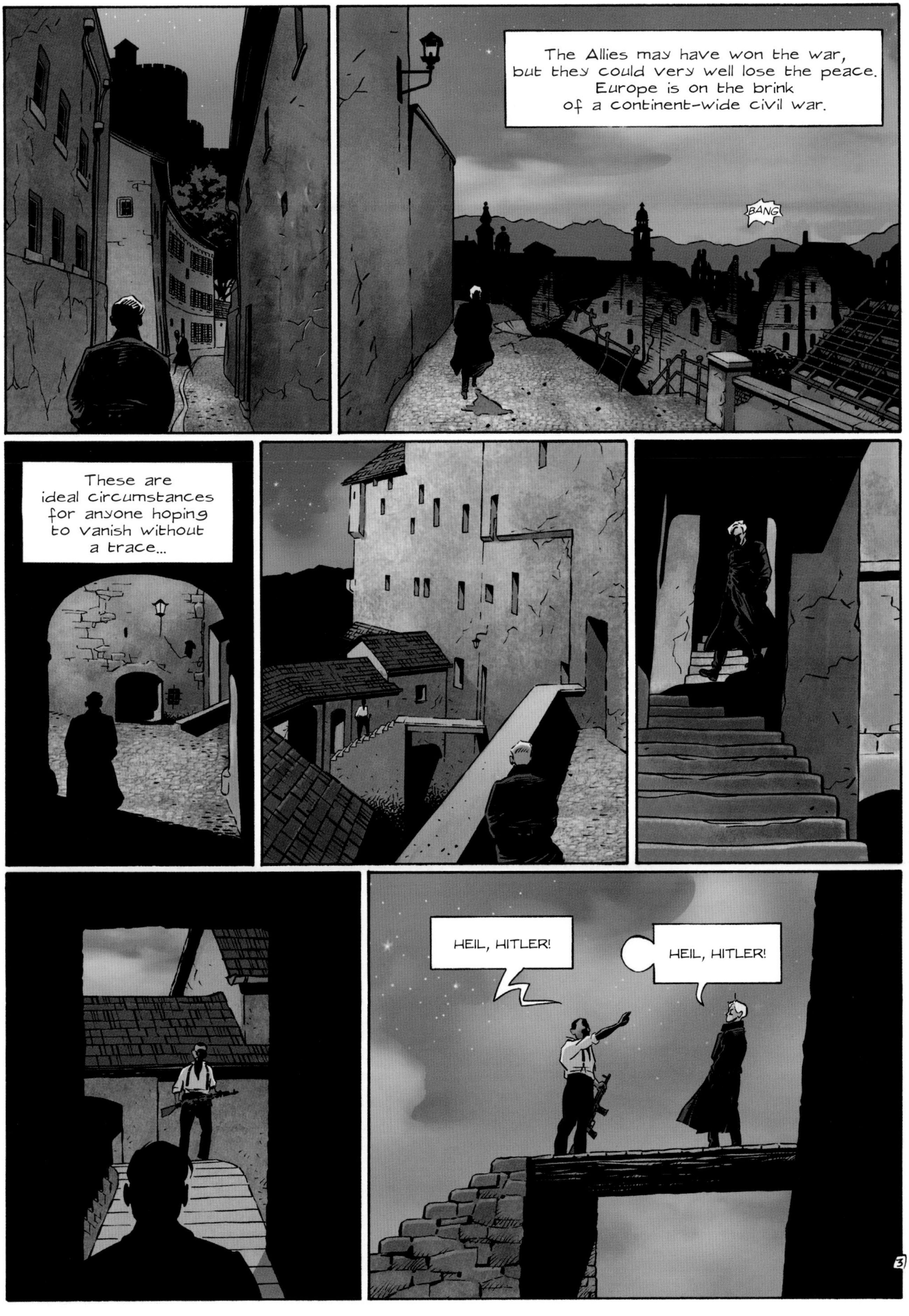

The Allies may have won the war, but they could very well lose the peace. Europe is on the brink of a continent-wide civil war.
BANG
These are ideal circumstances for anyone hoping to vanish without a trace...
HEIL, HITLER!
HEIL, HITLER!
3

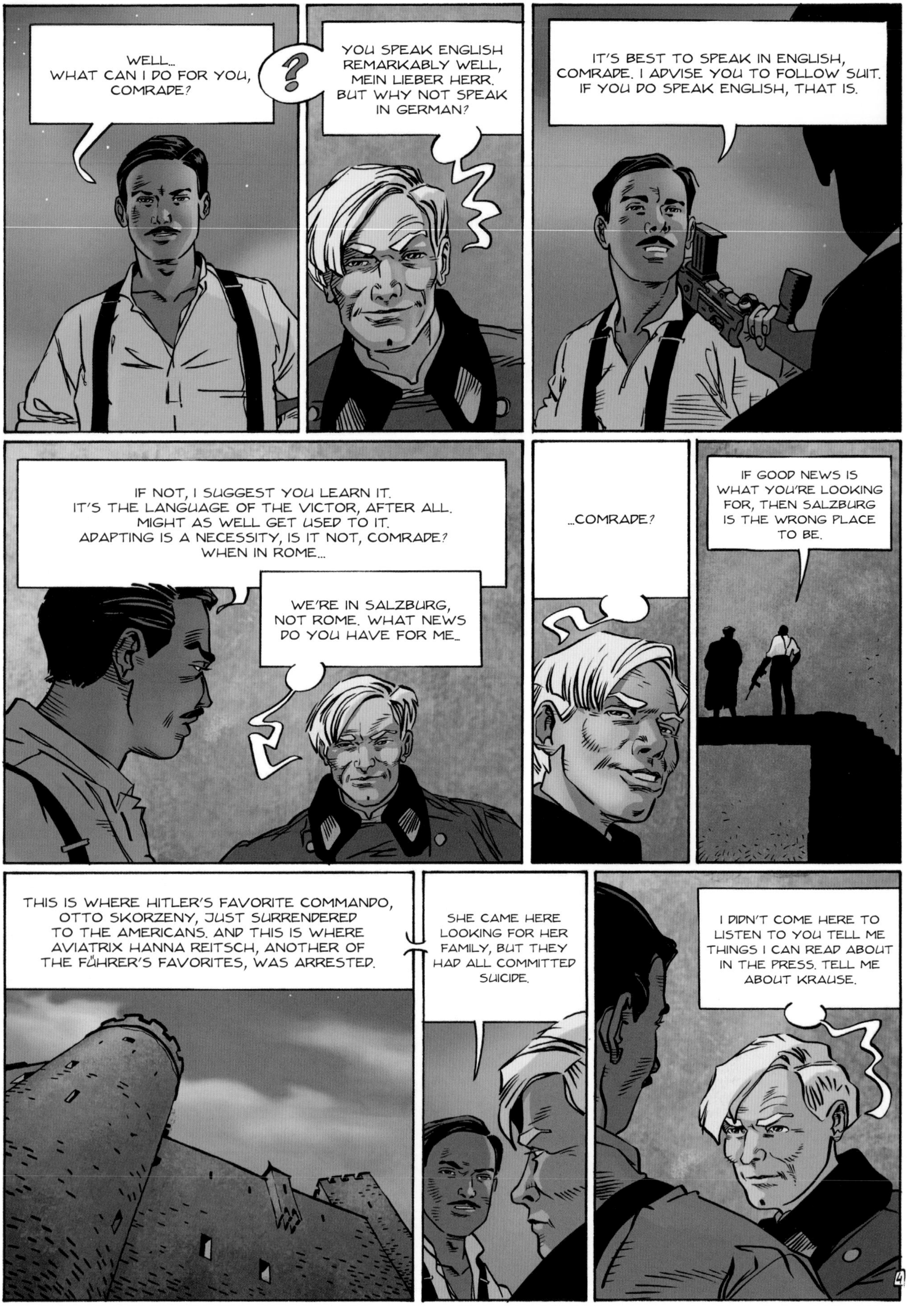
WELL... WHAT CAN I DO FOR YOU, COMRADE?
?
YOU SPEAK ENGLISH REMARKABLY WELL, MEIN LIEBER HERR. BUT WHY NOT SPEAK IN GERMAN?
IT'S BEST TO SPEAK IN ENGLISH, COMRADE. I ADVISE YOU TO FOLLOW SUIT. IF YOU DO SPEAK ENGLISH, THAT IS.
IF NOT, I SUGGEST YOU LEARN IT. IT'S THE LANGUAGE OF THE VICTOR, AFTER ALL. MIGHT AS WELL GET USED TO IT. ADAPTING IS A NECESSITY, IS IT NOT, COMRADE? WHEN IN ROME...
WE'RE IN SALZBURG, NOT ROME. WHAT NEWS DO YOU HAVE FOR ME...
...COMRADE?
IF GOOD NEWS IS WHAT YOU'RE LOOKING FOR, THEN SALZBURG IS THE WRONG PLACE TO BE.
THIS IS WHERE HITLER'S FAVORITE COMMANDO, OTTO SKORZENY, JUST SURRENDERED TO THE AMERICANS. AND THIS IS WHERE AVIATRIX HANNA REITSCH, ANOTHER OF THE FÜHRER'S FAVORITES, WAS ARRESTED.
SHE CAME HERE LOOKING FOR HER FAMILY, BUT THEY HAD ALL COMMITTED SUICIDE.
I DIDN'T COME HERE TO LISTEN TO YOU TELL ME THINGS I CAN READ ABOUT IN THE PRESS. TELL ME ABOUT KRAUSE.
4

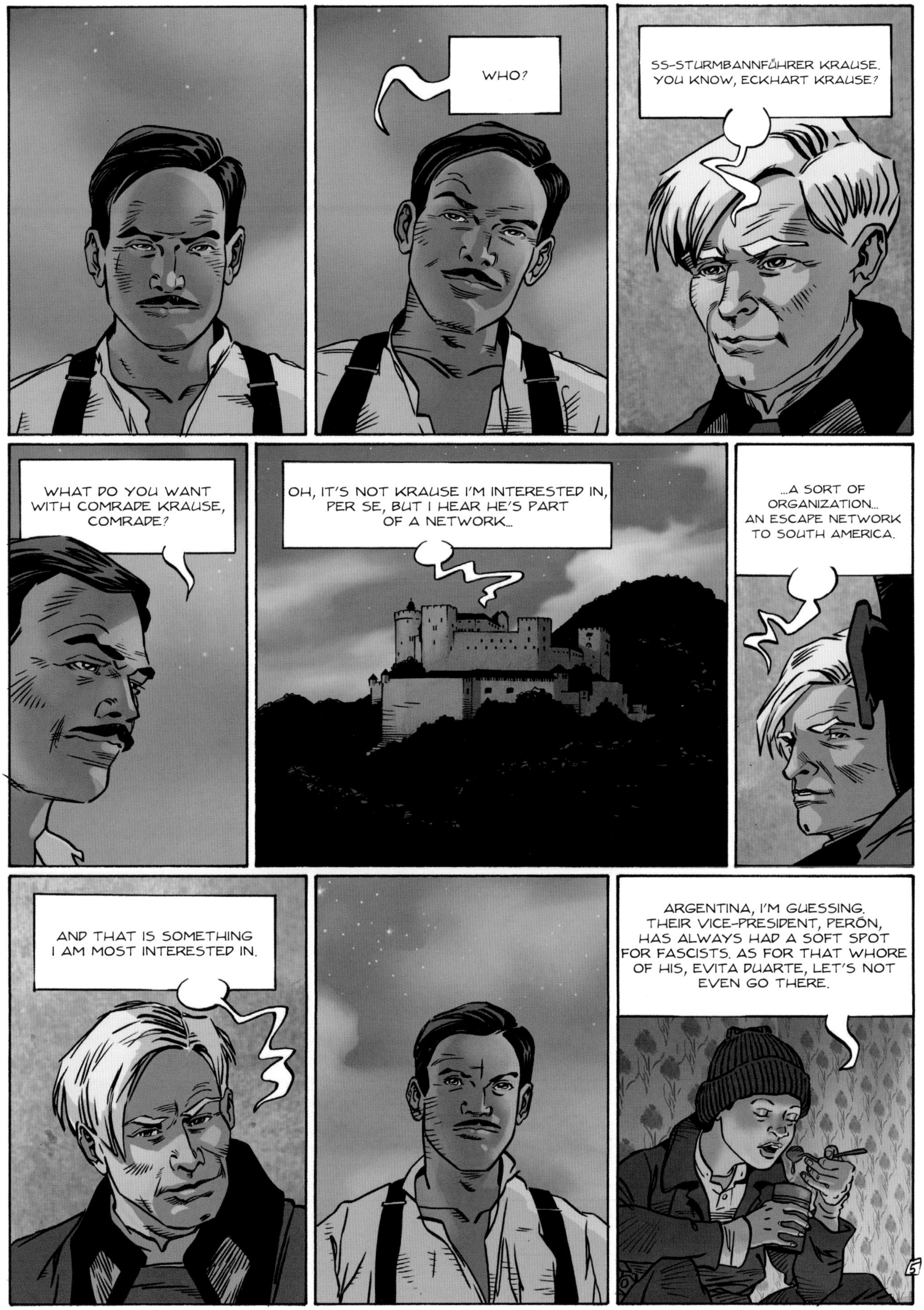
WHO?
SS-STURMBANNFÜHRER KRAUSE. YOU KNOW, ECKHART KRAUSE?
WHAT DO YOU WANT WITH COMRADE KRAUSE, COMRADE?
OH, IT'S NOT KRAUSE I'M INTERESTED IN, PER SE, BUT I HEAR HE'S PART OF A NETWORK...
...A SORT OF ORGANIZATION... AN ESCAPE NETWORK TO SOUTH AMERICA.
AND THAT IS SOMETHING I AM MOST INTERESTED IN.
ARGENTINA, I'M GUESSING. THEIR VICE-PRESIDENT, PERÓN, HAS ALWAYS HAD A SOFT SPOT FOR FASCISTS. AS FOR THAT WHORE OF HIS, EVITA DUARTE, LET'S NOT EVEN GO THERE.

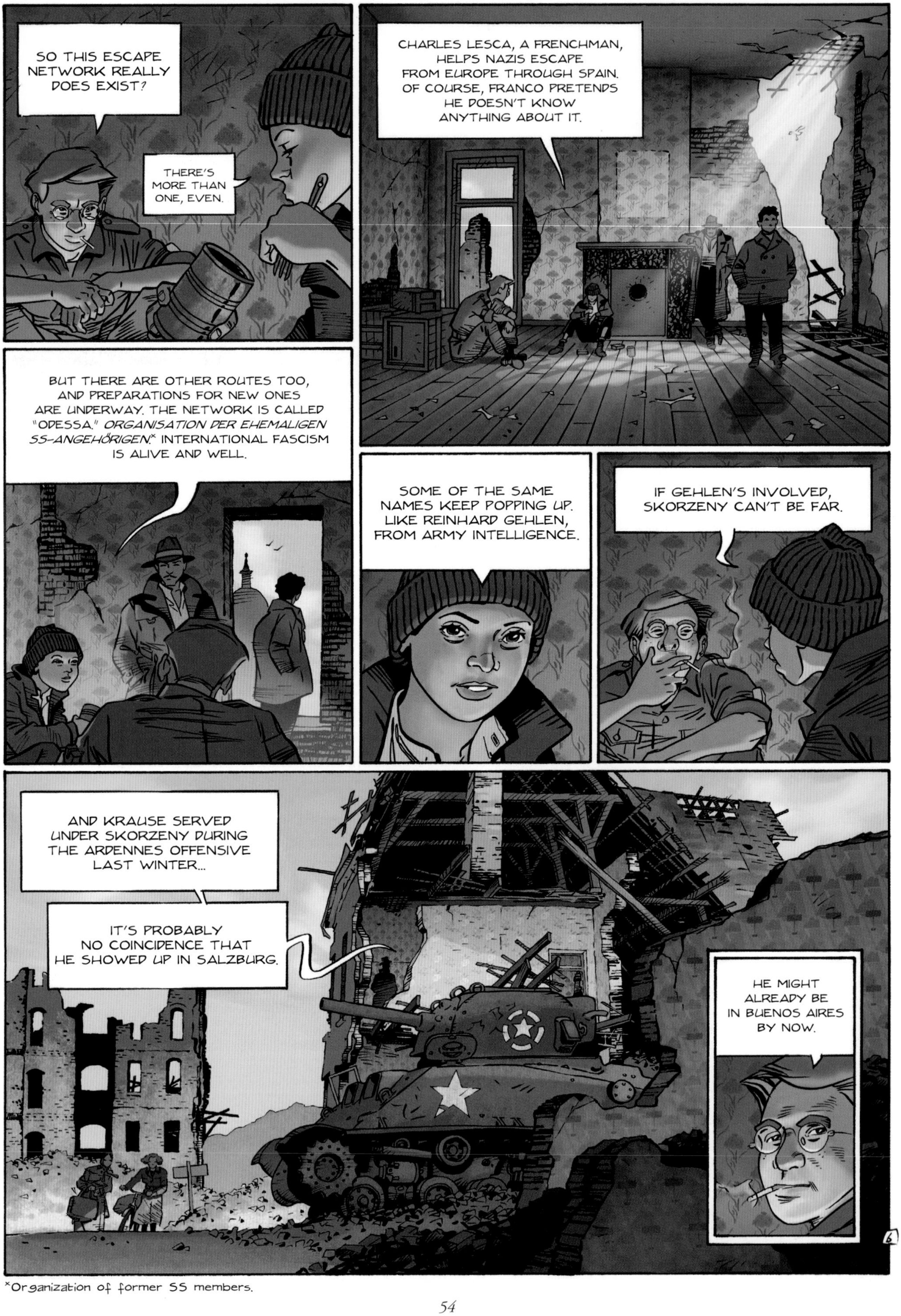
SO THIS ESCAPE NETWORK REALLY DOES EXIST?
THERE'S MORE THAN ONE, EVEN.
CHARLES LESCA, A FRENCHMAN, HELPS NAZIS ESCAPE FROM EUROPE THROUGH SPAIN. OF COURSE, FRANCO PRETENDS HE DOESN'T KNOW ANYTHING ABOUT IT.
BUT THERE ARE OTHER ROUTES TOO, AND PREPARATIONS FOR NEW ONES ARE UNDERWAY. THE NETWORK IS CALLED "ODESSA." *ORGANISATION DER EHEMALIGEN SS-ANGEHÖRIGEN.*˟ INTERNATIONAL FASCISM IS ALIVE AND WELL.
SOME OF THE SAME NAMES KEEP POPPING UP. LIKE REINHARD GEHLEN, FROM ARMY INTELLIGENCE.
IF GEHLEN'S INVOLVED, SKORZENY CAN'T BE FAR.
AND KRAUSE SERVED UNDER SKORZENY DURING THE ARDENNES OFFENSIVE LAST WINTER...
IT'S PROBABLY NO COINCIDENCE THAT HE SHOWED UP IN SALZBURG.
HE MIGHT ALREADY BE IN BUENOS AIRES BY NOW.
6

˟Organization of former SS members.

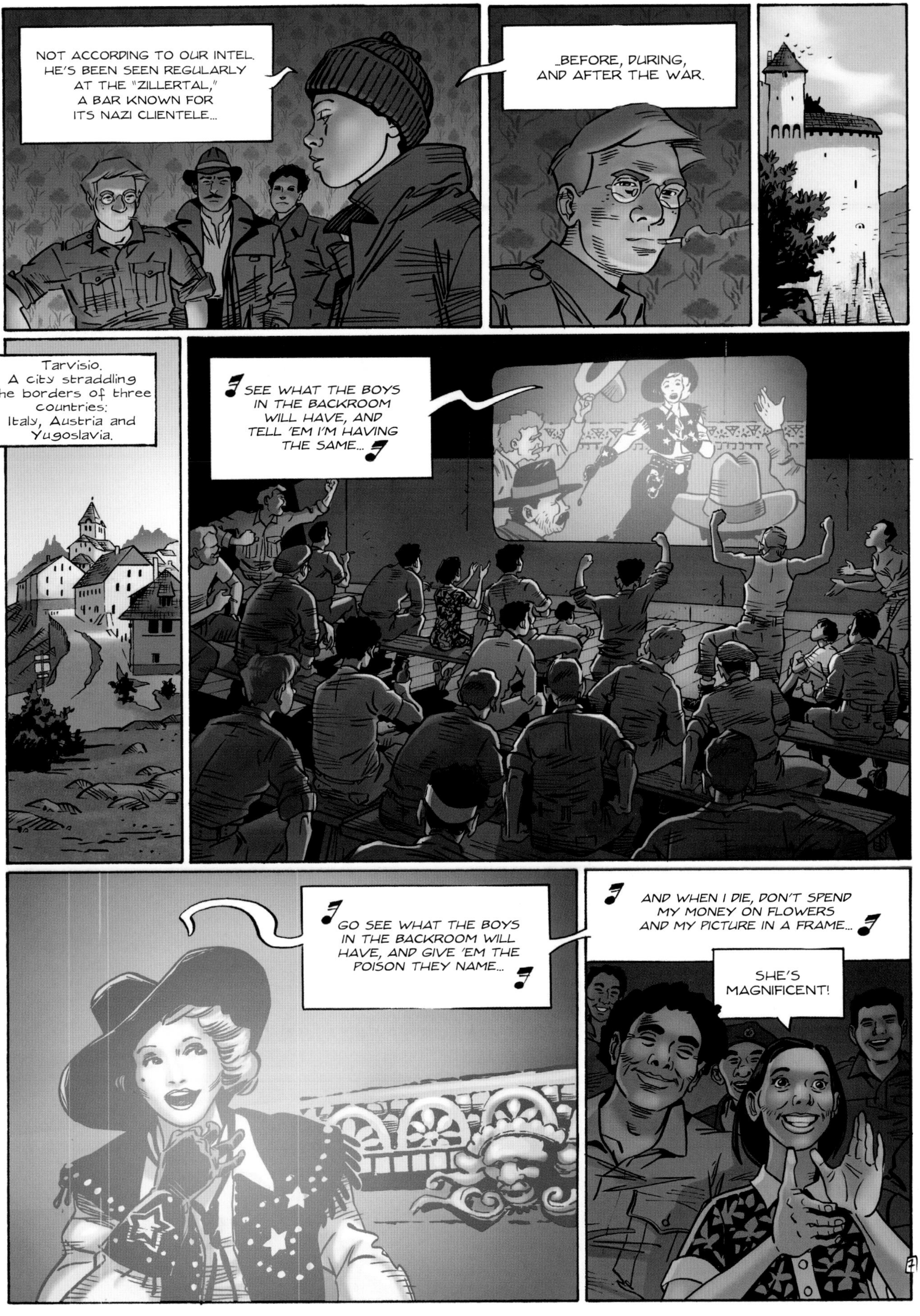
NOT ACCORDING TO OUR INTEL. HE'S BEEN SEEN REGULARLY AT THE "ZILLERTAL," A BAR KNOWN FOR ITS NAZI CLIENTELE...
...BEFORE, DURING, AND AFTER THE WAR.
Tarvisio. A city straddling the borders of three countries: Italy, Austria and Yugoslavia.
SEE WHAT THE BOYS IN THE BACKROOM WILL HAVE, AND TELL 'EM I'M HAVING THE SAME...
GO SEE WHAT THE BOYS IN THE BACKROOM WILL HAVE, AND GIVE 'EM THE POISON THEY NAME...
AND WHEN I DIE, DON'T SPEND MY MONEY ON FLOWERS AND MY PICTURE IN A FRAME...
SHE'S MAGNIFICENT!

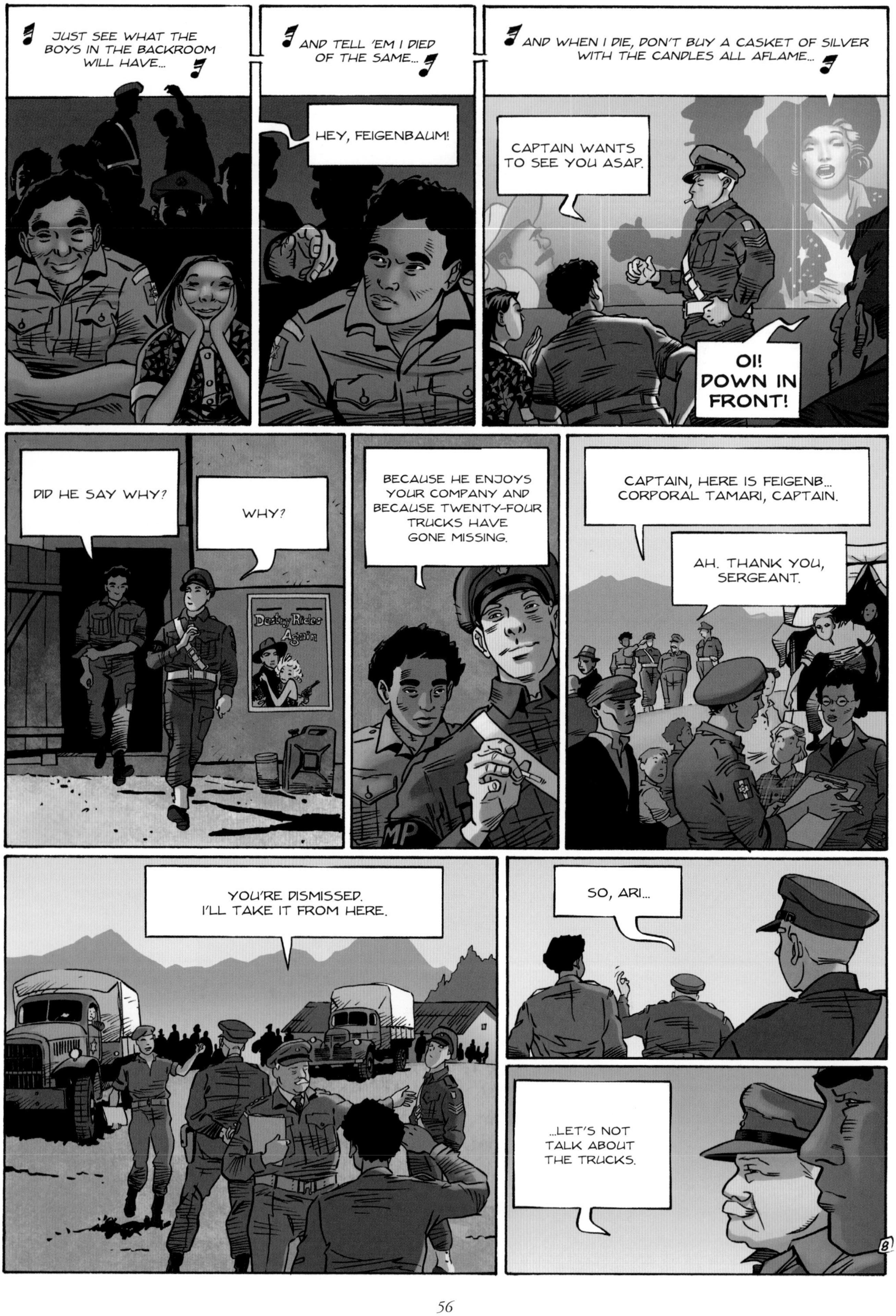

JUST SEE WHAT THE BOYS IN THE BACKROOM WILL HAVE...
AND TELL 'EM I DIED OF THE SAME...
HEY, FEIGENBAUM!
AND WHEN I DIE, DON'T BUY A CASKET OF SILVER WITH THE CANDLES ALL AFLAME...
CAPTAIN WANTS TO SEE YOU ASAP.
OI! DOWN IN FRONT!
DID HE SAY WHY?
WHY?
Destry Rides Again
BECAUSE HE ENJOYS YOUR COMPANY AND BECAUSE TWENTY-FOUR TRUCKS HAVE GONE MISSING.
MP
CAPTAIN, HERE IS FEIGENB... CORPORAL TAMARI, CAPTAIN.
AH. THANK YOU, SERGEANT.
YOU'RE DISMISSED. I'LL TAKE IT FROM HERE.
SO, ARI...
...LET'S NOT TALK ABOUT THE TRUCKS.

EVEN THOUGH THERE'S ENOUGH EQUIPMENT GOING MISSING TO SUPPLY A WHOLE ARMY, THAT'S NOT WHAT HAS LONDON WORRIED.

WESTMINSTER IS WONDERING WHAT ON EARTH IS HAPPENING IN THIS REMOTE PART OF EUROPE.

THEY'RE RECEIVING REPORTS OF ARMS AND HUMAN TRAFFICKING, FROM WHAT I CAN SEE. UNFORTUNATELY, IT DOESN'T SAY WHO WROTE THESE REPORTS.

BUT WHEN IT SUITS THEM, POLITICIANS CAN SHOW SURPRISING INITIATIVE.

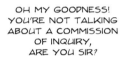

OH MY GOODNESS! YOU'RE NOT TALKING ABOUT A COMMISSION OF INQUIRY, ARE YOU SIR?

SPARE ME YOUR SARCASM, CORPORAL. IF ONLY THAT WERE TRUE! NO, THE BRIGADE IS BEING TRANSFERRED.

THEY'RE EXPECTING US IN ANTWERP BY AUGUST 1st.

ANTWERP?

YES... THE PORT THROUGH WHICH ALMOST ALL THE SUPPLIES FOR THE ALLIES TRANSIT.

MILLIONS OF TONS OF WEAPONS, FUEL, CLOTHING, AND SUPPLIES OF ALL SORTS...

THE WHOLE LOT OF IT GUARDED—WELL, IF YOU CAN CALL IT THAT—BY YOUNG CONSCRIPTS WITH ONLY ONE THING ON THEIR MIND: GOING HOME.

A CONSTANT, BARELY INSPECTED STREAM OF SHIPS, MERCHANDISE, AND PEOPLE COMING AND GOING. A HIVE OF ACTIVITY, BASICALLY.

I DON'T KNOW IF LONDON HAS REALLY THOUGHT THIS THROUGH... BUT AS ARMY MEN, WE HAVE NO CHOICE BUT TO OBEY THE ORDERS OF OUR SUPERIORS.

AND GLADLY, SIR, IN SOME CASES.

UH-HUH.

SPEAKING OF TROOP MOVEMENTS...

AS YOU KNOW, THE ACTUAL MILITARY SITUATION IN EUROPE DOES NOT COMPLETELY CORRESPOND TO THE BORDERS OUR POLITICIANS HAVE SET.

EVERYTHING IS STILL IN MOTION. THE ARMIES ARE ENTRENCHING THEMSELVES IN THEIR POSITIONS OR ESTABLISHING NEW ONES, IN THE HOPES OF HOLDING ON TO THEM.

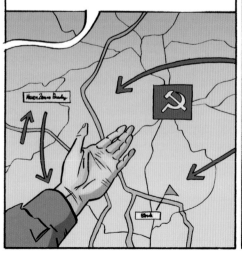

FOR EXAMPLE, UP UNTIL NOW, THE CITY OF GRAZ, A GOOD HUNDRED MILES FROM HERE, WAS OCCUPIED BY THE RUSSIANS.

OVER THE PAST FEW WEEKS, THE TOWN HAS SEEN AN INFLUX OF CAMP SURVIVORS FROM EASTERN EUROPE. IT'S AS IF SOMEONE HAD GIVEN THEM A MANDATE.

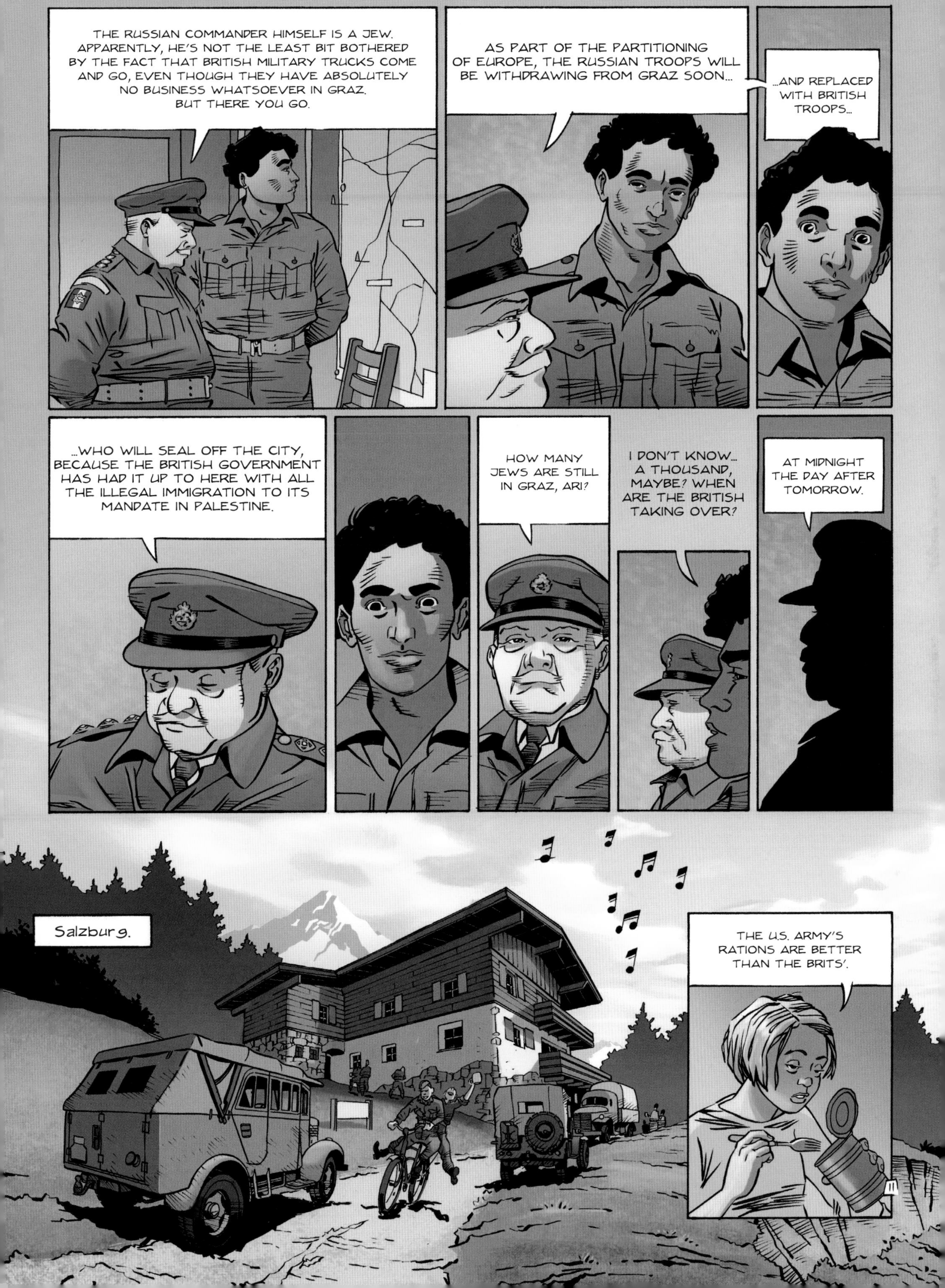
THE RUSSIAN COMMANDER HIMSELF IS A JEW. APPARENTLY, HE'S NOT THE LEAST BIT BOTHERED BY THE FACT THAT BRITISH MILITARY TRUCKS COME AND GO, EVEN THOUGH THEY HAVE ABSOLUTELY NO BUSINESS WHATSOEVER IN GRAZ. BUT THERE YOU GO.
AS PART OF THE PARTITIONING OF EUROPE, THE RUSSIAN TROOPS WILL BE WITHDRAWING FROM GRAZ SOON...
...AND REPLACED WITH BRITISH TROOPS...
...WHO WILL SEAL OFF THE CITY, BECAUSE THE BRITISH GOVERNMENT HAS HAD IT UP TO HERE WITH ALL THE ILLEGAL IMMIGRATION TO ITS MANDATE IN PALESTINE.
HOW MANY JEWS ARE STILL IN GRAZ, ARI?
I DON'T KNOW... A THOUSAND, MAYBE? WHEN ARE THE BRITISH TAKING OVER?
AT MIDNIGHT THE DAY AFTER TOMORROW.
Salzburg.
THE U.S. ARMY'S RATIONS ARE BETTER THAN THE BRITS'.
11

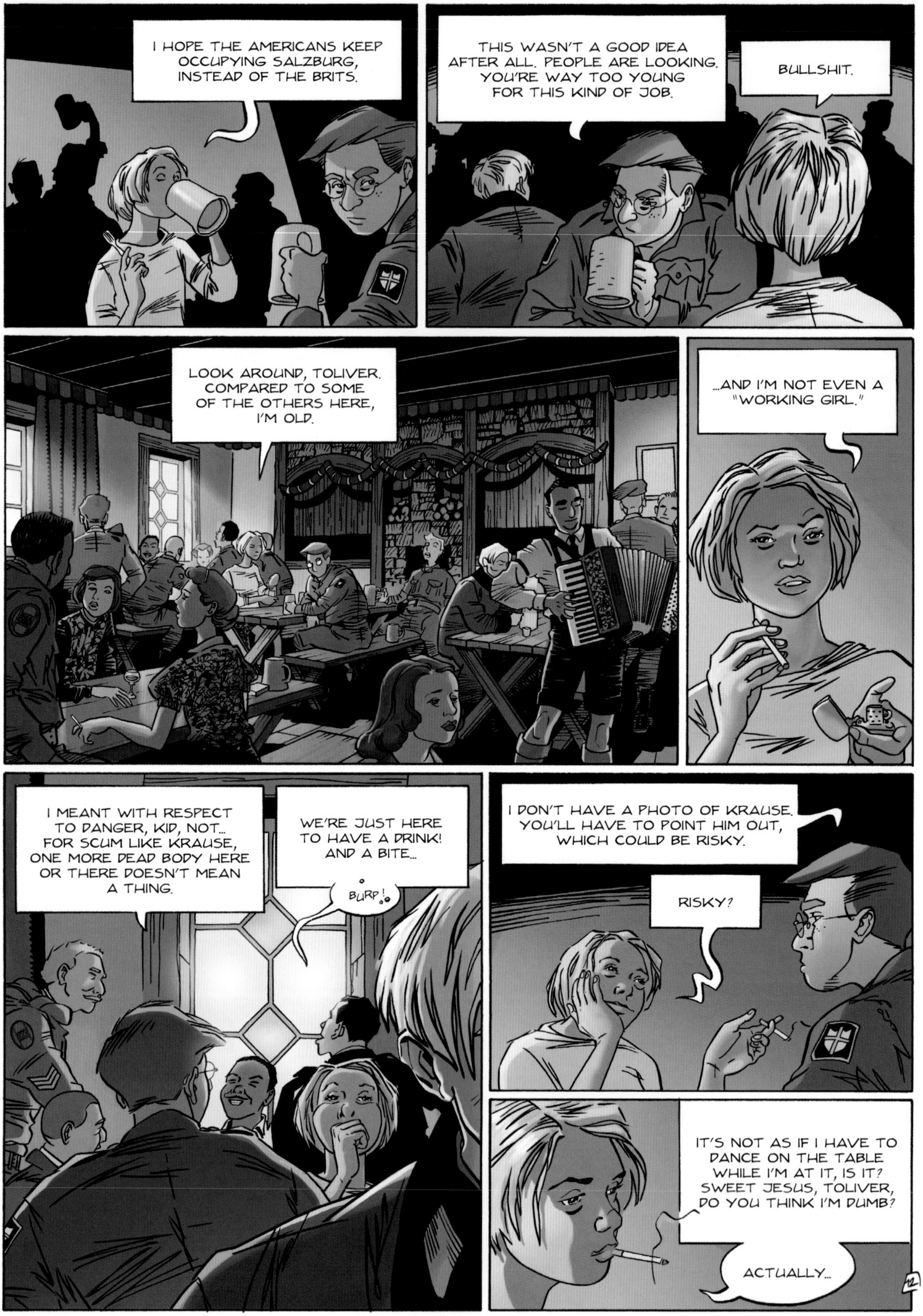
I HOPE THE AMERICANS KEEP OCCUPYING SALZBURG, INSTEAD OF THE BRITS.
THIS WASN'T A GOOD IDEA AFTER ALL. PEOPLE ARE LOOKING. YOU'RE WAY TOO YOUNG FOR THIS KIND OF JOB.
BULLSHIT.
LOOK AROUND, TOLIVER. COMPARED TO SOME OF THE OTHERS HERE, I'M OLD.
...AND I'M NOT EVEN A "WORKING GIRL."
I MEANT WITH RESPECT TO DANGER, KID, NOT... FOR SCUM LIKE KRAUSE, ONE MORE DEAD BODY HERE OR THERE DOESN'T MEAN A THING.
WE'RE JUST HERE TO HAVE A DRINK! AND A BITE...
BURP!
I DON'T HAVE A PHOTO OF KRAUSE. YOU'LL HAVE TO POINT HIM OUT, WHICH COULD BE RISKY.
RISKY?
IT'S NOT AS IF I HAVE TO DANCE ON THE TABLE WHILE I'M AT IT, IS IT? SWEET JESUS, TOLIVER, DO YOU THINK I'M DUMB?
ACTUALLY...

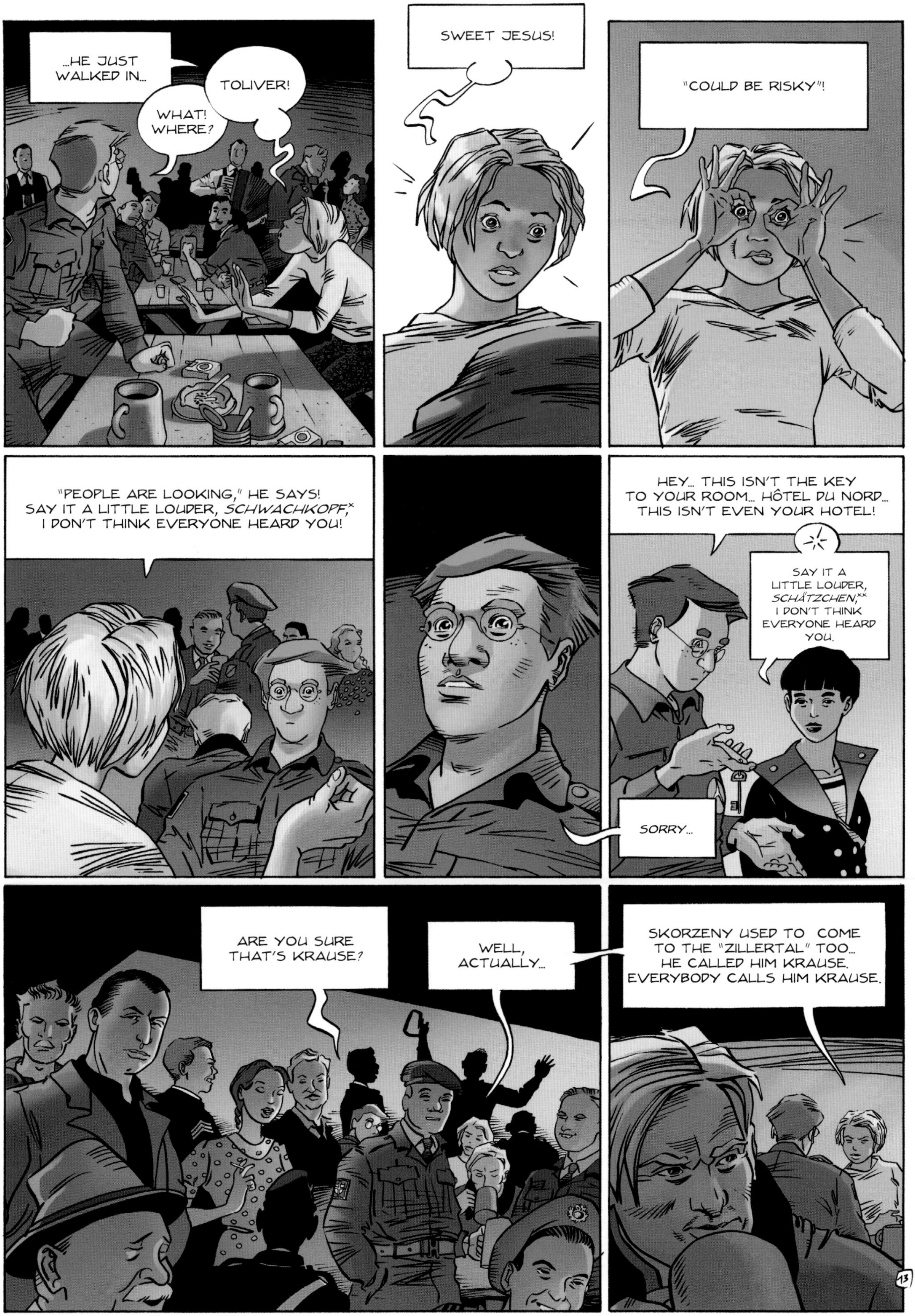
...HE JUST WALKED IN...
TOLIVER!
WHAT! WHERE?
SWEET JESUS!
"COULD BE RISKY"!
"PEOPLE ARE LOOKING," HE SAYS! SAY IT A LITTLE LOUDER, SCHWACHKOPF,^x I DON'T THINK EVERYONE HEARD YOU!
HEY... THIS ISN'T THE KEY TO YOUR ROOM... HÔTEL DU NORD... THIS ISN'T EVEN YOUR HOTEL!
SAY IT A LITTLE LOUDER, SCHÄTZCHEN,^xx I DON'T THINK EVERYONE HEARD YOU.
SORRY...
ARE YOU SURE THAT'S KRAUSE?
WELL, ACTUALLY...
SKORZENY USED TO COME TO THE "ZILLERTAL" TOO... HE CALLED HIM KRAUSE. EVERYBODY CALLS HIM KRAUSE.
13

^x You idiot.
^xx Darling.

I DOUBT THE KRAUSE I'M LOOKING FOR WOULD USE HIS REAL NAME. COULD BE DANGEROUS.

UNLESS THEY'RE AMONG *ALTE KAMERADEN*...*

HUH?

THEN IT WOULD MAKE SENSE. IN THAT CASE, IT'S BETTER FOR EVERYONE TO KNOW EXACTLY WHO'S WHO.

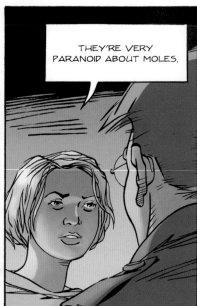

THEY'RE VERY PARANOID ABOUT MOLES.

Somewhere between Tarvisio and Graz...

WHOA!

CHECKPOINT.

HMM... BRITS, IT LOOKS LIKE.

*Old chums.

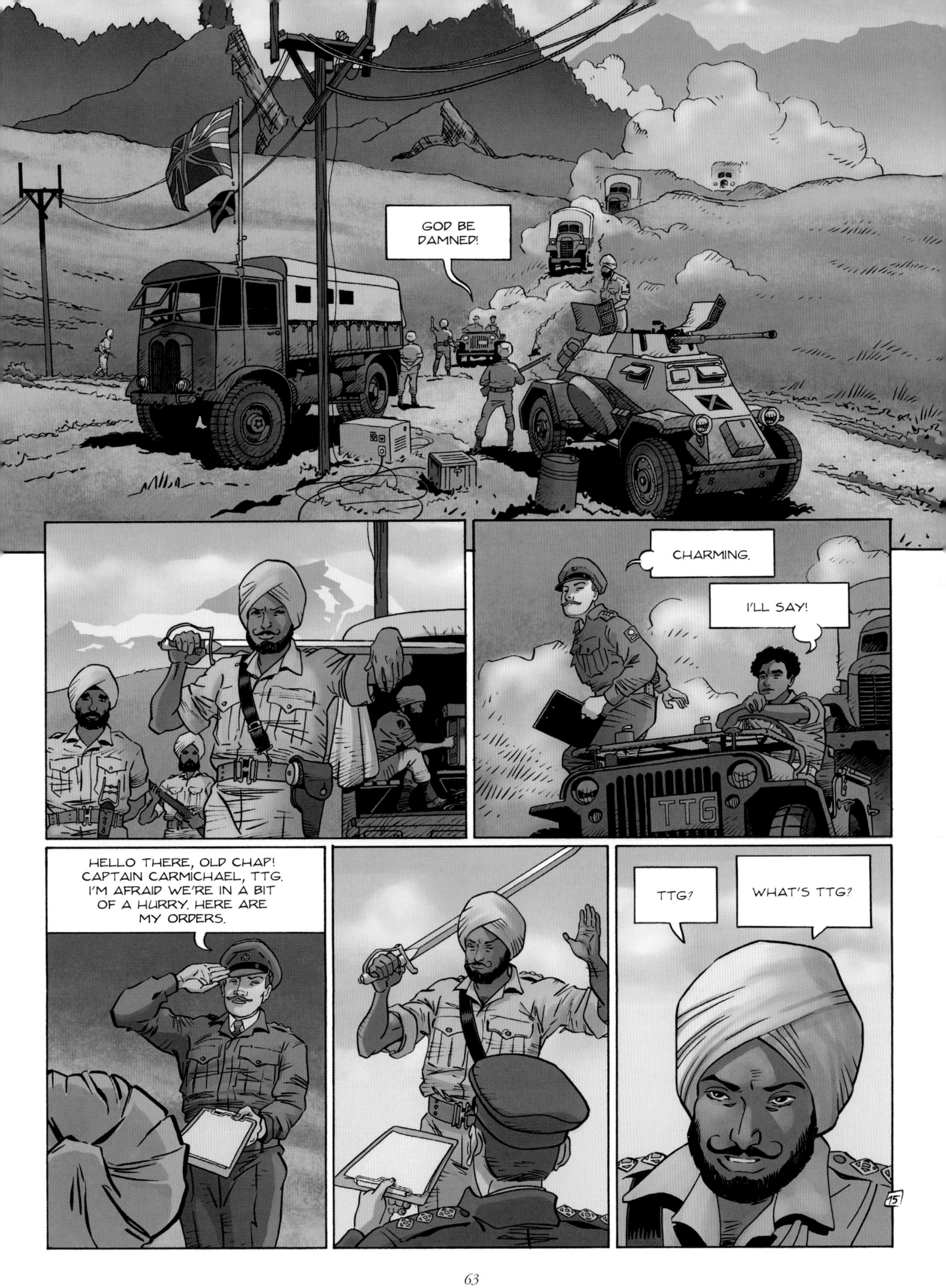
GOD BE DAMNED!
CHARMING.
I'LL SAY!
TTG
HELLO THERE, OLD CHAP! CAPTAIN CARMICHAEL, TTG. I'M AFRAID WE'RE IN A BIT OF A HURRY. HERE ARE MY ORDERS.
TTG?
WHAT'S TTG?
15

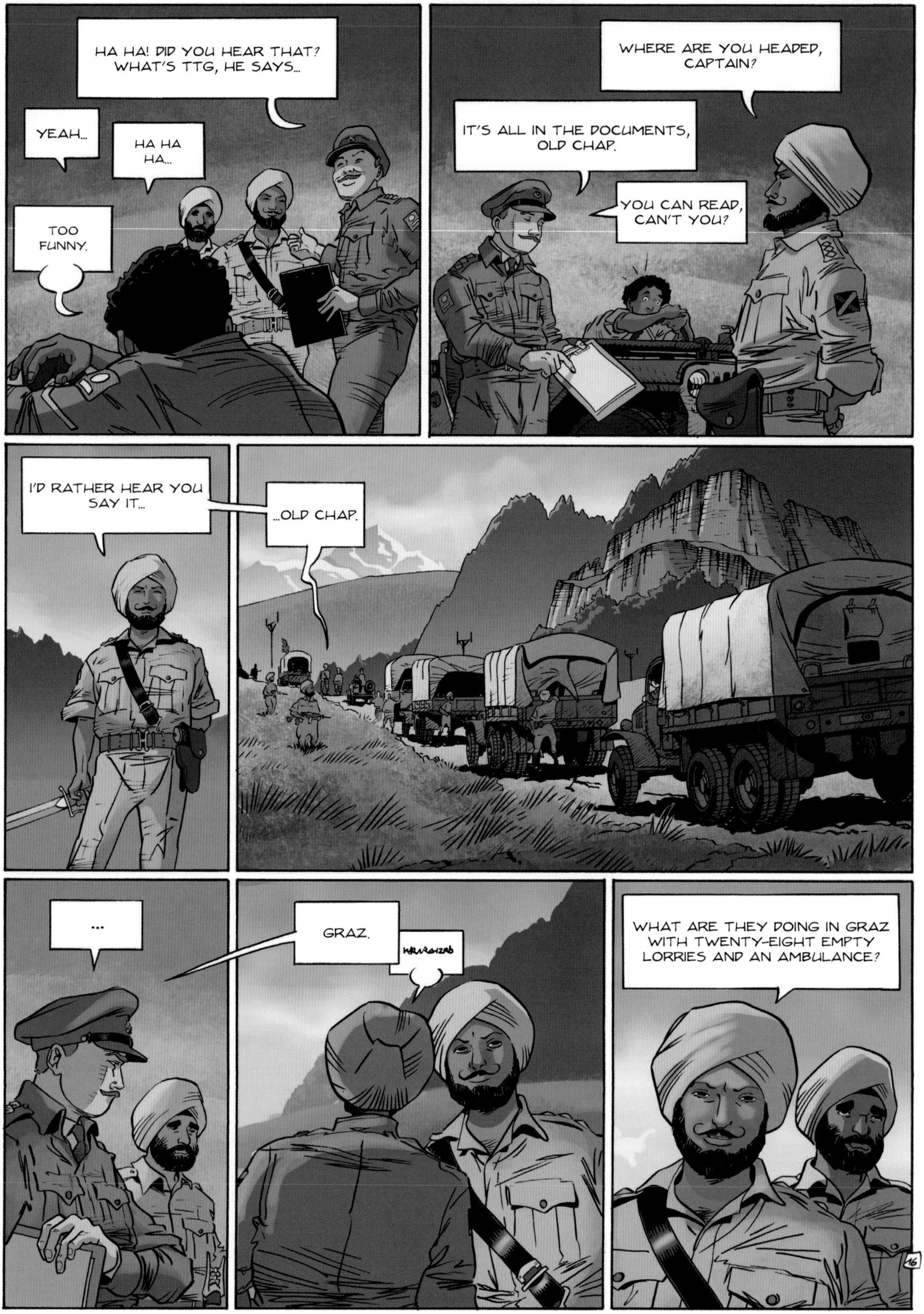
HA HA! DID YOU HEAR THAT? WHAT'S TTG, HE SAYS...
YEAH...
HA HA HA...
TOO FUNNY.
WHERE ARE YOU HEADED, CAPTAIN?
IT'S ALL IN THE DOCUMENTS, OLD CHAP.
YOU CAN READ, CAN'T YOU?
I'D RATHER HEAR YOU SAY IT...
...OLD CHAP.
...
GRAZ.
WHAT ARE THEY DOING IN GRAZ WITH TWENTY-EIGHT EMPTY LORRIES AND AN AMBULANCE?

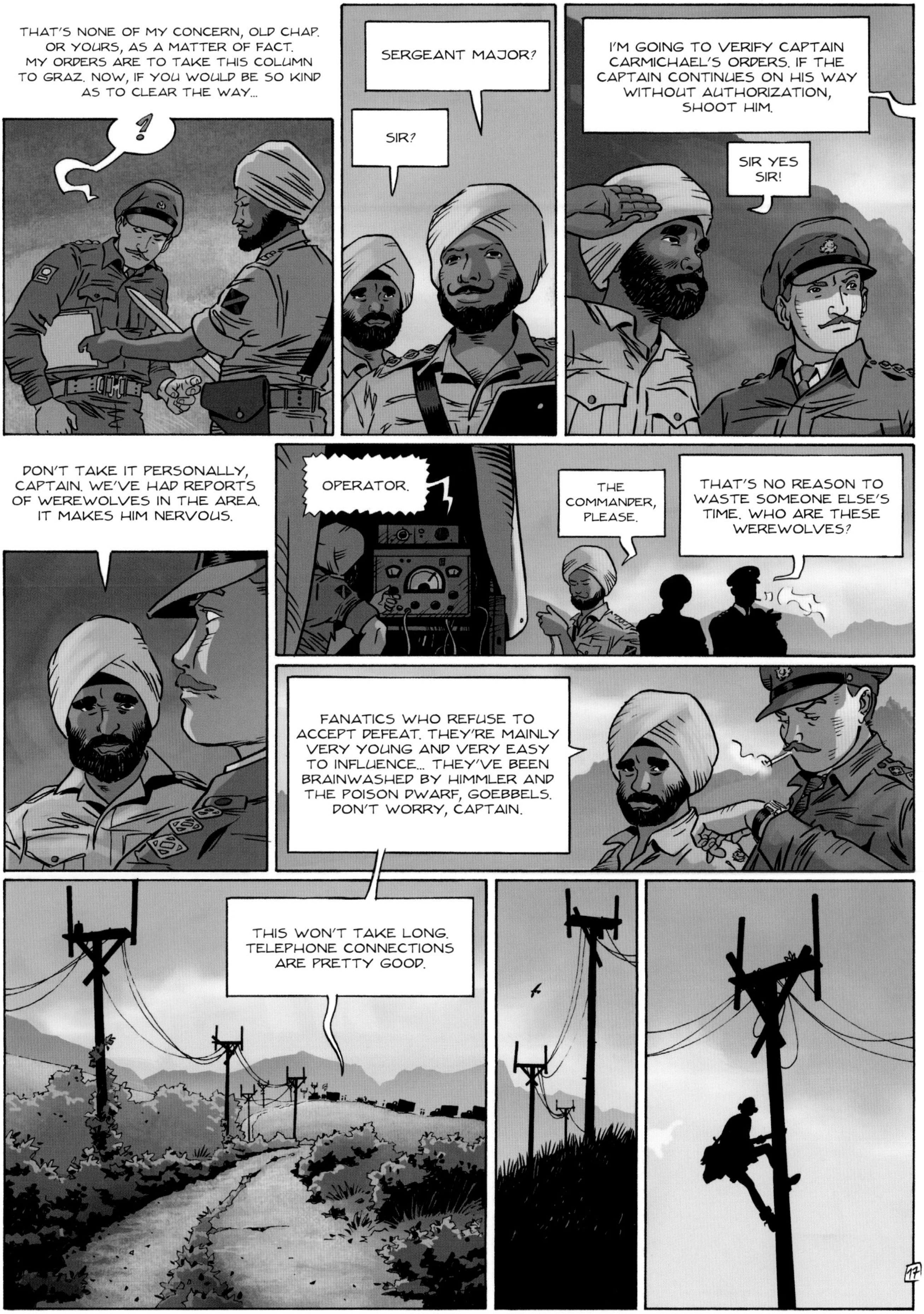
THAT'S NONE OF MY CONCERN, OLD CHAP. OR YOURS, AS A MATTER OF FACT. MY ORDERS ARE TO TAKE THIS COLUMN TO GRAZ. NOW, IF YOU WOULD BE SO KIND AS TO CLEAR THE WAY...
?
SERGEANT MAJOR?
SIR?
I'M GOING TO VERIFY CAPTAIN CARMICHAEL'S ORDERS. IF THE CAPTAIN CONTINUES ON HIS WAY WITHOUT AUTHORIZATION, SHOOT HIM.
SIR YES SIR!
DON'T TAKE IT PERSONALLY, CAPTAIN. WE'VE HAD REPORTS OF WEREWOLVES IN THE AREA. IT MAKES HIM NERVOUS.
OPERATOR.
THE COMMANDER, PLEASE.
THAT'S NO REASON TO WASTE SOMEONE ELSE'S TIME. WHO ARE THESE WEREWOLVES?
FANATICS WHO REFUSE TO ACCEPT DEFEAT. THEY'RE MAINLY VERY YOUNG AND VERY EASY TO INFLUENCE... THEY'VE BEEN BRAINWASHED BY HIMMLER AND THE POISON DWARF, GOEBBELS. DON'T WORRY, CAPTAIN.
THIS WON'T TAKE LONG. TELEPHONE CONNECTIONS ARE PRETTY GOOD.
17

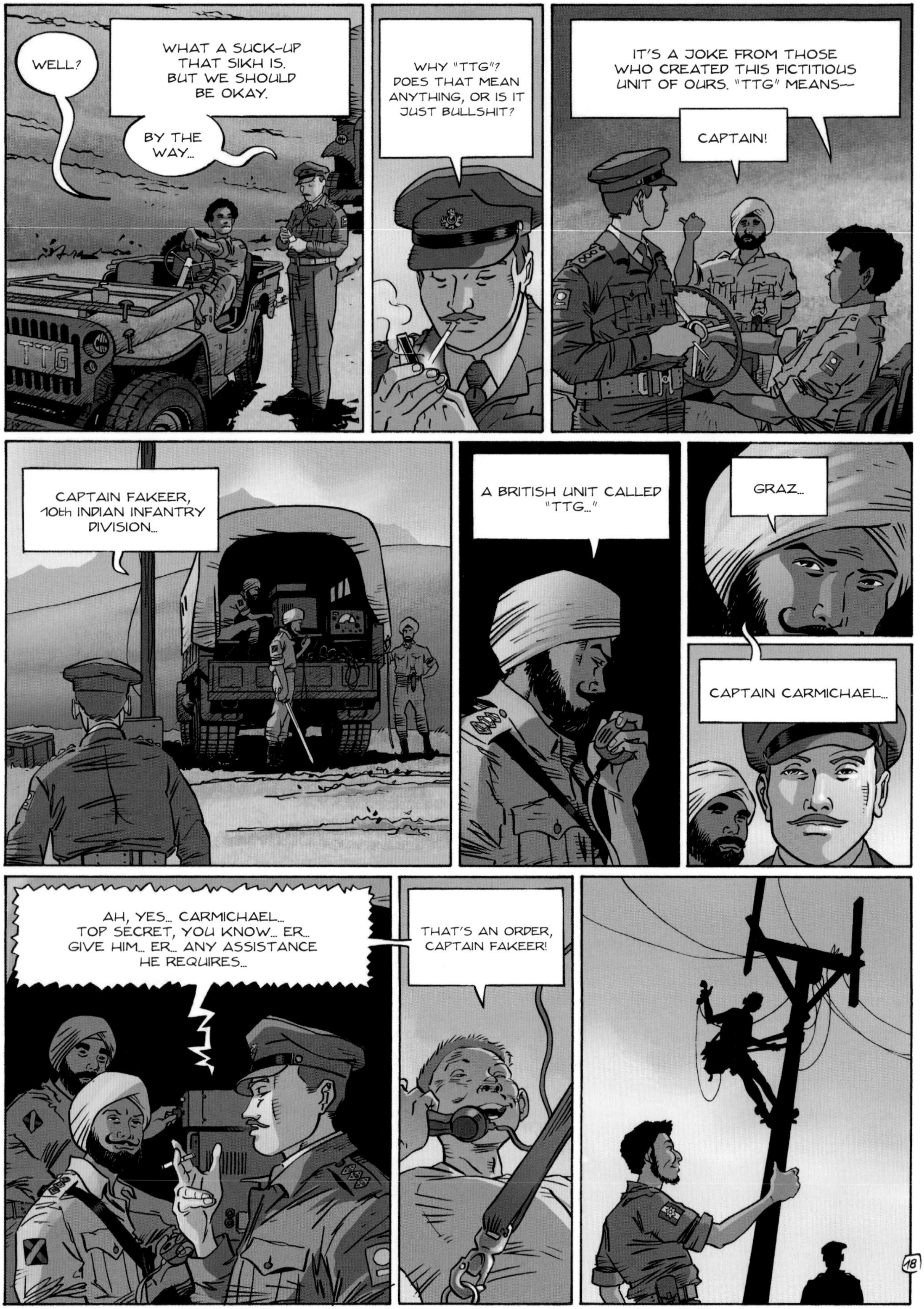
WELL?
WHAT A SUCK-UP THAT SIKH IS. BUT WE SHOULD BE OKAY.
BY THE WAY...
WHY "TTG"? DOES THAT MEAN ANYTHING, OR IS IT JUST BULLSHIT?
IT'S A JOKE FROM THOSE WHO CREATED THIS FICTITIOUS UNIT OF OURS. "TTG" MEANS--
CAPTAIN!
CAPTAIN FAKEER, 10th INDIAN INFANTRY DIVISION...
A BRITISH UNIT CALLED "TTG..."
GRAZ...
CAPTAIN CARMICHAEL...
AH, YES... CARMICHAEL... TOP SECRET, YOU KNOW... ER... GIVE HIM... ER... ANY ASSISTANCE HE REQUIRES...
THAT'S AN ORDER, CAPTAIN FAKEER!
TTG
18

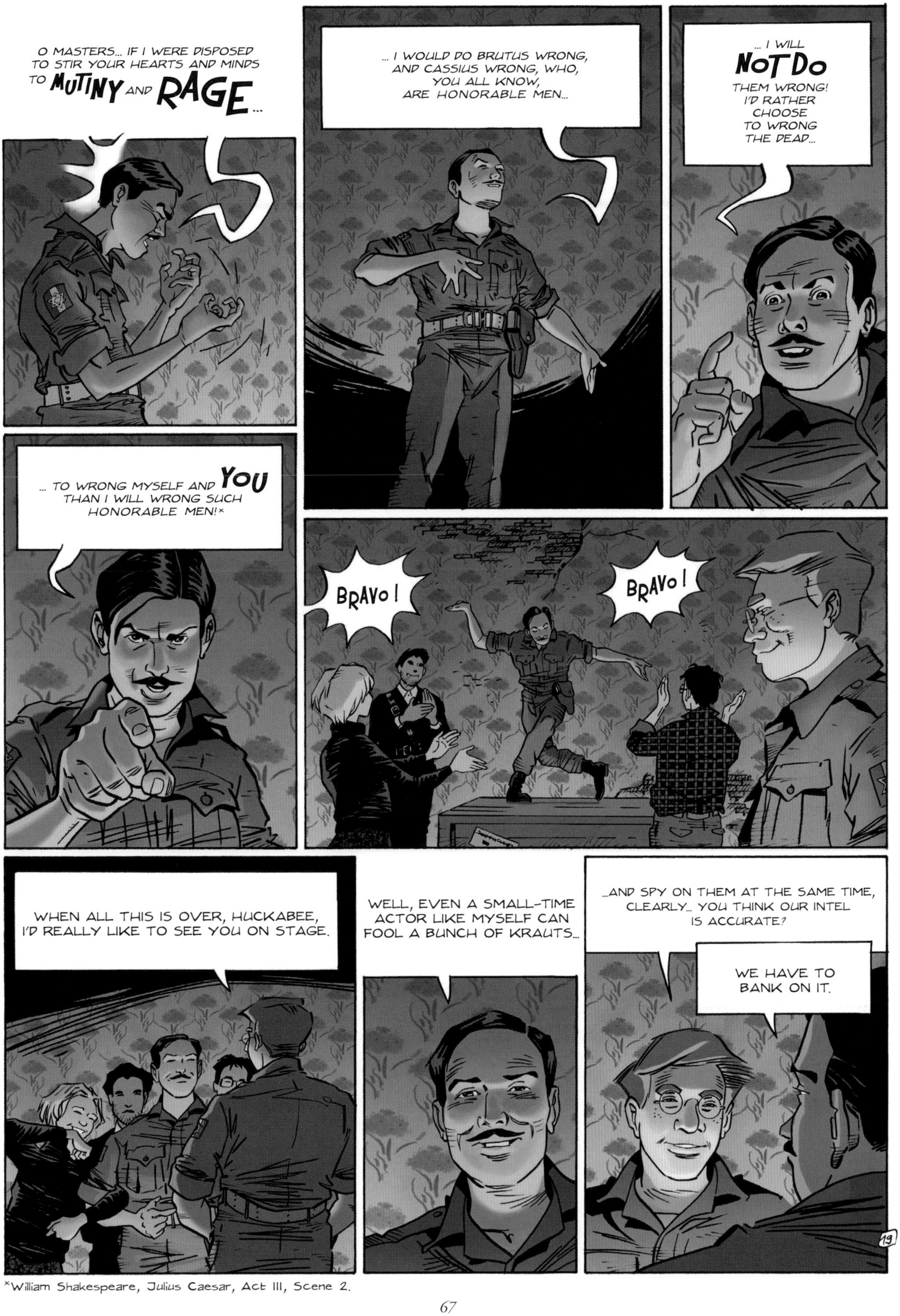
O MASTERS... IF I WERE DISPOSED TO STIR YOUR HEARTS AND MINDS TO MUTINY AND RAGE...
... I WOULD DO BRUTUS WRONG, AND CASSIUS WRONG, WHO, YOU ALL KNOW, ARE HONORABLE MEN...
... I WILL NOT DO THEM WRONG! I'D RATHER CHOOSE TO WRONG THE DEAD...
... TO WRONG MYSELF AND YOU THAN I WILL WRONG SUCH HONORABLE MEN!*
BRAVO!
BRAVO!
WHEN ALL THIS IS OVER, HUCKABEE, I'D REALLY LIKE TO SEE YOU ON STAGE.
WELL, EVEN A SMALL-TIME ACTOR LIKE MYSELF CAN FOOL A BUNCH OF KRAUTS...
...AND SPY ON THEM AT THE SAME TIME, CLEARLY... YOU THINK OUR INTEL IS ACCURATE?
WE HAVE TO BANK ON IT.
19

*William Shakespeare, Julius Caesar, Act III, Scene 2.

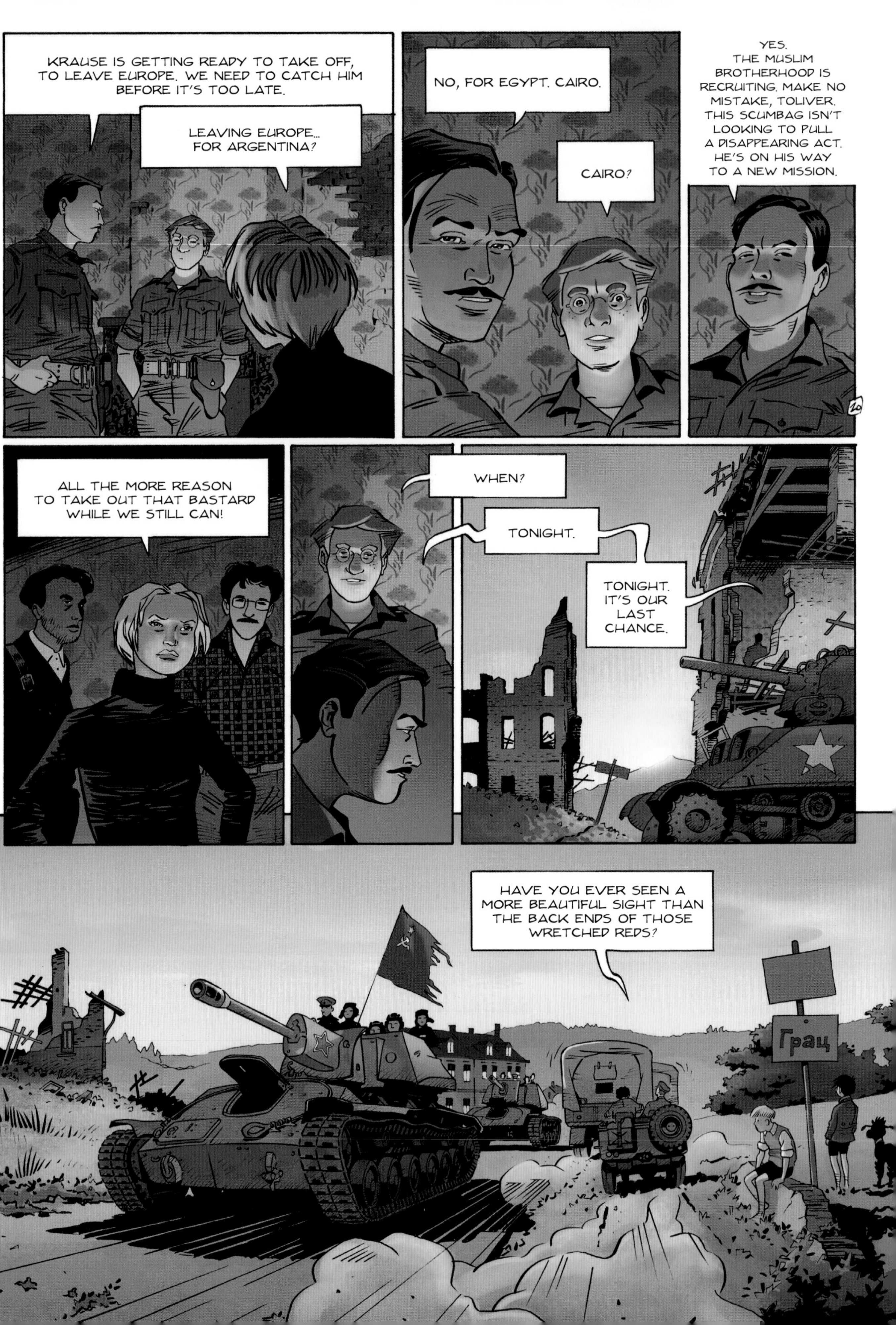
KRAUSE IS GETTING READY TO TAKE OFF, TO LEAVE EUROPE. WE NEED TO CATCH HIM BEFORE IT'S TOO LATE.
LEAVING EUROPE... FOR ARGENTINA?
NO, FOR EGYPT. CAIRO.
CAIRO?
YES. THE MUSLIM BROTHERHOOD IS RECRUITING. MAKE NO MISTAKE, TOLIVER. THIS SCUMBAG ISN'T LOOKING TO PULL A DISAPPEARING ACT. HE'S ON HIS WAY TO A NEW MISSION.
ALL THE MORE REASON TO TAKE OUT THAT BASTARD WHILE WE STILL CAN!
WHEN?
TONIGHT.
TONIGHT. IT'S OUR LAST CHANCE.
HAVE YOU EVER SEEN A MORE BEAUTIFUL SIGHT THAN THE BACK ENDS OF THOSE WRETCHED REDS?
Грац

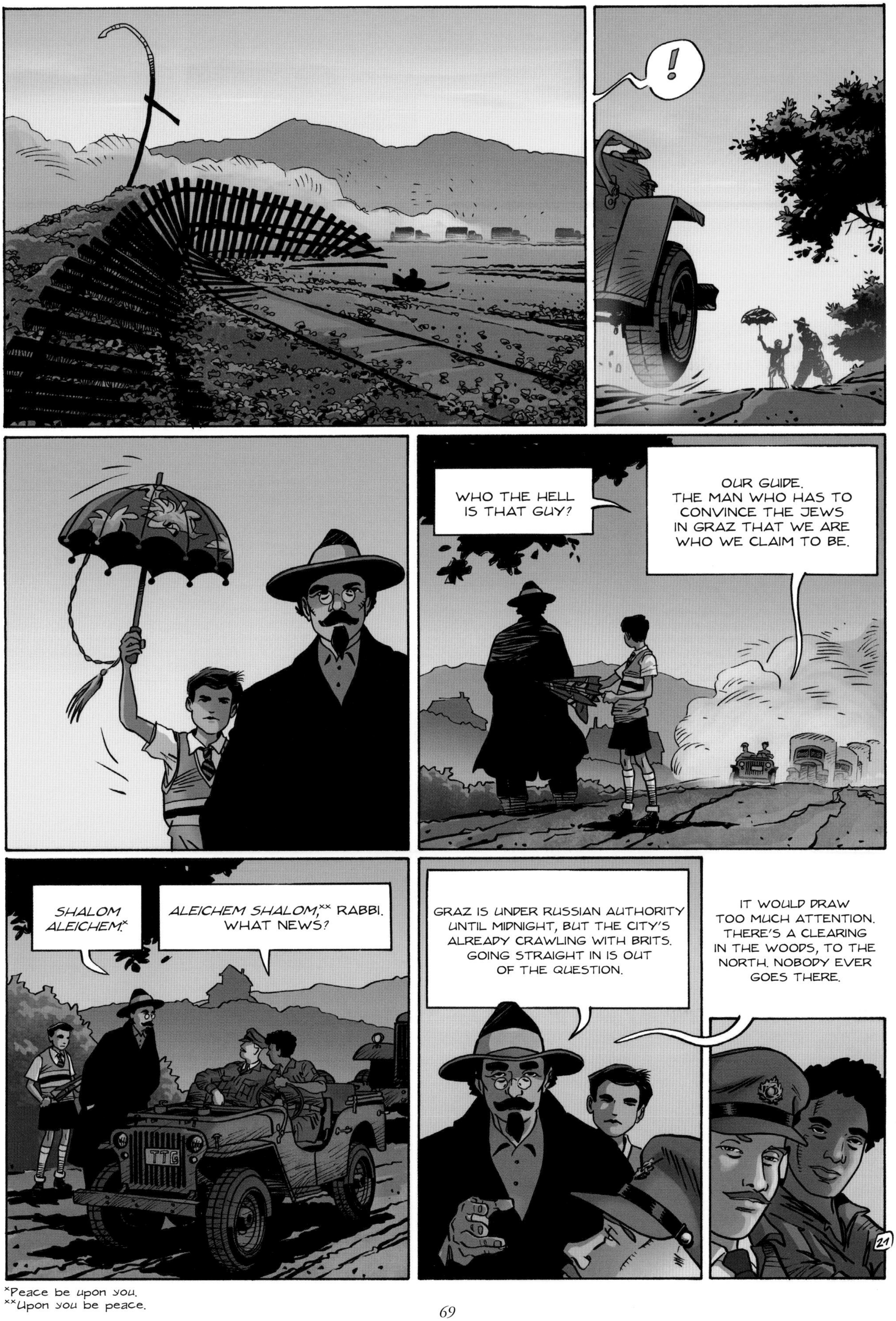
!
WHO THE HELL IS THAT GUY?
OUR GUIDE. THE MAN WHO HAS TO CONVINCE THE JEWS IN GRAZ THAT WE ARE WHO WE CLAIM TO BE.
SHALOM ALEICHEM.[x]
ALEICHEM SHALOM,[xx] RABBI. WHAT NEWS?
GRAZ IS UNDER RUSSIAN AUTHORITY UNTIL MIDNIGHT, BUT THE CITY'S ALREADY CRAWLING WITH BRITS. GOING STRAIGHT IN IS OUT OF THE QUESTION.
IT WOULD DRAW TOO MUCH ATTENTION. THERE'S A CLEARING IN THE WOODS, TO THE NORTH. NOBODY EVER GOES THERE.
21

[x]Peace be upon you.
[xx]Upon you be peace.

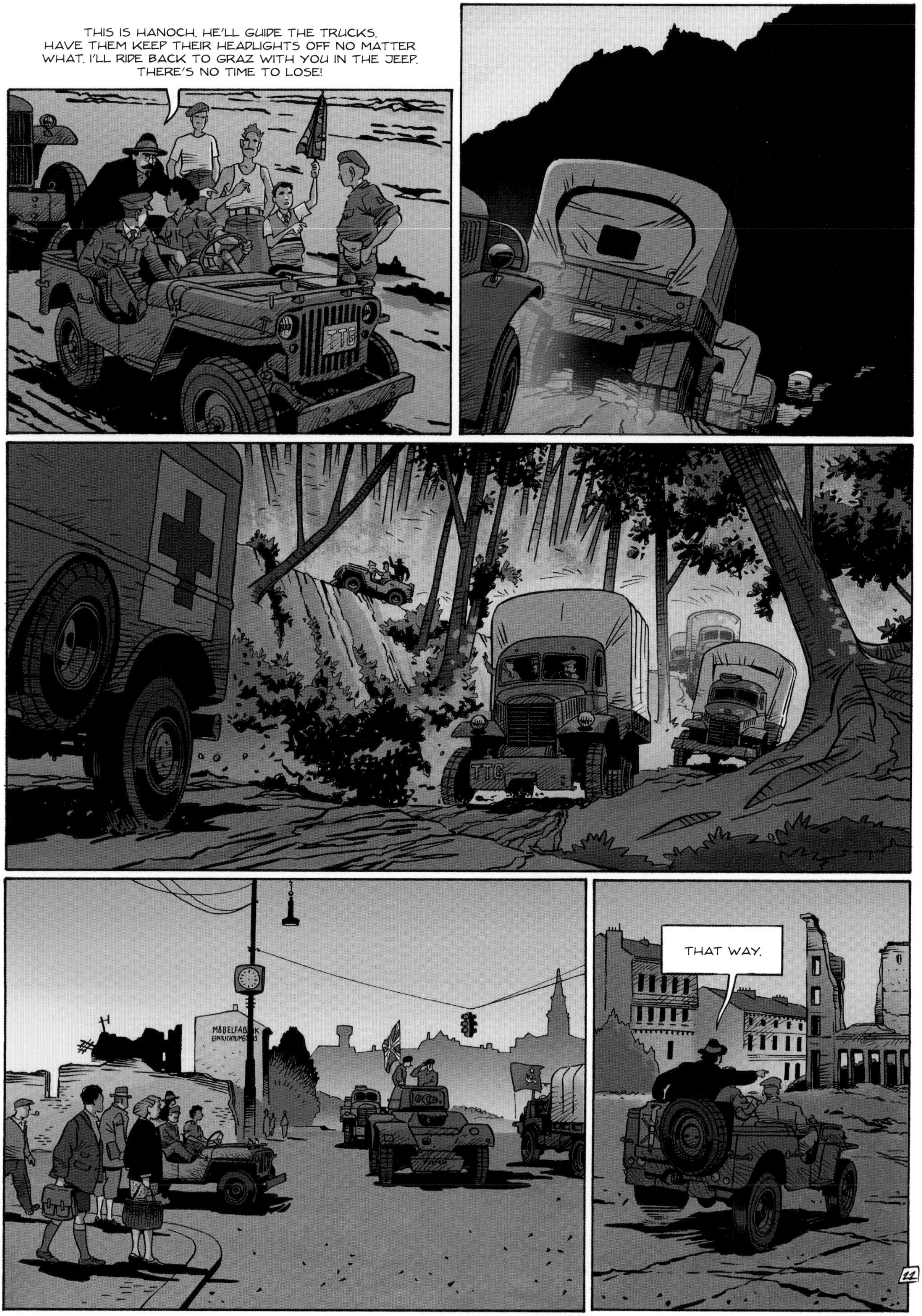
THIS IS HANOCH. HE'LL GUIDE THE TRUCKS. HAVE THEM KEEP THEIR HEADLIGHTS OFF NO MATTER WHAT. I'LL RIDE BACK TO GRAZ WITH YOU IN THE JEEP. THERE'S NO TIME TO LOSE!
TTG
TTG
MÖBELFABRIK
EINRICHTUNGSHAUS
THAT WAY.
22

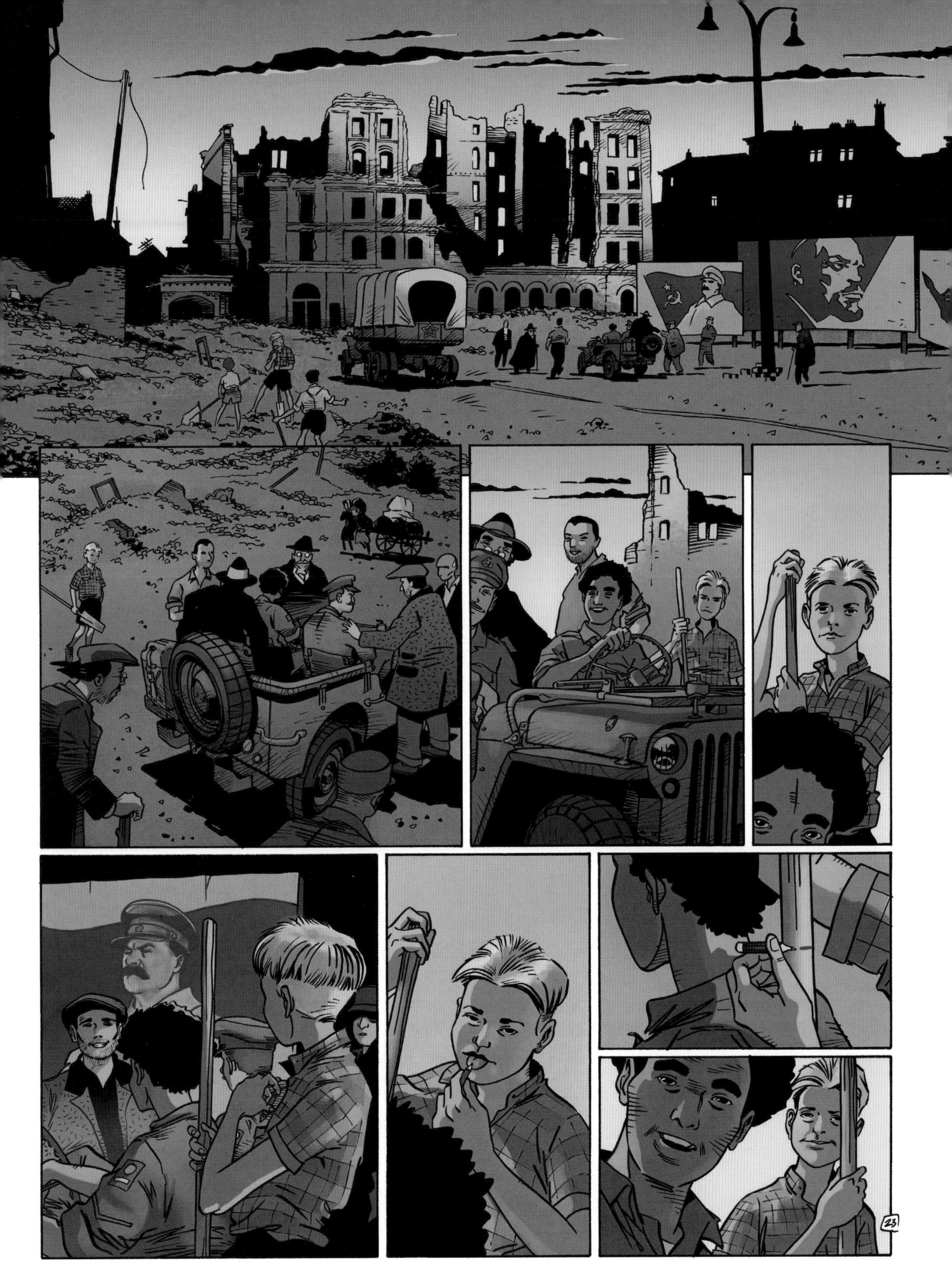
23

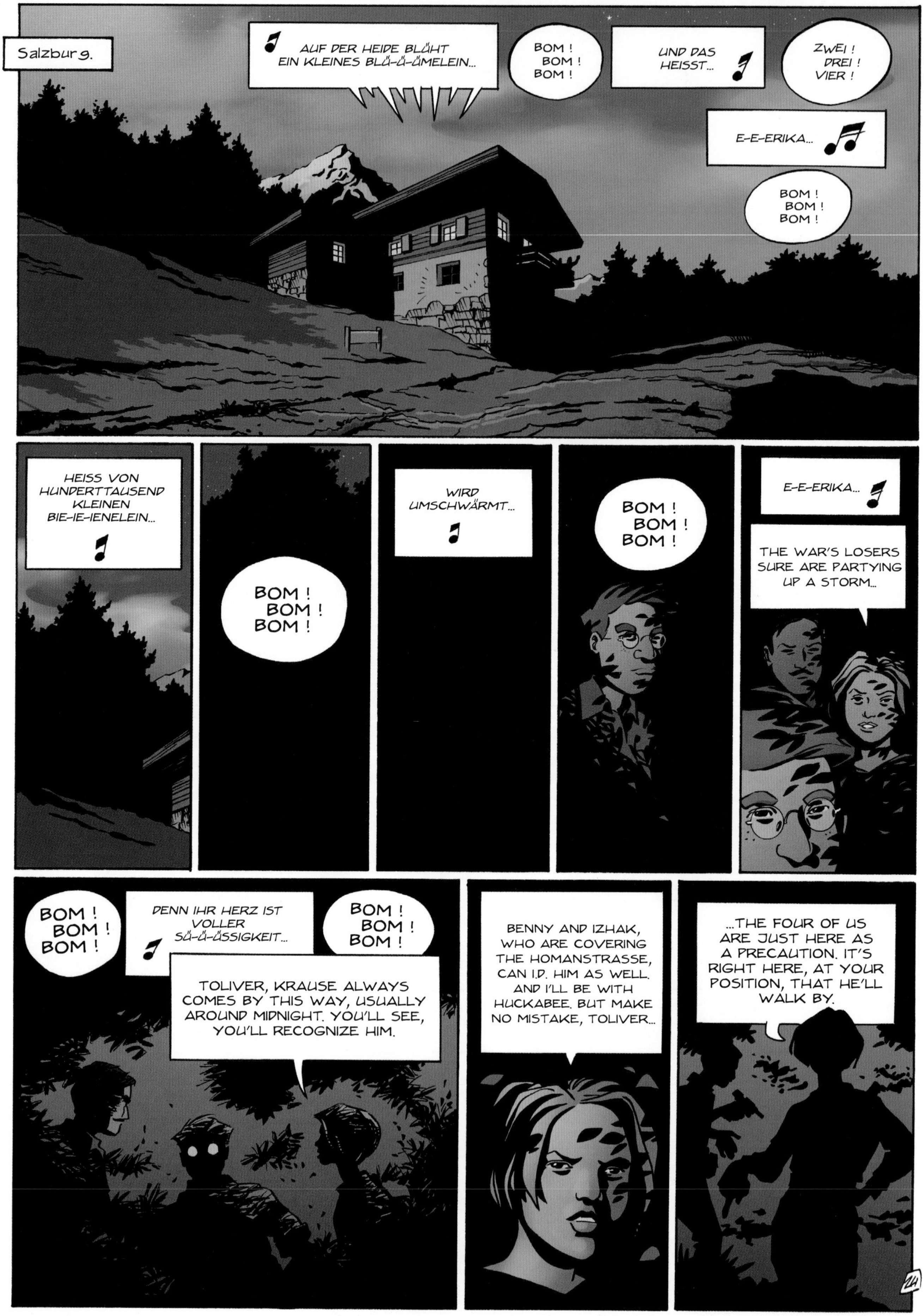
Salzburg.
AUF DER HEIDE BLÜHT EIN KLEINES BLÜ-Ü-ÜMELEIN...
BOM ! BOM ! BOM !
UND DAS HEISST...
ZWEI ! DREI ! VIER !
E-E-ERIKA...
BOM ! BOM ! BOM !
HEISS VON HUNDERTTAUSEND KLEINEN BIE-IE-IENELEIN...
BOM ! BOM ! BOM !
WIRD UMSCHWÄRMT...
BOM ! BOM ! BOM !
E-E-ERIKA...
THE WAR'S LOSERS SURE ARE PARTYING UP A STORM...
BOM ! BOM ! BOM !
DENN IHR HERZ IST VOLLER SÜ-Ü-ÜSSIGKEIT...
BOM ! BOM ! BOM !
TOLIVER, KRAUSE ALWAYS COMES BY THIS WAY, USUALLY AROUND MIDNIGHT. YOU'LL SEE, YOU'LL RECOGNIZE HIM.
BENNY AND IZHAK, WHO ARE COVERING THE HOMANSTRASSE, CAN I.D. HIM AS WELL. AND I'LL BE WITH HUCKABEE. BUT MAKE NO MISTAKE, TOLIVER...
...THE FOUR OF US ARE JUST HERE AS A PRECAUTION. IT'S RIGHT HERE, AT YOUR POSITION, THAT HE'LL WALK BY.
24

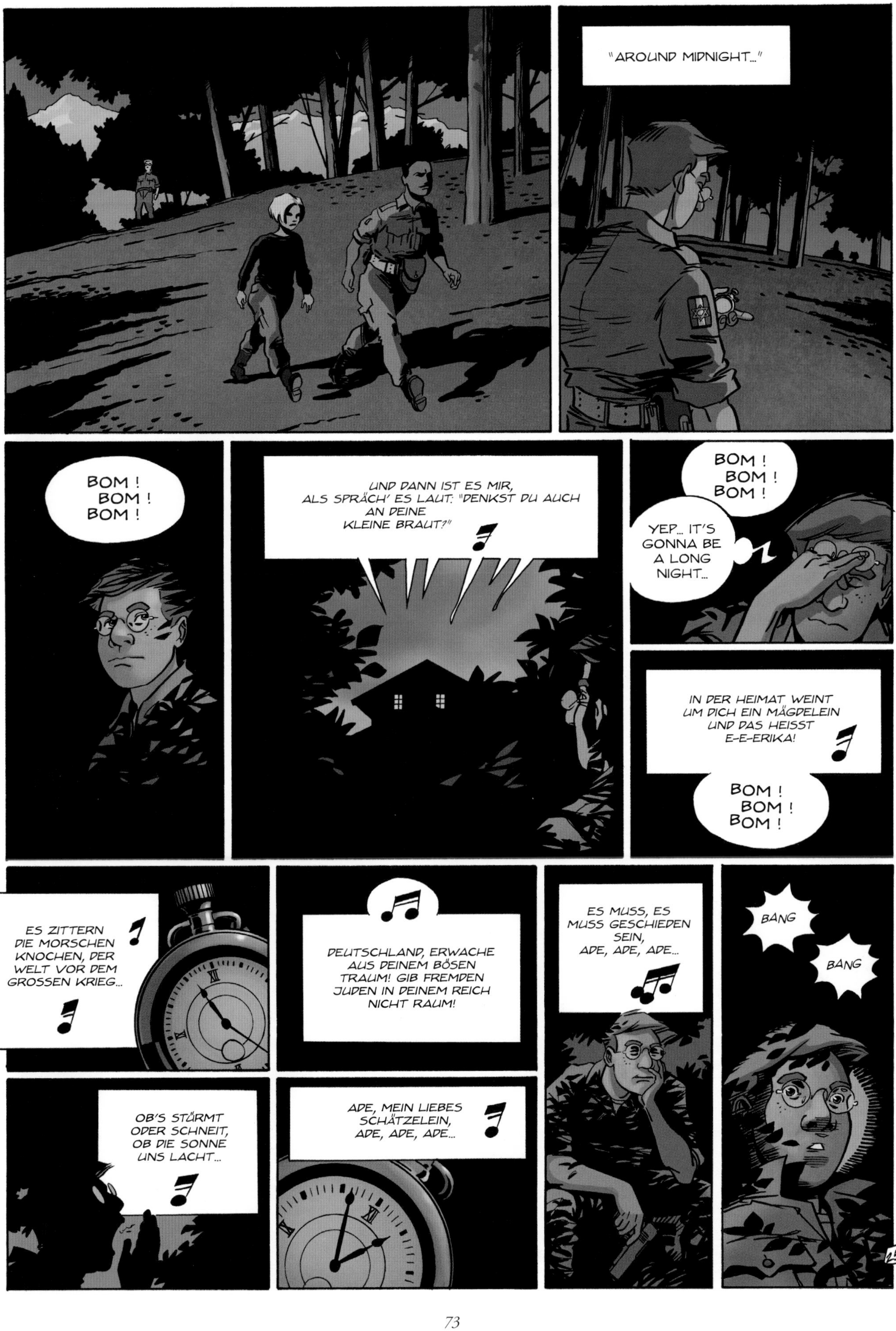

"AROUND MIDNIGHT..."
BOM ! BOM ! BOM !
UND DANN IST ES MIR, ALS SPRÄCH' ES LAUT: "DENKST DU AUCH AN DEINE KLEINE BRAUT?"
BOM ! BOM ! BOM !
YEP... IT'S GONNA BE A LONG NIGHT...
IN DER HEIMAT WEINT UM DICH EIN MÄGDELEIN UND DAS HEISST E-E-ERIKA!
BOM ! BOM ! BOM !
ES ZITTERN DIE MORSCHEN KNOCHEN, DER WELT VOR DEM GROSSEN KRIEG...
DEUTSCHLAND, ERWACHE AUS DEINEM BÖSEN TRAUM! GIB FREMDEN JUDEN IN DEINEM REICH NICHT RAUM!
OB'S STÜRMT ODER SCHNEIT, OB DIE SONNE UNS LACHT...
ADE, MEIN LIEBES SCHÄTZELEIN, ADE, ADE, ADE...
ES MUSS, ES MUSS GESCHIEDEN SEIN, ADE, ADE, ADE...
BANG
BANG
25

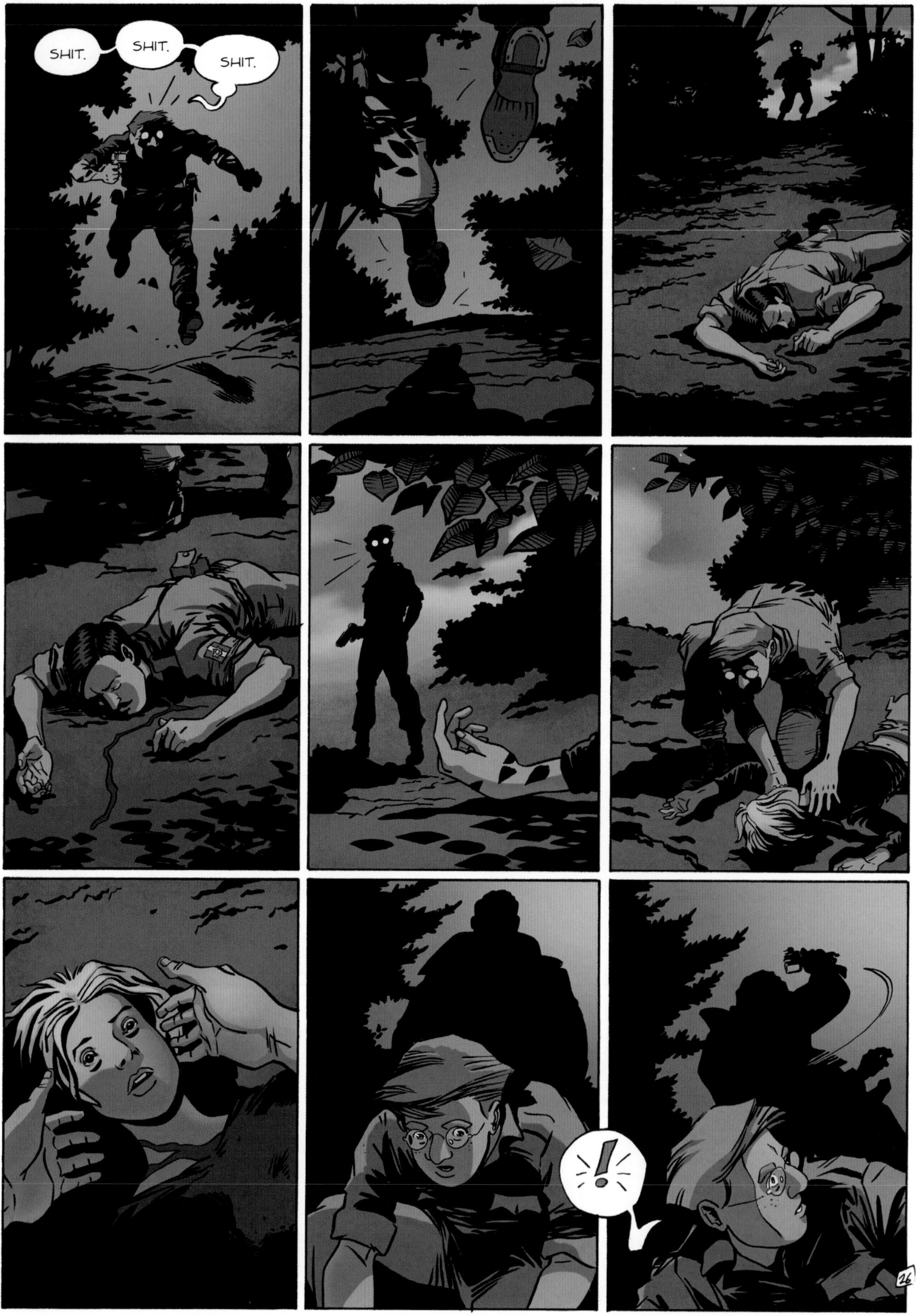
SHIT.
SHIT.
SHIT.
!
26

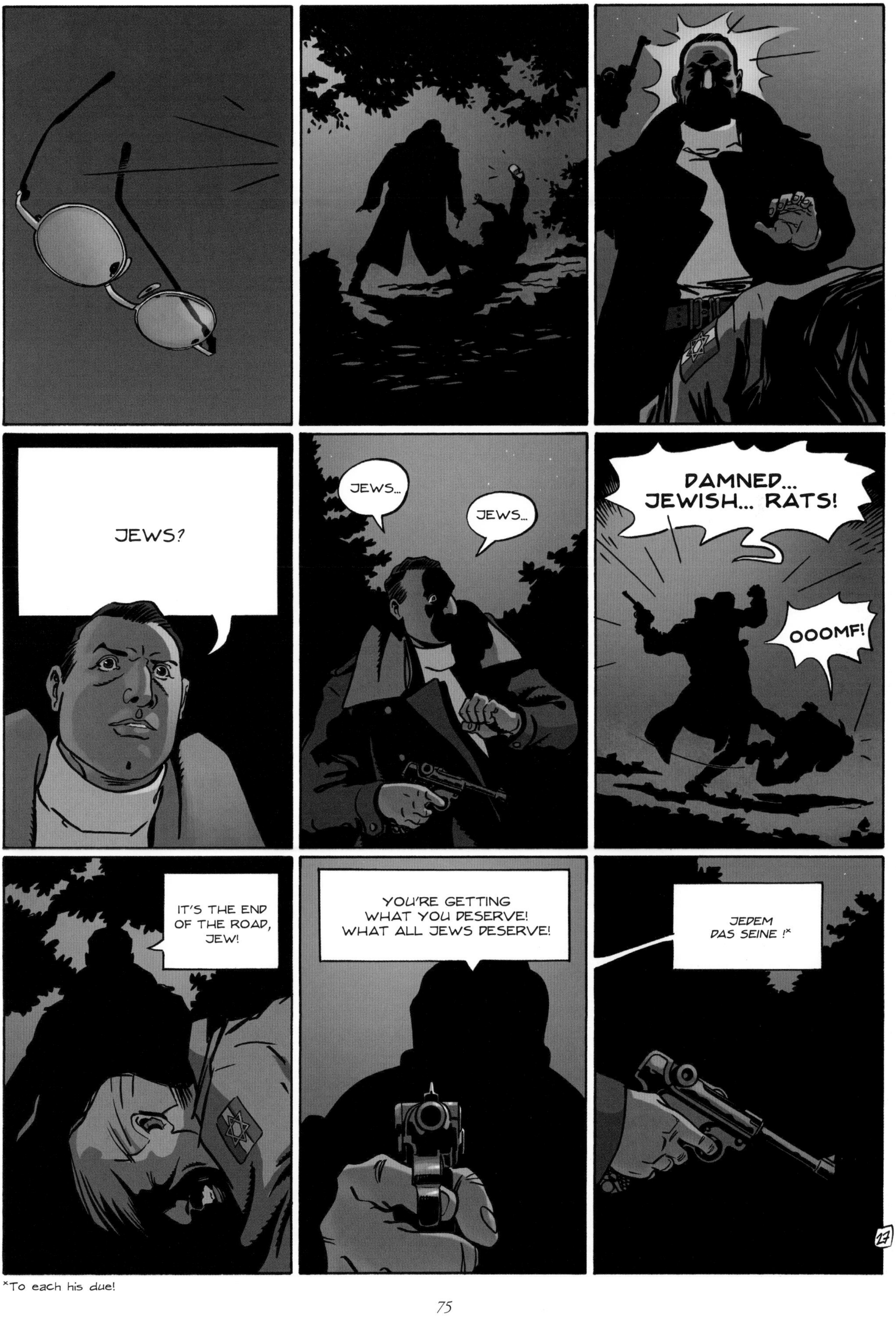
JEWS?
JEWS...
JEWS...
DAMNED... JEWISH... RATS!
OOOMF!
IT'S THE END OF THE ROAD, JEW!
YOU'RE GETTING WHAT YOU DESERVE! WHAT ALL JEWS DESERVE!
JEDEM DAS SEINE !*
17

*To each his due!

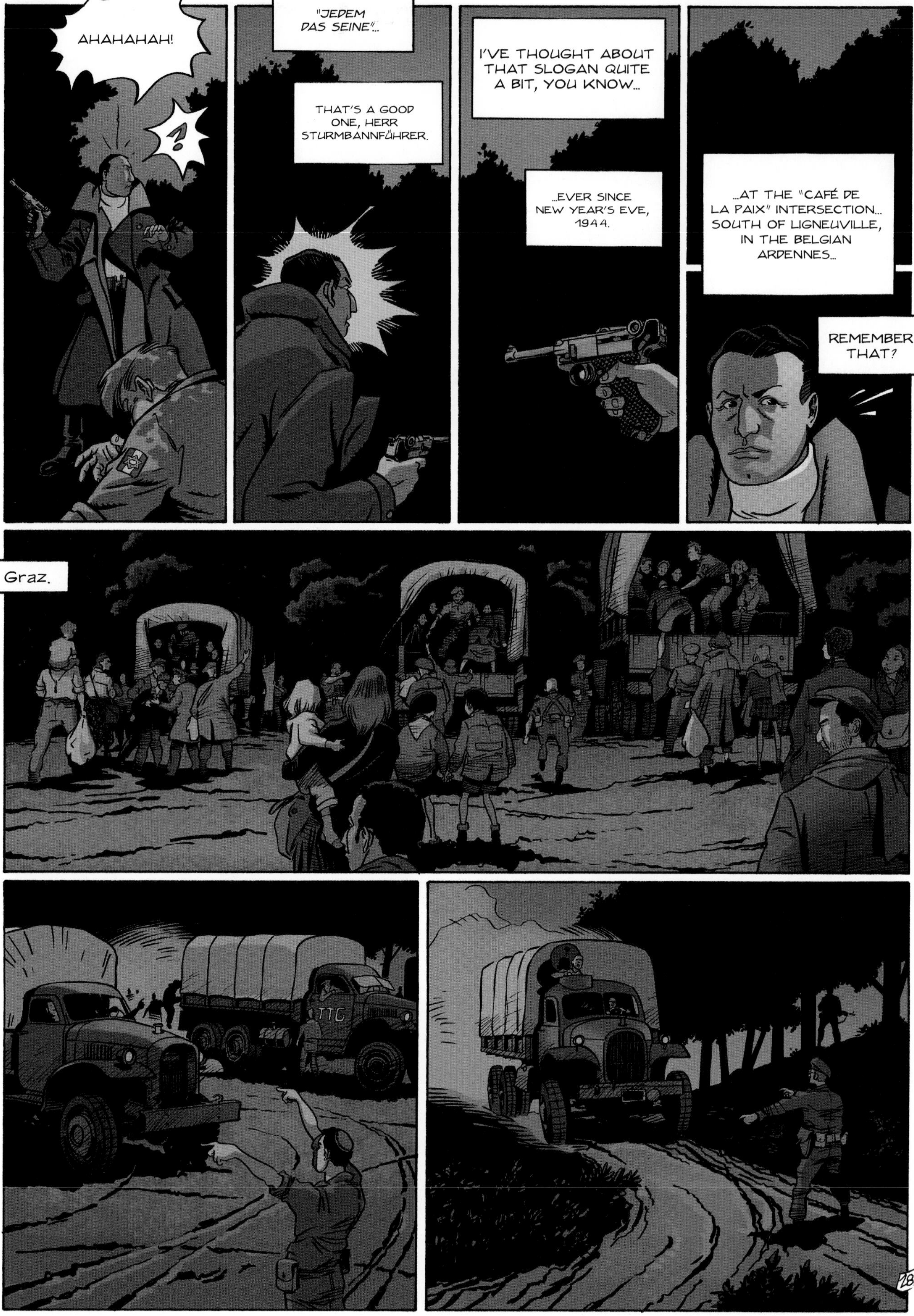
AHAHAHAH!
?
"JEDEM DAS SEINE"...
THAT'S A GOOD ONE, HERR STURMBANNFÜHRER.
I'VE THOUGHT ABOUT THAT SLOGAN QUITE A BIT, YOU KNOW...
...EVER SINCE NEW YEAR'S EVE, 1944.
...AT THE "CAFÉ DE LA PAIX" INTERSECTION... SOUTH OF LIGNEUVILLE, IN THE BELGIAN ARDENNES...
REMEMBER THAT?
Graz.
TTG
28

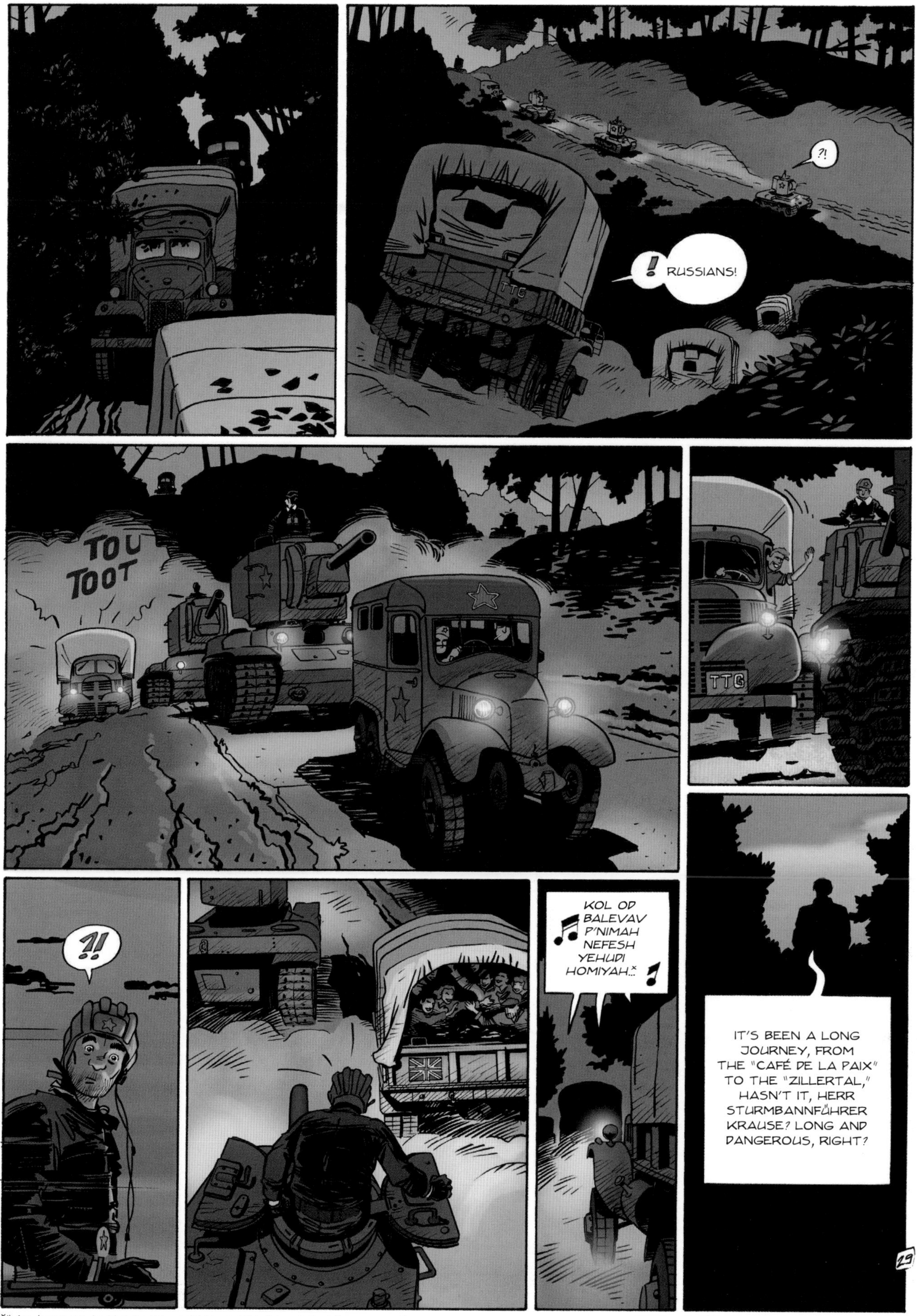
?!
RUSSIANS!
TOU TOOT
TTG
?!
KOL OD BALEVAV P'NIMAH NEFESH YEHUDI HOMIYAH...*
IT'S BEEN A LONG JOURNEY, FROM THE "CAFÉ DE LA PAIX" TO THE "ZILLERTAL," HASN'T IT, HERR STURMBANNFÜHRER KRAUSE? LONG AND DANGEROUS, RIGHT?
29

*"As long as in the heart, within, a Jewish soul still yearns..."

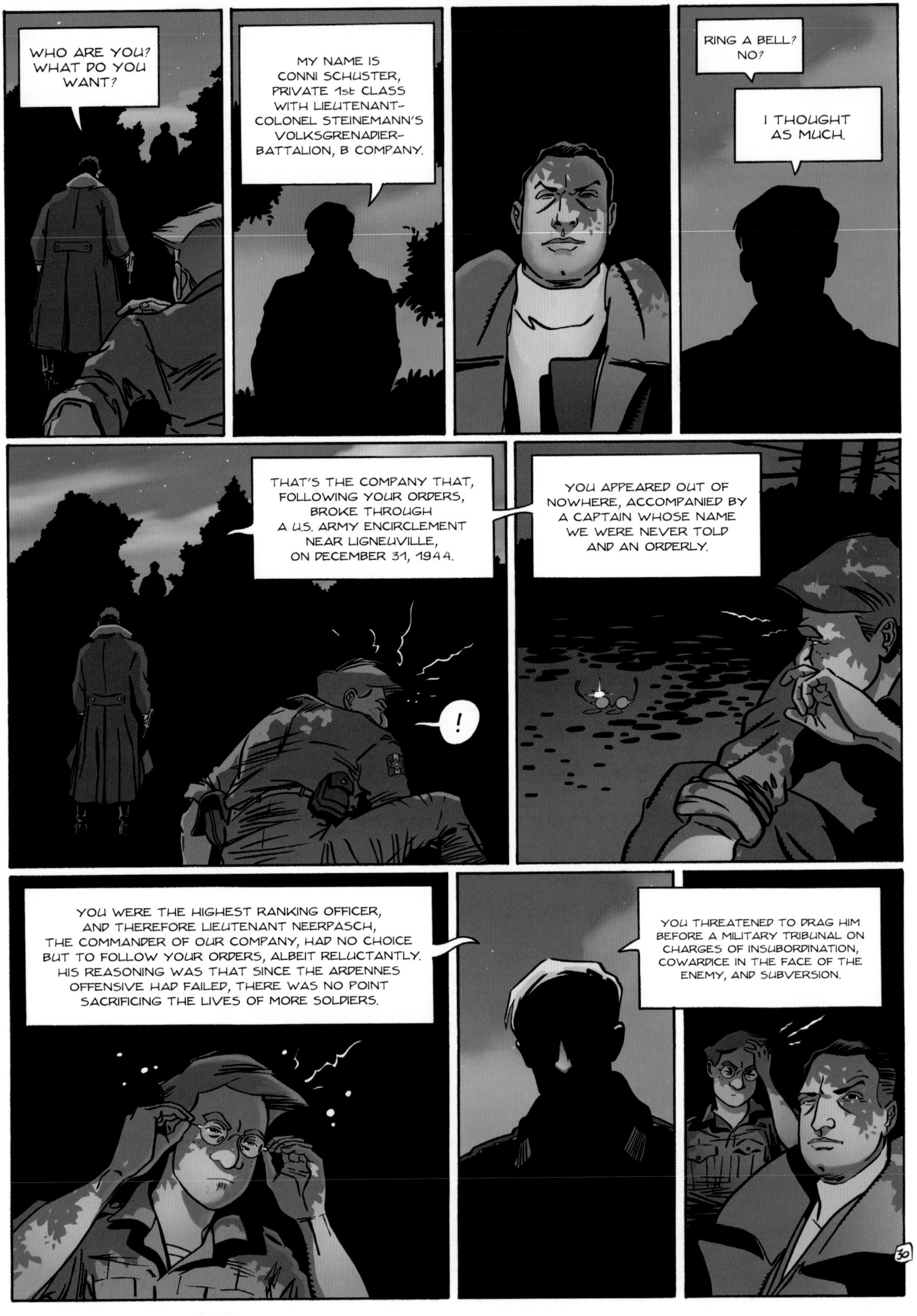
WHO ARE YOU? WHAT DO YOU WANT?
MY NAME IS CONNI SCHUSTER, PRIVATE 1st CLASS WITH LIEUTENANT-COLONEL STEINEMANN'S VOLKSGRENADIER-BATTALION, B COMPANY.
RING A BELL? NO?
I THOUGHT AS MUCH.
THAT'S THE COMPANY THAT, FOLLOWING YOUR ORDERS, BROKE THROUGH A U.S. ARMY ENCIRCLEMENT NEAR LIGNEUVILLE, ON DECEMBER 31, 1944.
!
YOU APPEARED OUT OF NOWHERE, ACCOMPANIED BY A CAPTAIN WHOSE NAME WE WERE NEVER TOLD AND AN ORDERLY.
YOU WERE THE HIGHEST RANKING OFFICER, AND THEREFORE LIEUTENANT NEERPASCH, THE COMMANDER OF OUR COMPANY, HAD NO CHOICE BUT TO FOLLOW YOUR ORDERS, ALBEIT RELUCTANTLY. HIS REASONING WAS THAT SINCE THE ARDENNES OFFENSIVE HAD FAILED, THERE WAS NO POINT SACRIFICING THE LIVES OF MORE SOLDIERS.
YOU THREATENED TO DRAG HIM BEFORE A MILITARY TRIBUNAL ON CHARGES OF INSUBORDINATION, COWARDICE IN THE FACE OF THE ENEMY, AND SUBVERSION.
30

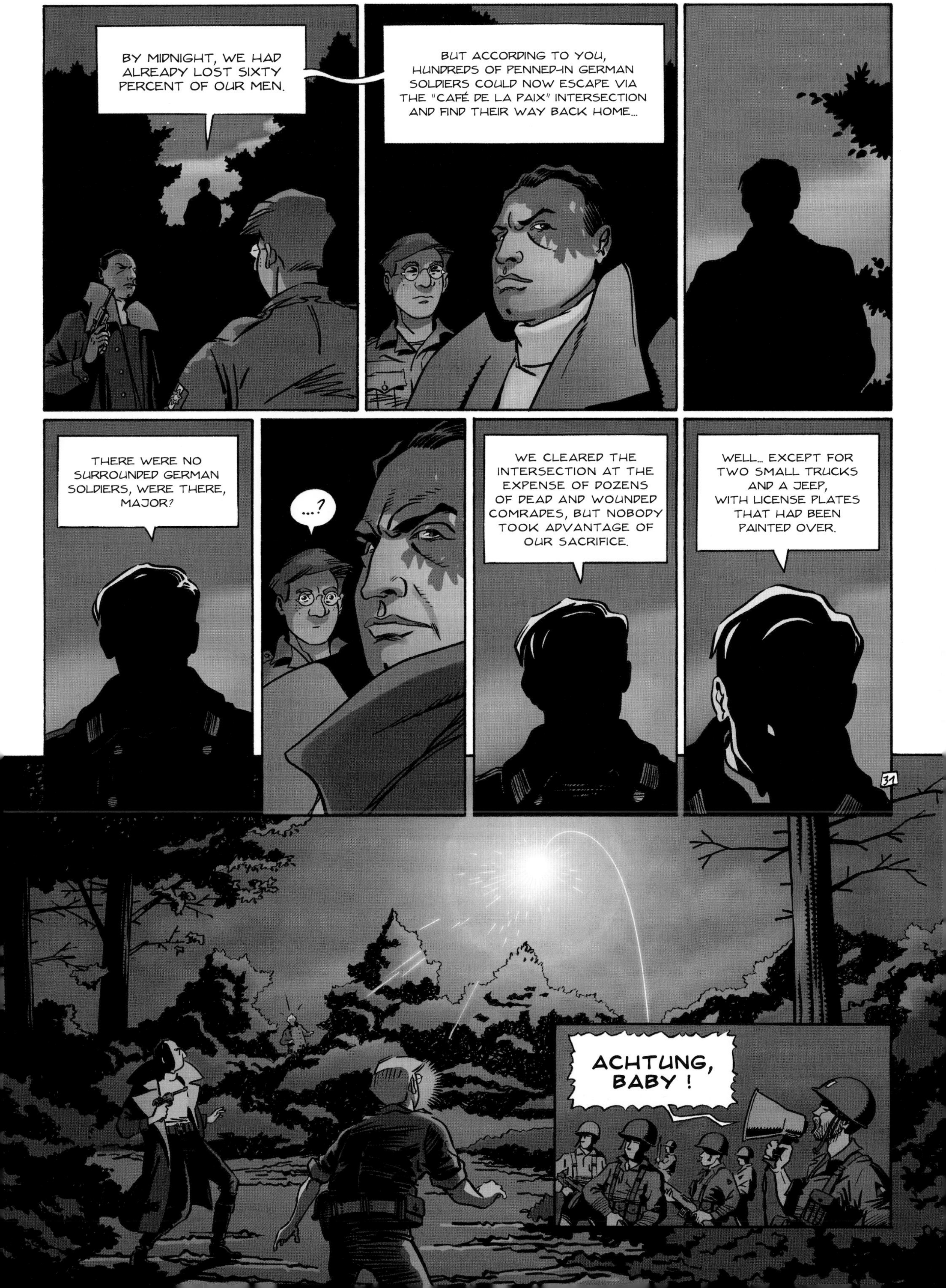
BY MIDNIGHT, WE HAD ALREADY LOST SIXTY PERCENT OF OUR MEN.
BUT ACCORDING TO YOU, HUNDREDS OF PENNED-IN GERMAN SOLDIERS COULD NOW ESCAPE VIA THE "CAFÉ DE LA PAIX" INTERSECTION AND FIND THEIR WAY BACK HOME...
THERE WERE NO SURROUNDED GERMAN SOLDIERS, WERE THERE, MAJOR?
...?
WE CLEARED THE INTERSECTION AT THE EXPENSE OF DOZENS OF DEAD AND WOUNDED COMRADES, BUT NOBODY TOOK ADVANTAGE OF OUR SACRIFICE.
WELL... EXCEPT FOR TWO SMALL TRUCKS AND A JEEP, WITH LICENSE PLATES THAT HAD BEEN PAINTED OVER.
ACHTUNG, BABY !

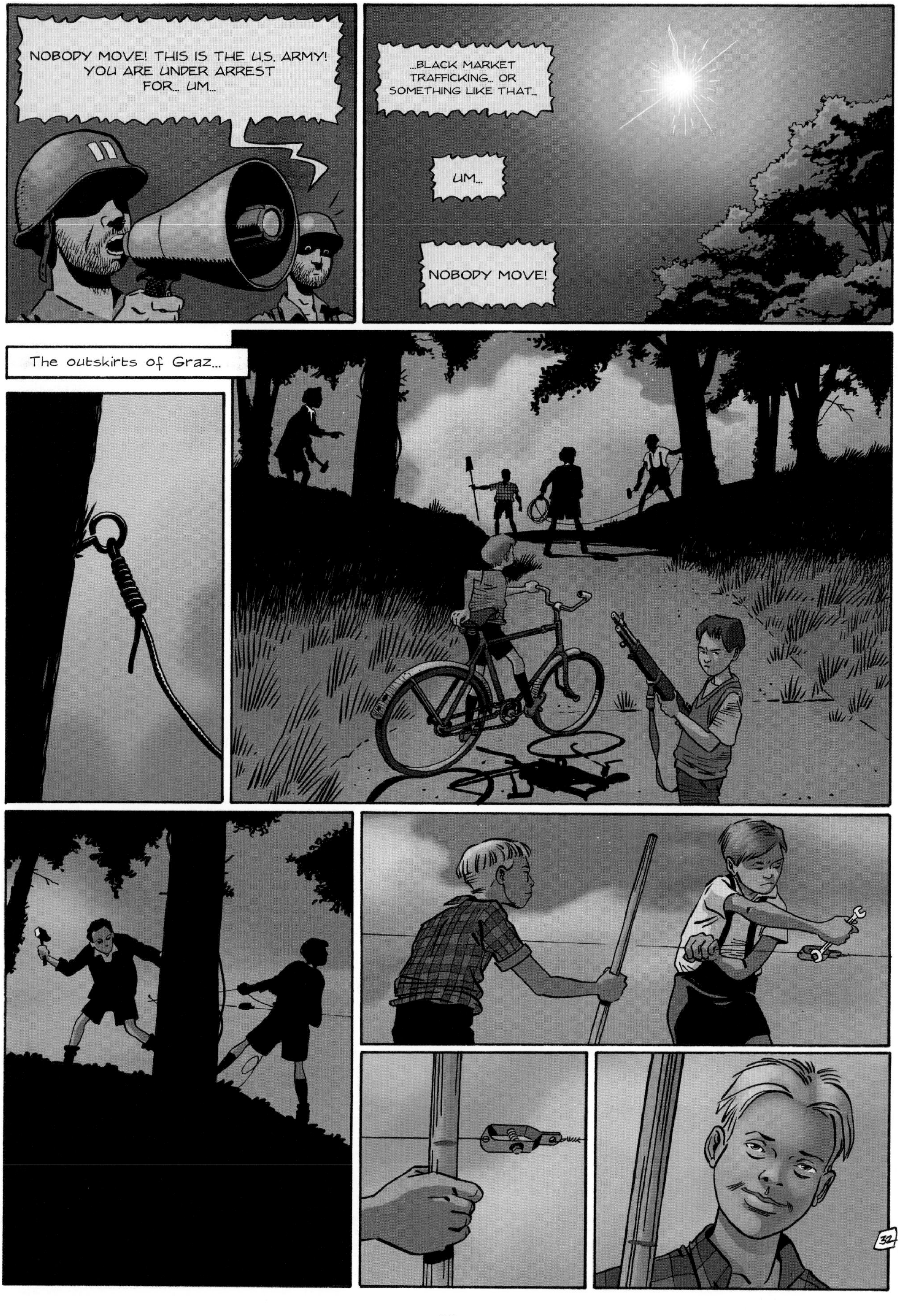
NOBODY MOVE! THIS IS THE U.S. ARMY! YOU ARE UNDER ARREST FOR... UM...
...BLACK MARKET TRAFFICKING... OR SOMETHING LIKE THAT...
UM...
NOBODY MOVE!
The outskirts of Graz...
32

HA HA HA, DID YOU HEAR THAT? WHAT'S THE TTG, HE SAYS...

CAPTAIN CARMICHAEL...

WHO ARE THOSE CIVILIANS IN YOUR TRUCKS, CAPTAIN?

CIVILIANS?

PRISONERS OF WAR, OLD CHAP, PRISONERS OF WAR!

?!

WE CAN'T GO ON LIKE THIS. THESE CHECKPOINTS ARE COSTING US A LOT OF TIME, AND EVEN CARMICHAEL WON'T BE ABLE TO BULLSHIT HIS WAY OUT OF IT EACH TIME.

WE HAVE TO FIND A DIFFERENT WAY IN. AROUND THE BRITS.

WON'T BE EASY. THEY'RE ADVANCING ON GRAZ FROM ALL SIDES.

NOT FROM THE EAST. WE HAVE TO GO AROUND THEM. WE'RE BETTER OFF WITH THE RUSSIANS THAN WE ARE WITH THE BRITS. THE RUSSIANS WILL MOST LIKELY LET A BRITISH COLUMN THROUGH WITHOUT MAKING A FUSS.

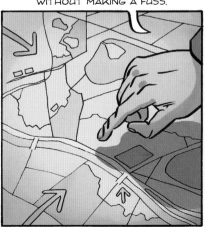

SHLOMO, YOU TAKE THE AMBULANCE AND TRY THIS ROUTE.

ARI... JEEP THREE... THIS ROAD HERE.

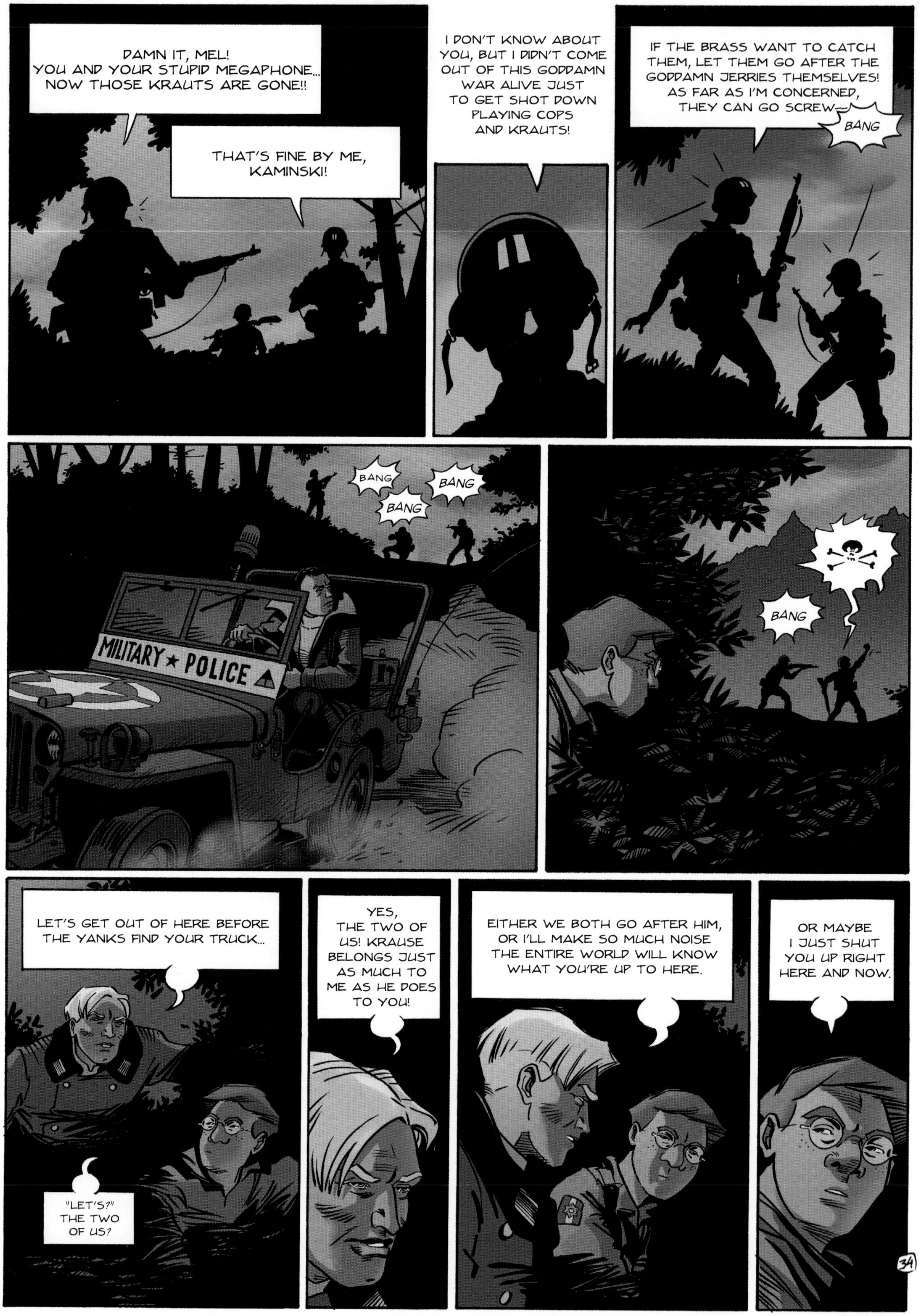
DAMN IT, MEL! YOU AND YOUR STUPID MEGAPHONE... NOW THOSE KRAUTS ARE GONE!!
THAT'S FINE BY ME, KAMINSKI!
I DON'T KNOW ABOUT YOU, BUT I DIDN'T COME OUT OF THIS GODDAMN WAR ALIVE JUST TO GET SHOT DOWN PLAYING COPS AND KRAUTS!
IF THE BRASS WANT TO CATCH THEM, LET THEM GO AFTER THE GODDAMN JERRIES THEMSELVES! AS FAR AS I'M CONCERNED, THEY CAN GO SCREW—
BANG
BANG
BANG
BANG
MILITARY ★ POLICE
BANG
LET'S GET OUT OF HERE BEFORE THE YANKS FIND YOUR TRUCK...
"LET'S?" THE TWO OF US?
YES, THE TWO OF US! KRAUSE BELONGS JUST AS MUCH TO ME AS HE DOES TO YOU!
EITHER WE BOTH GO AFTER HIM, OR I'LL MAKE SO MUCH NOISE THE ENTIRE WORLD WILL KNOW WHAT YOU'RE UP TO HERE.
OR MAYBE I JUST SHUT YOU UP RIGHT HERE AND NOW.
34

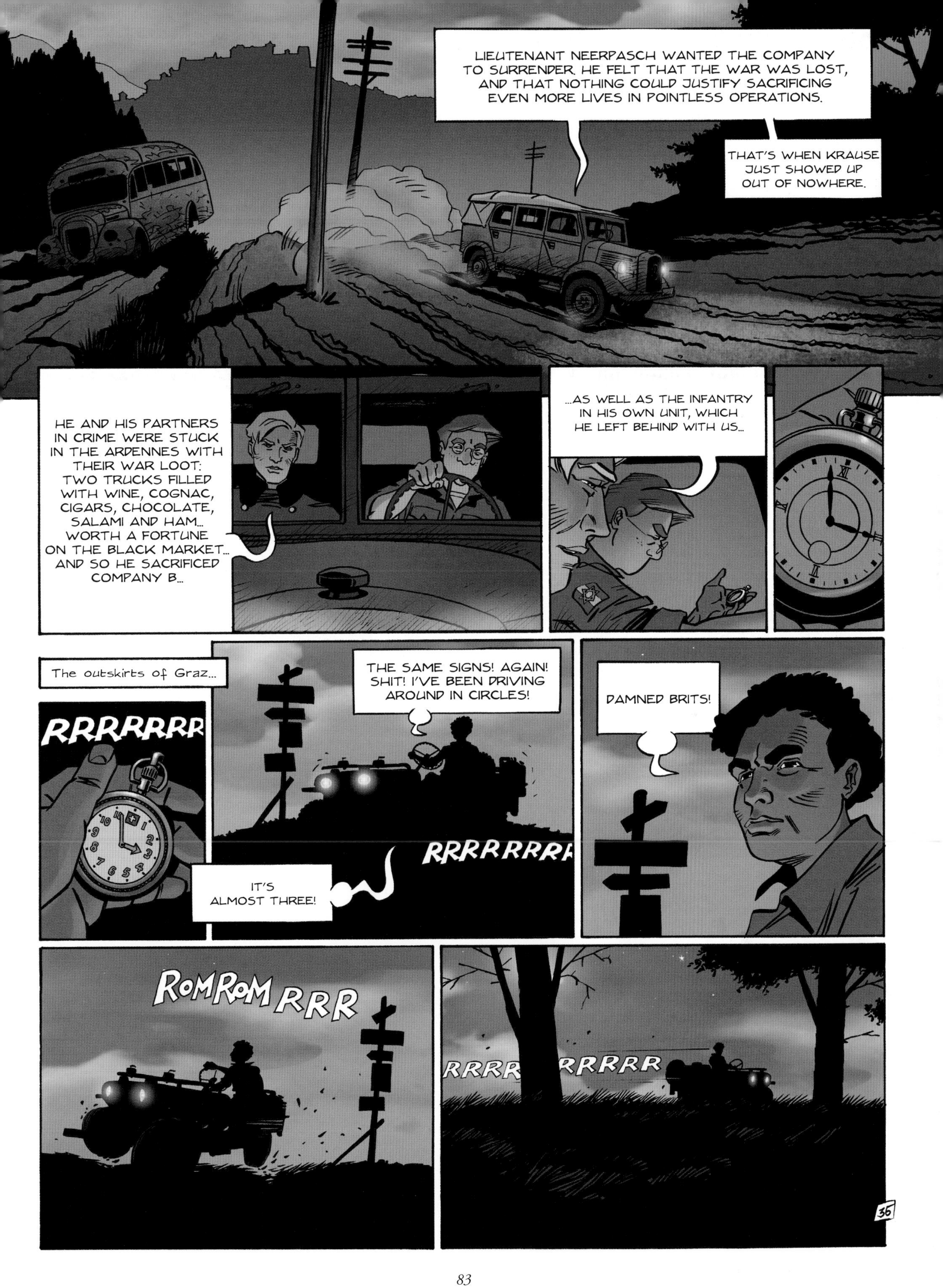
LIEUTENANT NEERPASCH WANTED THE COMPANY TO SURRENDER. HE FELT THAT THE WAR WAS LOST, AND THAT NOTHING COULD JUSTIFY SACRIFICING EVEN MORE LIVES IN POINTLESS OPERATIONS.
THAT'S WHEN KRAUSE JUST SHOWED UP OUT OF NOWHERE.
HE AND HIS PARTNERS IN CRIME WERE STUCK IN THE ARDENNES WITH THEIR WAR LOOT: TWO TRUCKS FILLED WITH WINE, COGNAC, CIGARS, CHOCOLATE, SALAMI AND HAM... WORTH A FORTUNE ON THE BLACK MARKET... AND SO HE SACRIFICED COMPANY B...
...AS WELL AS THE INFANTRY IN HIS OWN UNIT, WHICH HE LEFT BEHIND WITH US...
The outskirts of Graz...
RRRRRRR
THE SAME SIGNS! AGAIN! SHIT! I'VE BEEN DRIVING AROUND IN CIRCLES!
RRRRRRRR
IT'S ALMOST THREE!
DAMNED BRITS!
ROMROM RRR
RRRR RRRRR
35

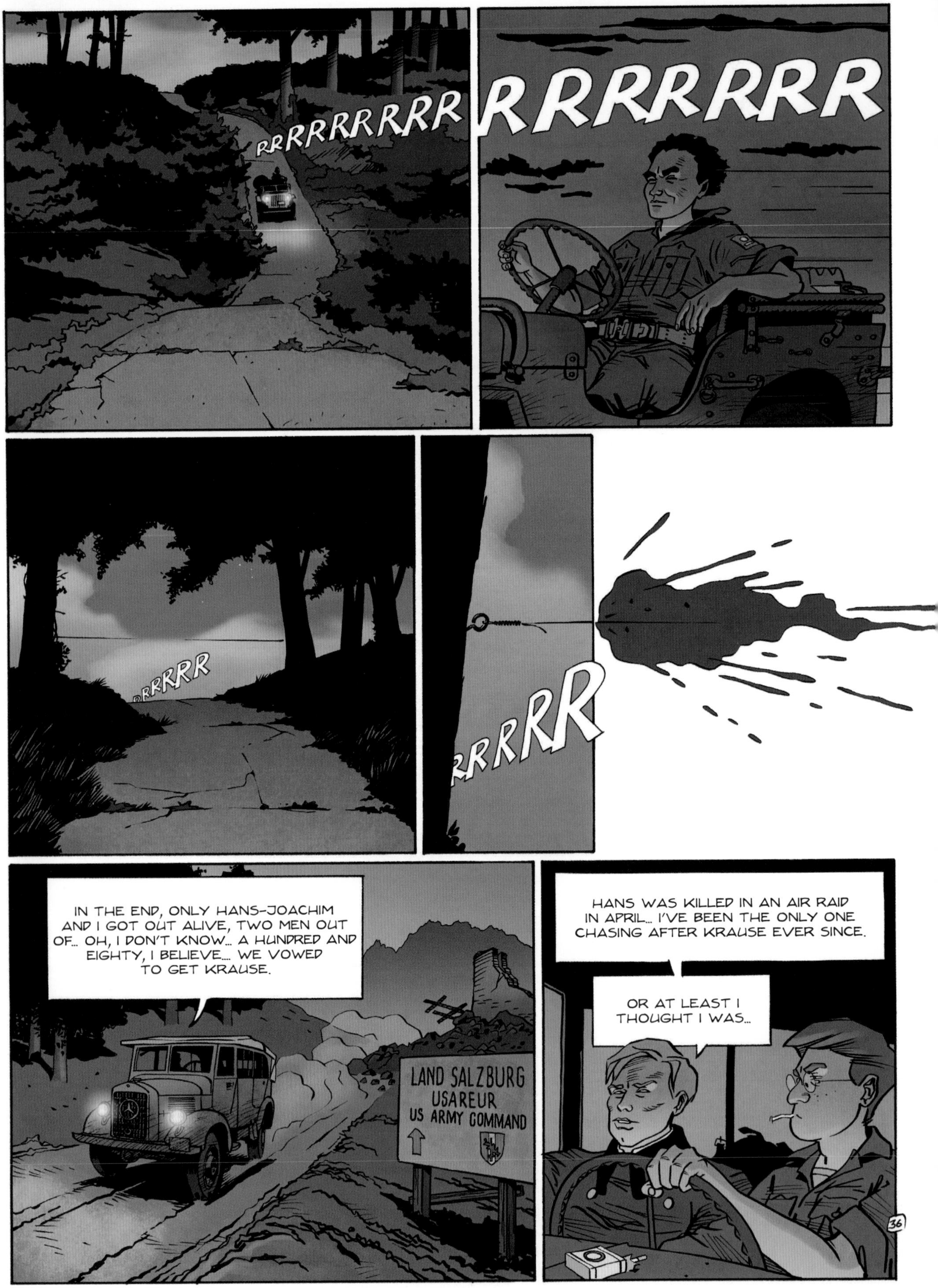

RRRRRRRRRR
RRRRRRR
RRRRR
RRRRR
IN THE END, ONLY HANS-JOACHIM AND I GOT OUT ALIVE, TWO MEN OUT OF... OH, I DON'T KNOW... A HUNDRED AND EIGHTY, I BELIEVE.... WE VOWED TO GET KRAUSE.
LAND SALZBURG
USAREUR
US ARMY COMMAND
HANS WAS KILLED IN AN AIR RAID IN APRIL... I'VE BEEN THE ONLY ONE CHASING AFTER KRAUSE EVER SINCE.
OR AT LEAST I THOUGHT I WAS...
36

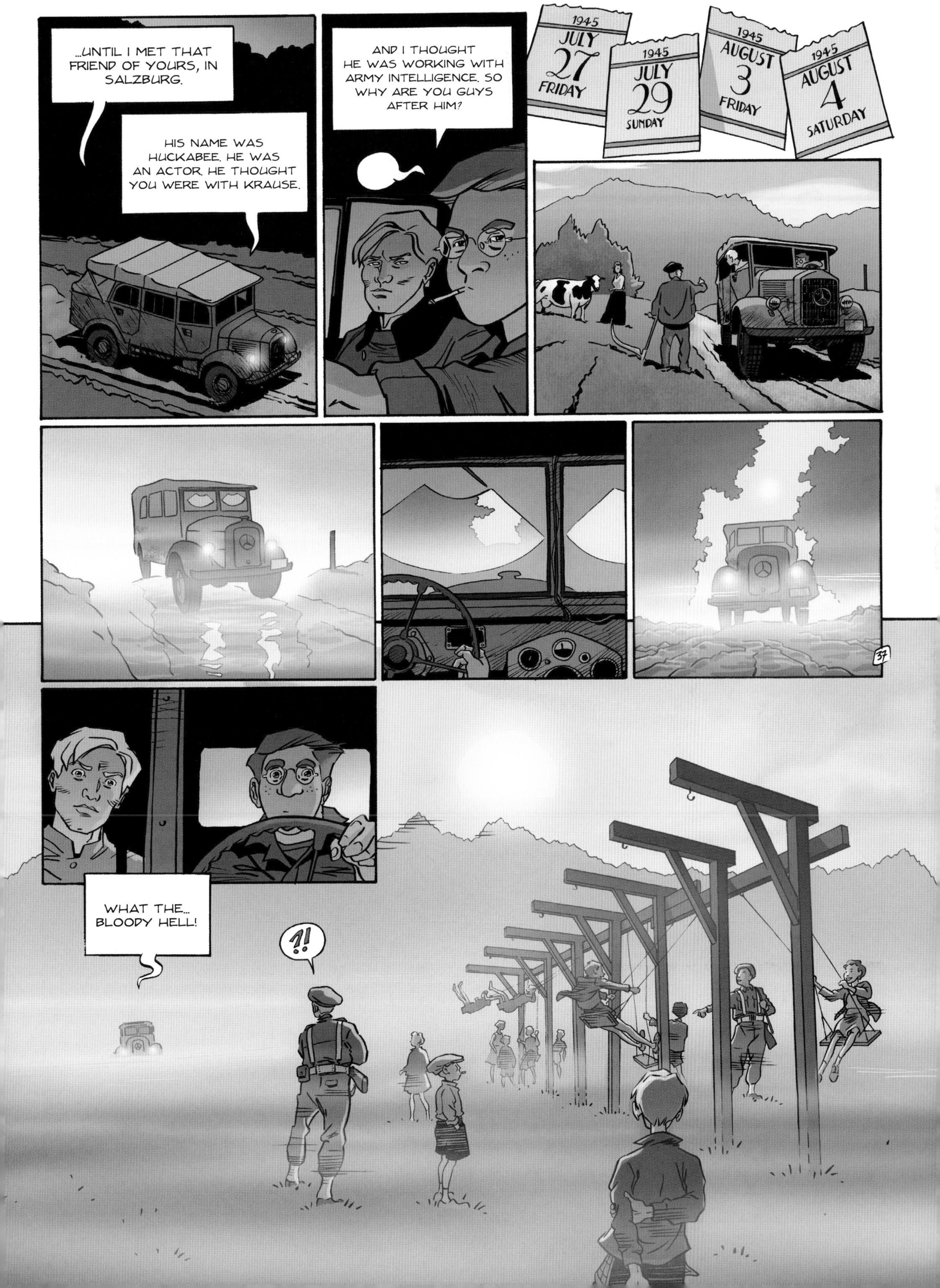
...UNTIL I MET THAT FRIEND OF YOURS, IN SALZBURG.
HIS NAME WAS HUCKABEE. HE WAS AN ACTOR. HE THOUGHT YOU WERE WITH KRAUSE.
AND I THOUGHT HE WAS WORKING WITH ARMY INTELLIGENCE. SO WHY ARE YOU GUYS AFTER HIM?
1945 JULY 27 FRIDAY
1945 JULY 29 SUNDAY
1945 AUGUST 3 FRIDAY
1945 AUGUST 4 SATURDAY
37
WHAT THE... BLOODY HELL!
?!

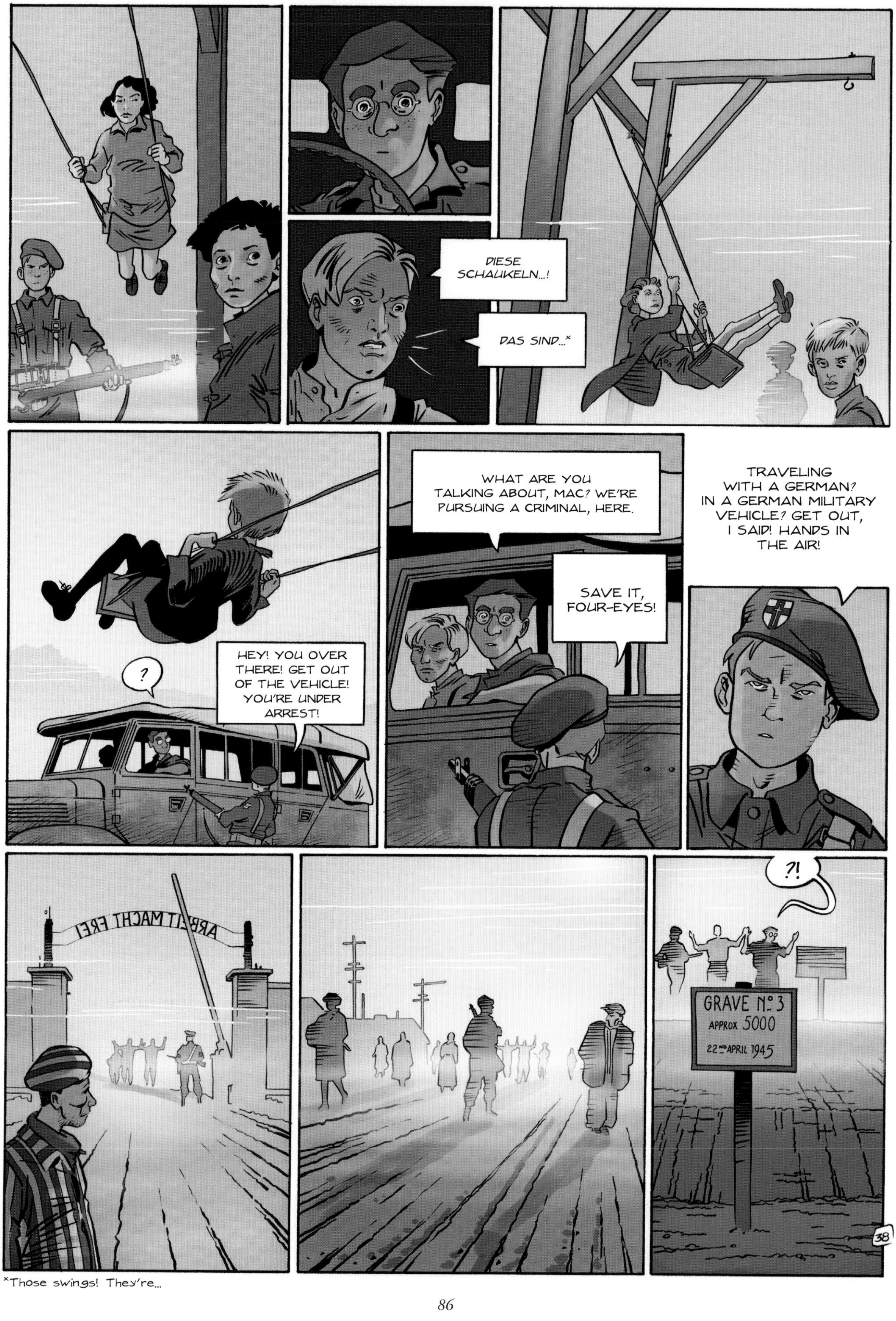
DIESE SCHAUKELN...!
DAS SIND...*
HEY! YOU OVER THERE! GET OUT OF THE VEHICLE! YOU'RE UNDER ARREST!
?
WHAT ARE YOU TALKING ABOUT, MAC? WE'RE PURSUING A CRIMINAL, HERE.
SAVE IT, FOUR-EYES!
TRAVELING WITH A GERMAN? IN A GERMAN MILITARY VEHICLE? GET OUT, I SAID! HANDS IN THE AIR!
ARBEIT MACHT FREI
?!
GRAVE No. 3
APPROX 5000
22nd APRIL 1945
38

*Those swings! They're...

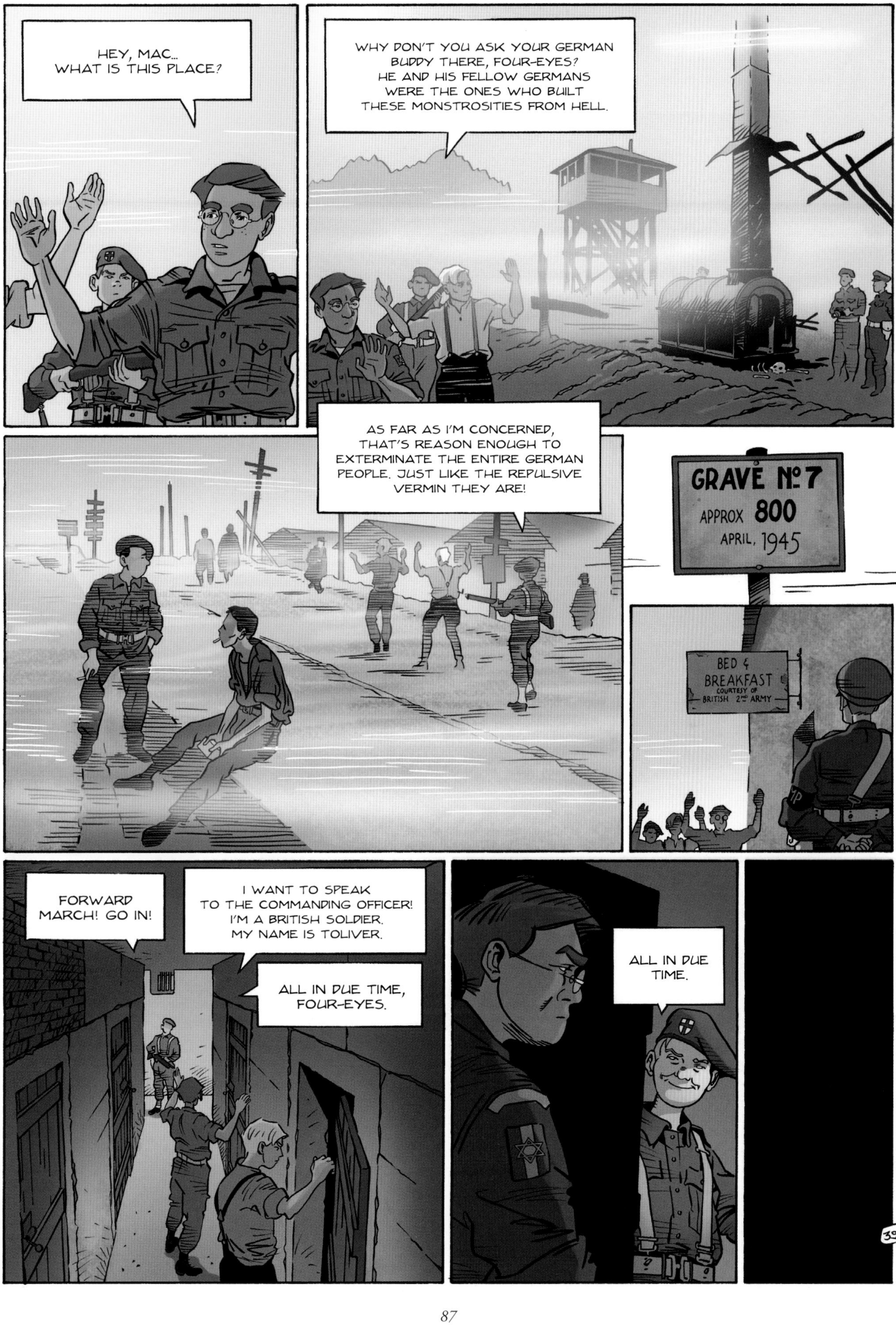
HEY, MAC... WHAT IS THIS PLACE?
WHY DON'T YOU ASK YOUR GERMAN BUDDY THERE, FOUR-EYES? HE AND HIS FELLOW GERMANS WERE THE ONES WHO BUILT THESE MONSTROSITIES FROM HELL.
AS FAR AS I'M CONCERNED, THAT'S REASON ENOUGH TO EXTERMINATE THE ENTIRE GERMAN PEOPLE. JUST LIKE THE REPULSIVE VERMIN THEY ARE!
GRAVE No. 7 APPROX 800 APRIL, 1945
BED & BREAKFAST COURTESY OF BRITISH 2ND ARMY
FORWARD MARCH! GO IN!
I WANT TO SPEAK TO THE COMMANDING OFFICER! I'M A BRITISH SOLDIER. MY NAME IS TOLIVER.
ALL IN DUE TIME, FOUR-EYES.
ALL IN DUE TIME.
39

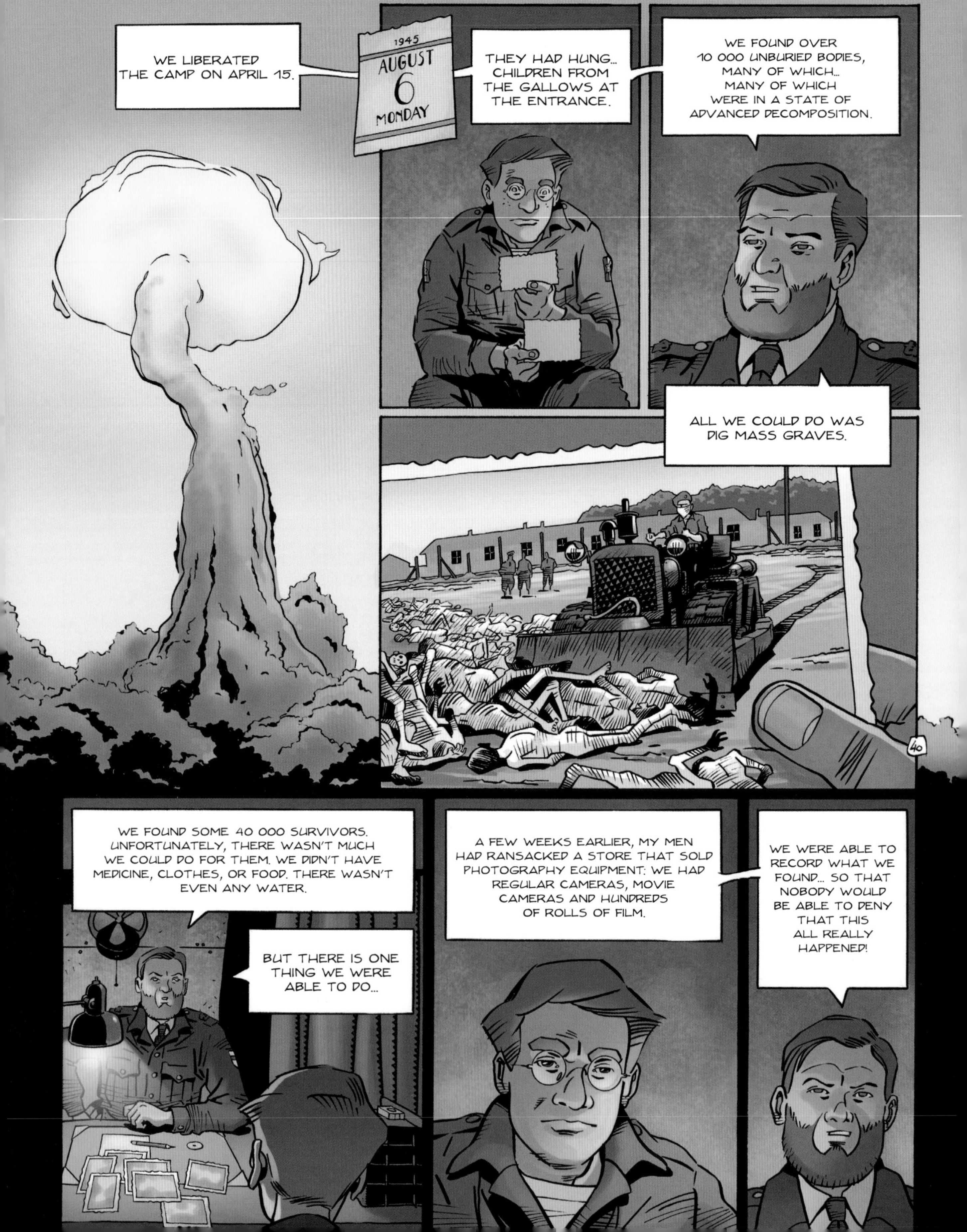
WE LIBERATED THE CAMP ON APRIL 15.
1945 AUGUST 6 MONDAY
THEY HAD HUNG... CHILDREN FROM THE GALLOWS AT THE ENTRANCE.
WE FOUND OVER 10 000 UNBURIED BODIES, MANY OF WHICH... MANY OF WHICH WERE IN A STATE OF ADVANCED DECOMPOSITION.
ALL WE COULD DO WAS DIG MASS GRAVES.
40
WE FOUND SOME 40 000 SURVIVORS. UNFORTUNATELY, THERE WASN'T MUCH WE COULD DO FOR THEM. WE DIDN'T HAVE MEDICINE, CLOTHES, OR FOOD. THERE WASN'T EVEN ANY WATER.
BUT THERE IS ONE THING WE WERE ABLE TO DO...
A FEW WEEKS EARLIER, MY MEN HAD RANSACKED A STORE THAT SOLD PHOTOGRAPHY EQUIPMENT: WE HAD REGULAR CAMERAS, MOVIE CAMERAS AND HUNDREDS OF ROLLS OF FILM.
WE WERE ABLE TO RECORD WHAT WE FOUND... SO THAT NOBODY WOULD BE ABLE TO DENY THAT THIS ALL REALLY HAPPENED!

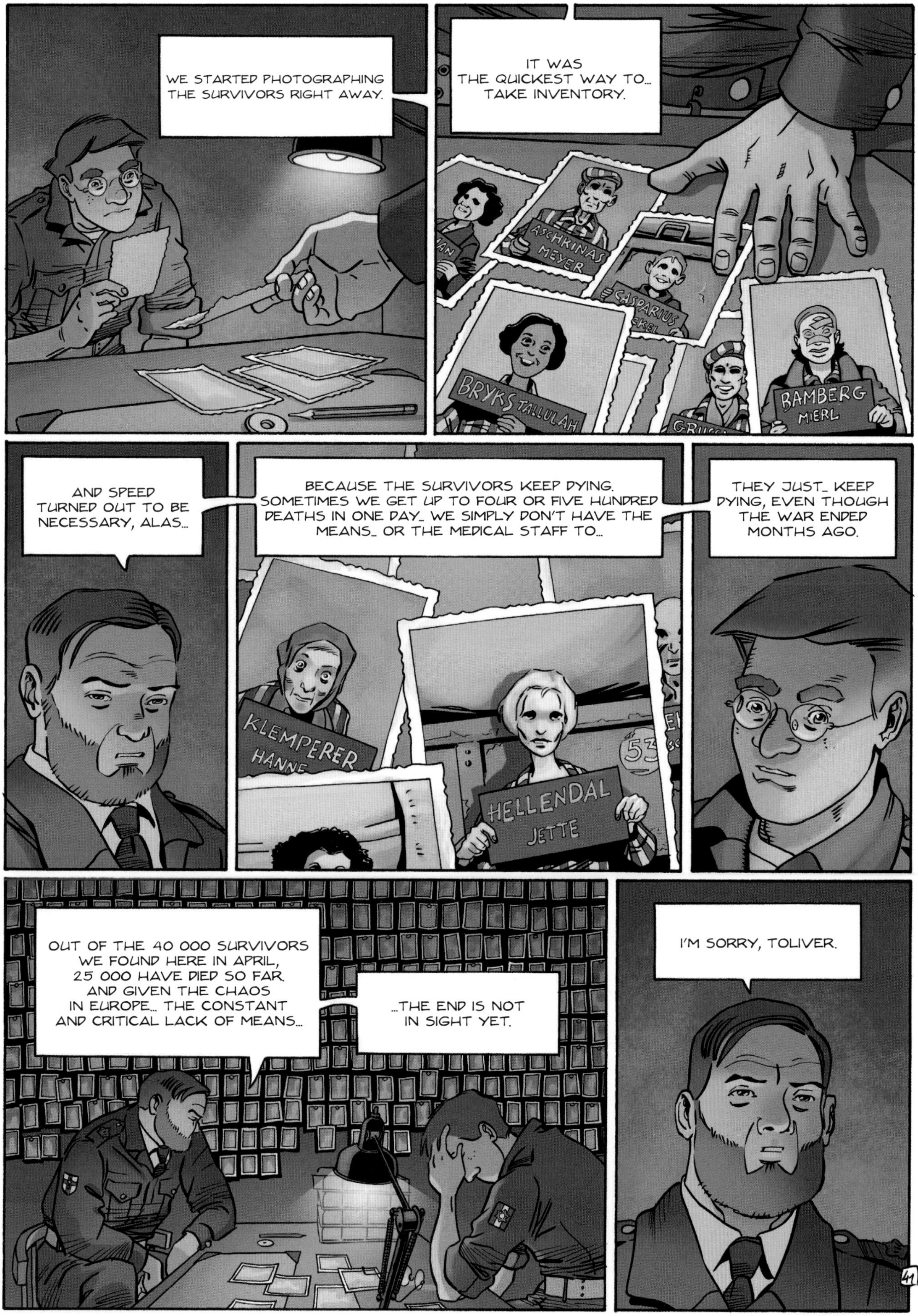
WE STARTED PHOTOGRAPHING THE SURVIVORS RIGHT AWAY.
IT WAS THE QUICKEST WAY TO... TAKE INVENTORY.
ASCHKINAS MEYER
CASPARIUS
BRYKS TALLULAH
BAMBERG MIERL
AND SPEED TURNED OUT TO BE NECESSARY, ALAS...
BECAUSE THE SURVIVORS KEEP DYING. SOMETIMES WE GET UP TO FOUR OR FIVE HUNDRED DEATHS IN ONE DAY... WE SIMPLY DON'T HAVE THE MEANS... OR THE MEDICAL STAFF TO...
THEY JUST... KEEP DYING, EVEN THOUGH THE WAR ENDED MONTHS AGO.
KLEMPERER HANNE
HELLENDAL JETTE
OUT OF THE 40 000 SURVIVORS WE FOUND HERE IN APRIL, 25 000 HAVE DIED SO FAR. AND GIVEN THE CHAOS IN EUROPE... THE CONSTANT AND CRITICAL LACK OF MEANS...
...THE END IS NOT IN SIGHT YET.
I'M SORRY, TOLIVER.
41

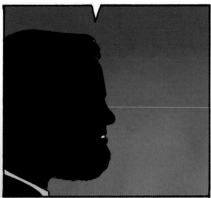

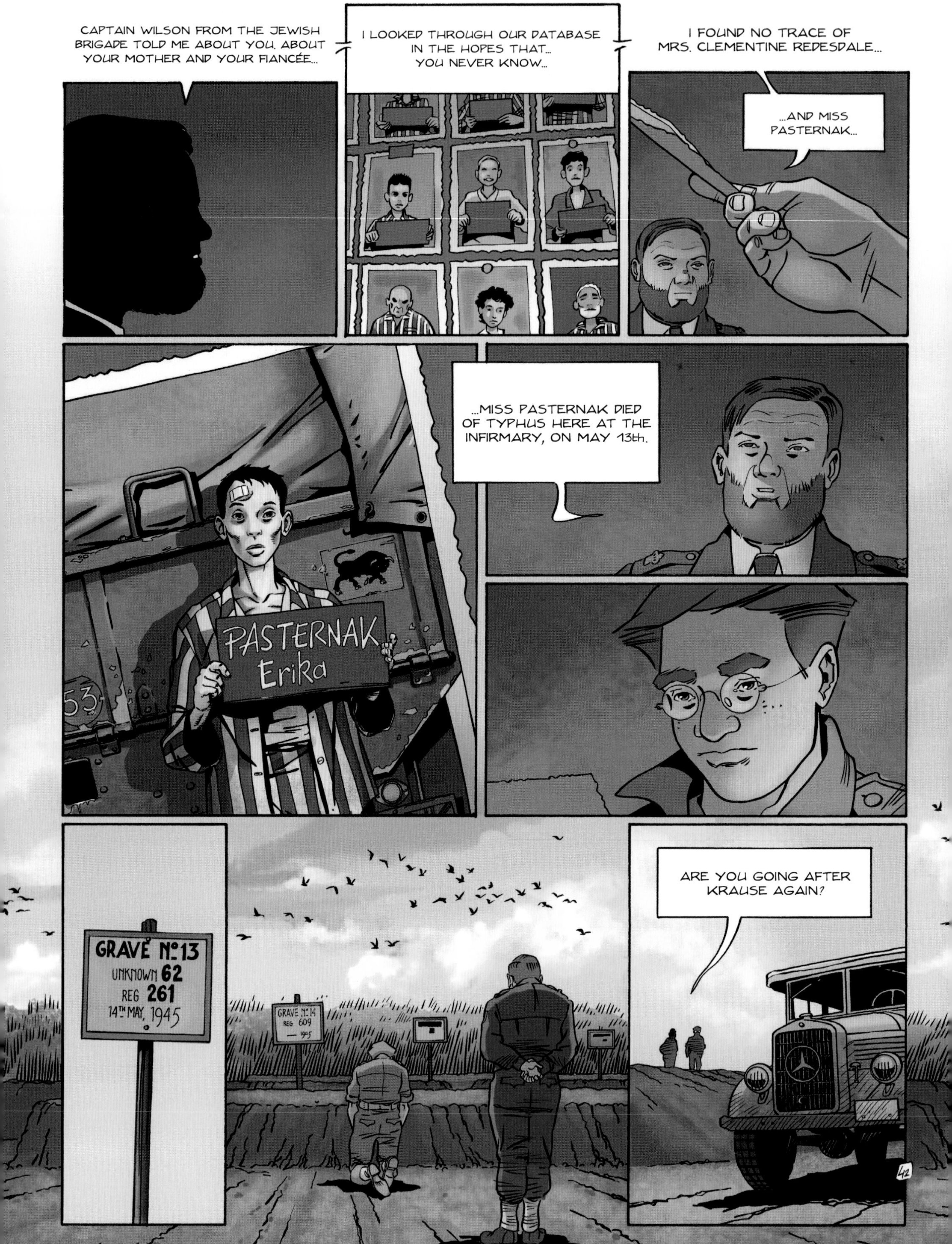
CAPTAIN WILSON FROM THE JEWISH BRIGADE TOLD ME ABOUT YOU. ABOUT YOUR MOTHER AND YOUR FIANCÉE...
I LOOKED THROUGH OUR DATABASE IN THE HOPES THAT... YOU NEVER KNOW...
I FOUND NO TRACE OF MRS. CLEMENTINE REDESDALE...
...AND MISS PASTERNAK...
PASTERNAK Erika
...MISS PASTERNAK DIED OF TYPHUS HERE AT THE INFIRMARY, ON MAY 13th.
GRAVE N°13
UNKNOWN 62
REG 261
14TH MAY, 1945
GRAVE N°14
REG 609
— 1945
ARE YOU GOING AFTER KRAUSE AGAIN?
42

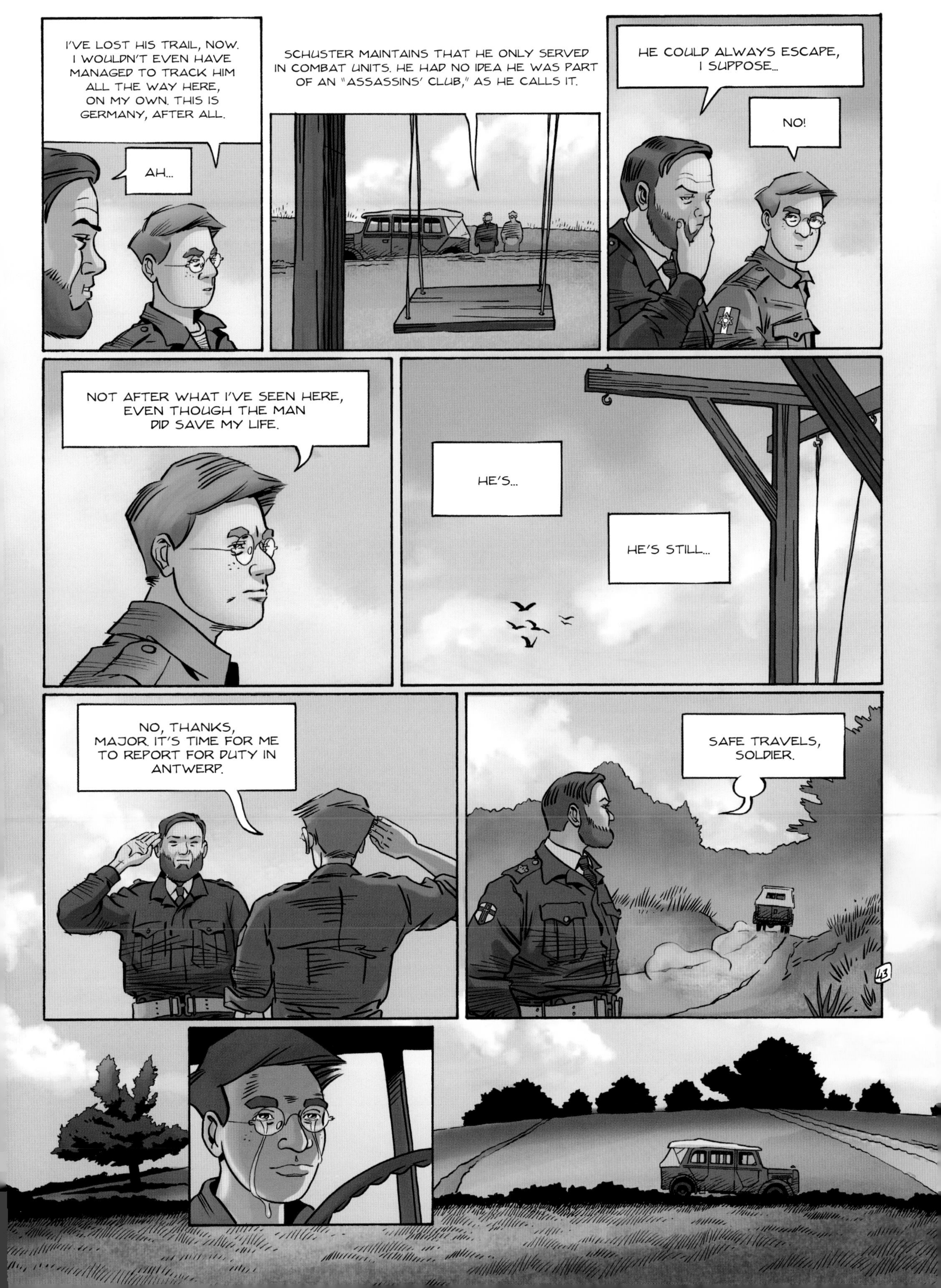

I'VE LOST HIS TRAIL, NOW. I WOULDN'T EVEN HAVE MANAGED TO TRACK HIM ALL THE WAY HERE, ON MY OWN. THIS IS GERMANY, AFTER ALL.
AH...
SCHUSTER MAINTAINS THAT HE ONLY SERVED IN COMBAT UNITS. HE HAD NO IDEA HE WAS PART OF AN "ASSASSINS' CLUB," AS HE CALLS IT.
HE COULD ALWAYS ESCAPE, I SUPPOSE...
NO!
NOT AFTER WHAT I'VE SEEN HERE, EVEN THOUGH THE MAN DID SAVE MY LIFE.
HE'S...
HE'S STILL...
NO, THANKS, MAJOR. IT'S TIME FOR ME TO REPORT FOR DUTY IN ANTWERP.
SAFE TRAVELS, SOLDIER.
43

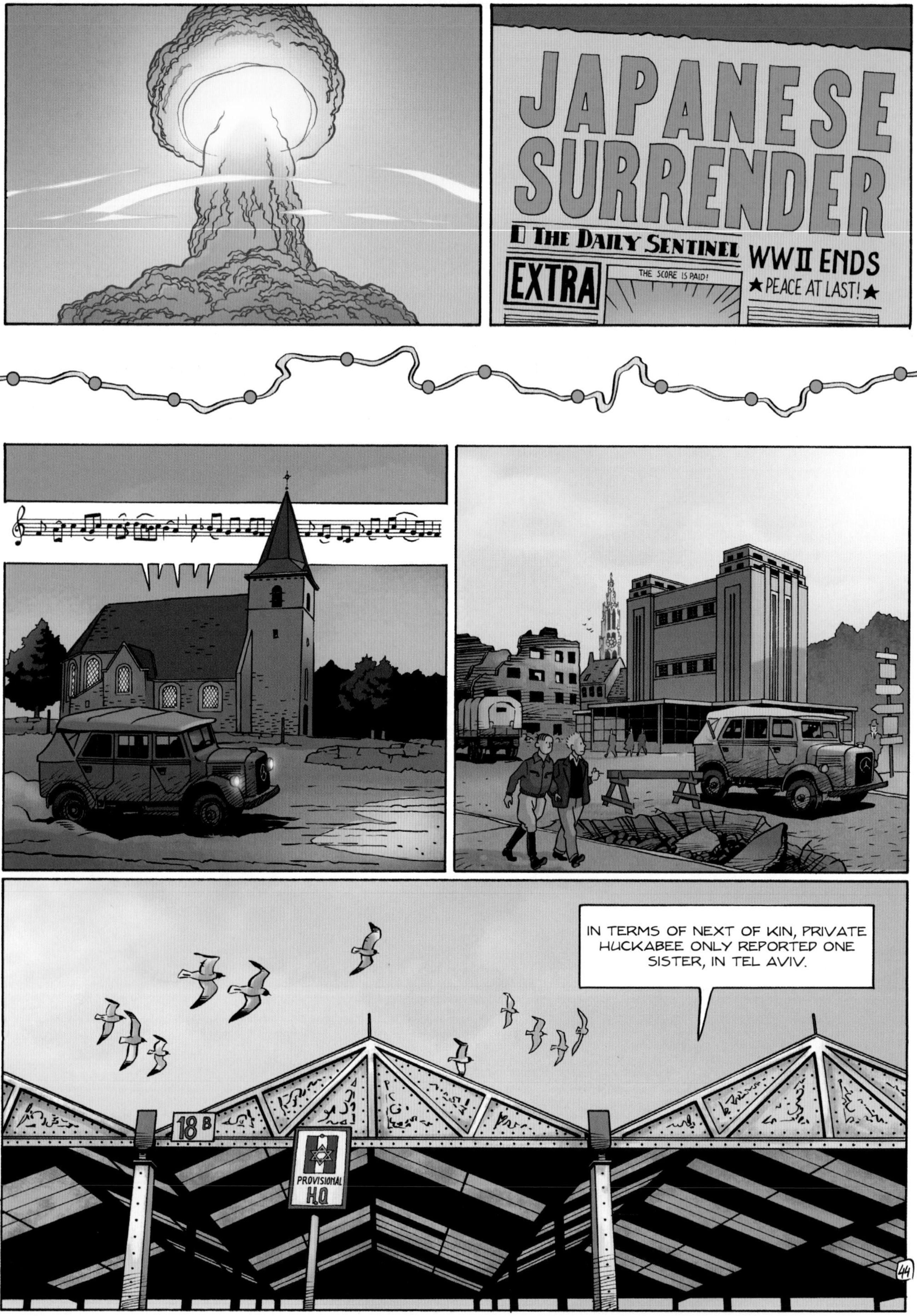
JAPANESE SURRENDER
THE DAILY SENTINEL
EXTRA
THE SCORE IS PAID!
WWII ENDS
★PEACE AT LAST!★
IN TERMS OF NEXT OF KIN, PRIVATE HUCKABEE ONLY REPORTED ONE SISTER, IN TEL AVIV.
18 B
PROVISIONAL H.Q
44

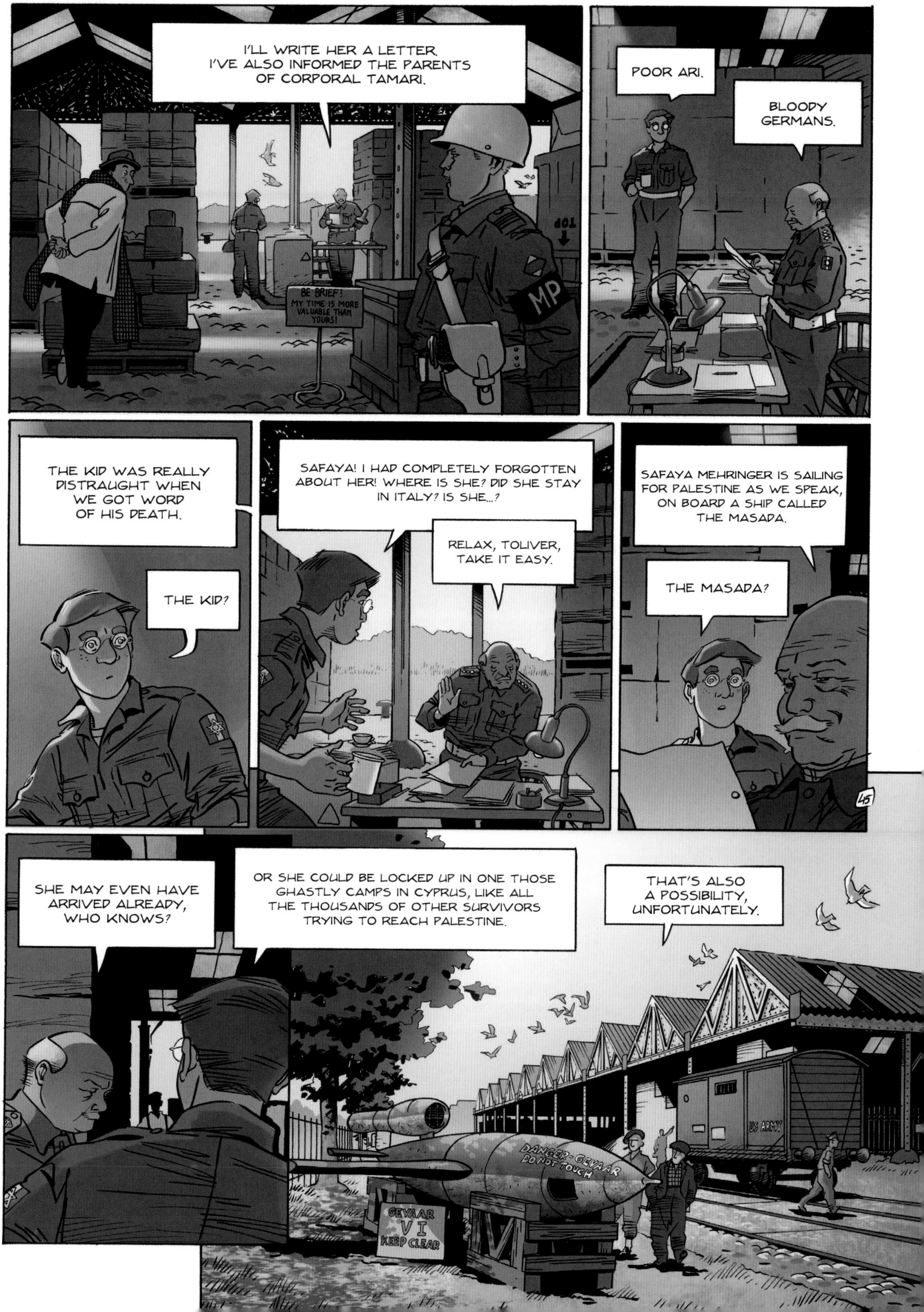
I'LL WRITE HER A LETTER. I'VE ALSO INFORMED THE PARENTS OF CORPORAL TAMARI.
BE BRIEF! MY TIME IS MORE VALUABLE THAN YOURS!
TOP
MP
POOR ARI.
BLOODY GERMANS.
THE KID WAS REALLY DISTRAUGHT WHEN WE GOT WORD OF HIS DEATH.
THE KID?
SAFAYA! I HAD COMPLETELY FORGOTTEN ABOUT HER! WHERE IS SHE? DID SHE STAY IN ITALY? IS SHE...?
RELAX, TOLIVER, TAKE IT EASY.
SAFAYA MEHRINGER IS SAILING FOR PALESTINE AS WE SPEAK, ON BOARD A SHIP CALLED THE MASADA.
THE MASADA?
SHE MAY EVEN HAVE ARRIVED ALREADY, WHO KNOWS?
OR SHE COULD BE LOCKED UP IN ONE THOSE GHASTLY CAMPS IN CYPRUS, LIKE ALL THE THOUSANDS OF OTHER SURVIVORS TRYING TO REACH PALESTINE.
THAT'S ALSO A POSSIBILITY, UNFORTUNATELY.
DANGER-GEVAAR DO NOT TOUCH
GEVAAR V1 KEEP CLEAR
US ARMY

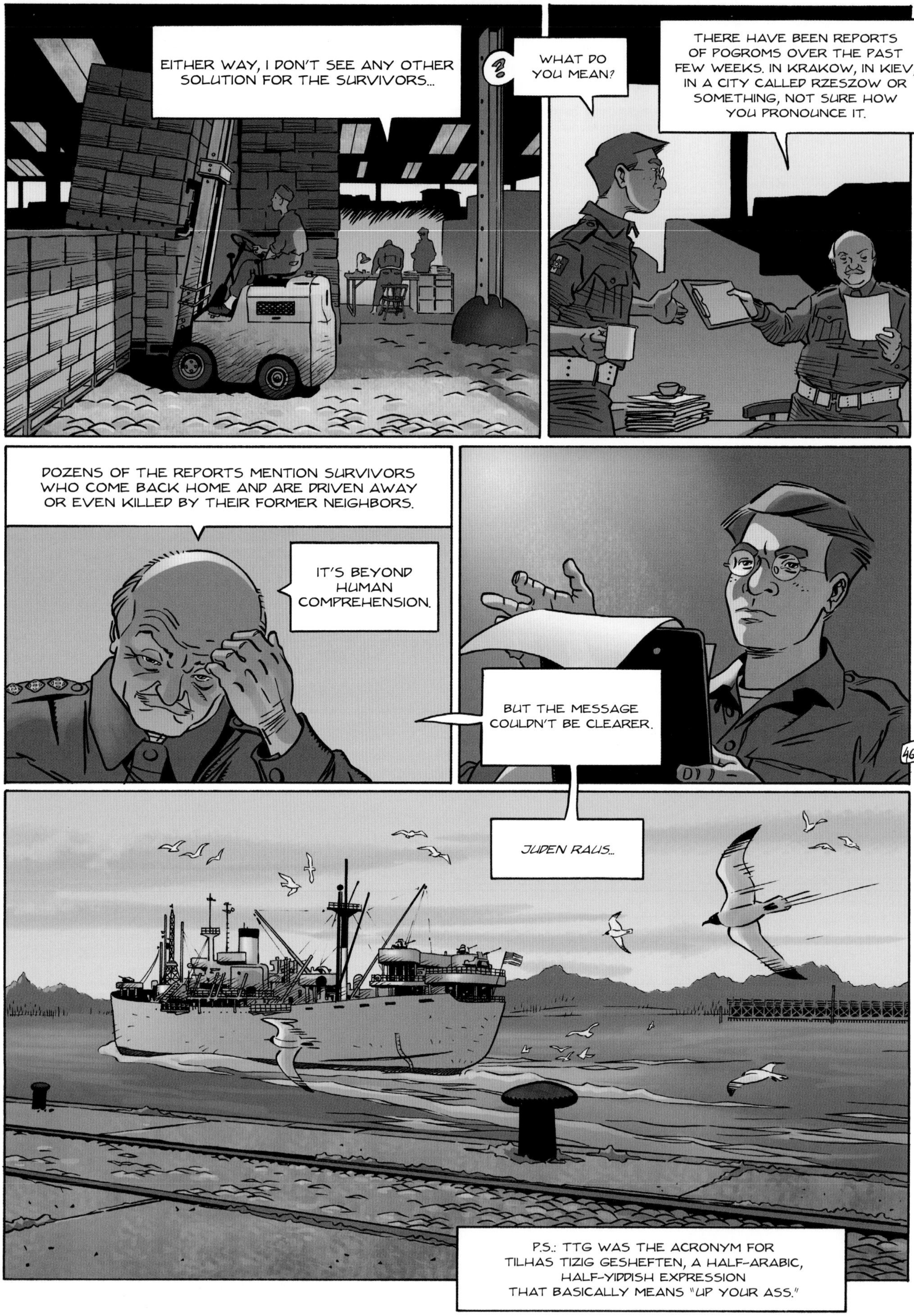
EITHER WAY, I DON'T SEE ANY OTHER SOLUTION FOR THE SURVIVORS...
?
WHAT DO YOU MEAN?
THERE HAVE BEEN REPORTS OF POGROMS OVER THE PAST FEW WEEKS. IN KRAKOW, IN KIEV, IN A CITY CALLED RZESZOW OR SOMETHING, NOT SURE HOW YOU PRONOUNCE IT.
DOZENS OF THE REPORTS MENTION SURVIVORS WHO COME BACK HOME AND ARE DRIVEN AWAY OR EVEN KILLED BY THEIR FORMER NEIGHBORS.
IT'S BEYOND HUMAN COMPREHENSION.
BUT THE MESSAGE COULDN'T BE CLEARER.
JUDEN RAUS...
P.S.: TTG WAS THE ACRONYM FOR TILHAS TIZIG GESHEFTEN, A HALF-ARABIC, HALF-YIDDISH EXPRESSION THAT BASICALLY MEANS "UP YOUR ASS."

MARVANO

THE JEWISH BRIGADE

3. HATIKVAH

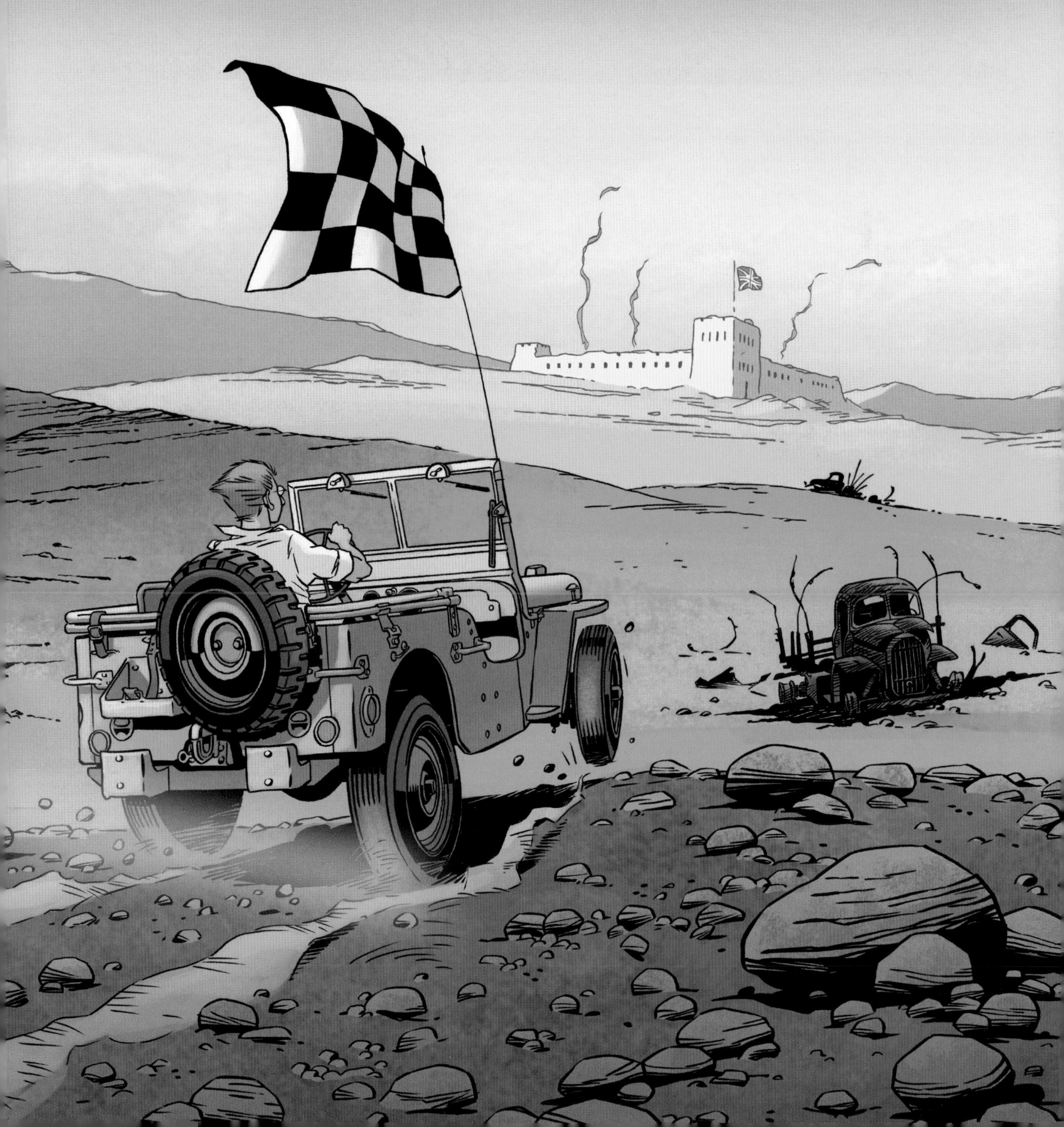

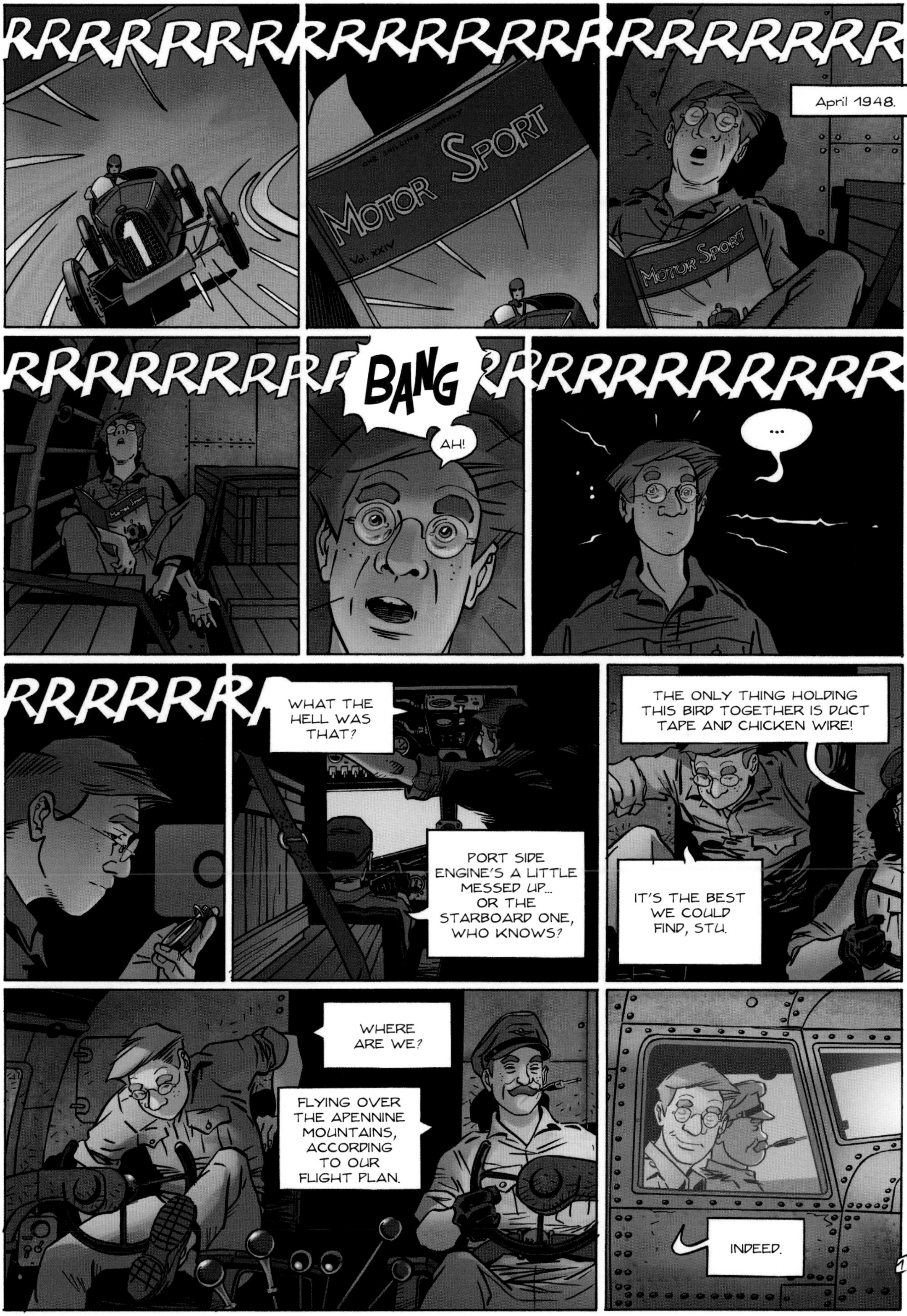
RRRRRRRRRRRRRRRRRRRRRRRRRRRRR
MOTOR SPORT
Vol. XXIV
April 1948.
RRRRRRRRRRRRRRRRRRRRRRRRRRR
BANG
AH!
...
RRRRRR
WHAT THE HELL WAS THAT?
PORT SIDE ENGINE'S A LITTLE MESSED UP... OR THE STARBOARD ONE, WHO KNOWS?
THE ONLY THING HOLDING THIS BIRD TOGETHER IS DUCT TAPE AND CHICKEN WIRE!
IT'S THE BEST WE COULD FIND, STU.
WHERE ARE WE?
FLYING OVER THE APENNINE MOUNTAINS, ACCORDING TO OUR FLIGHT PLAN.
INDEED.
1

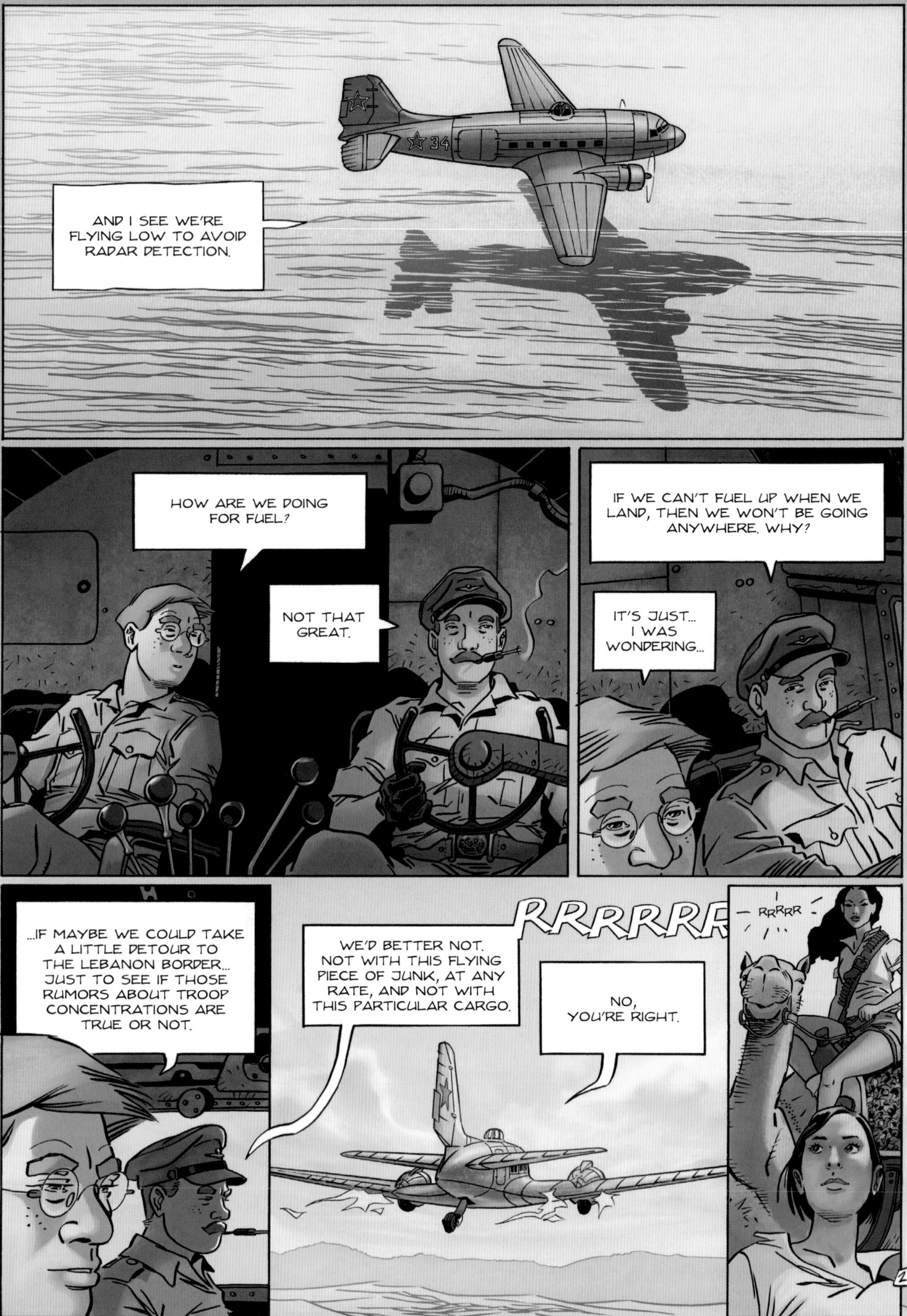
AND I SEE WE'RE FLYING LOW TO AVOID RADAR DETECTION.
HOW ARE WE DOING FOR FUEL?
NOT THAT GREAT.
IF WE CAN'T FUEL UP WHEN WE LAND, THEN WE WON'T BE GOING ANYWHERE. WHY?
IT'S JUST... I WAS WONDERING...
...IF MAYBE WE COULD TAKE A LITTLE DETOUR TO THE LEBANON BORDER... JUST TO SEE IF THOSE RUMORS ABOUT TROOP CONCENTRATIONS ARE TRUE OR NOT.
RRRRRR
WE'D BETTER NOT. NOT WITH THIS FLYING PIECE OF JUNK, AT ANY RATE, AND NOT WITH THIS PARTICULAR CARGO.
NO, YOU'RE RIGHT.
RRRRR
2

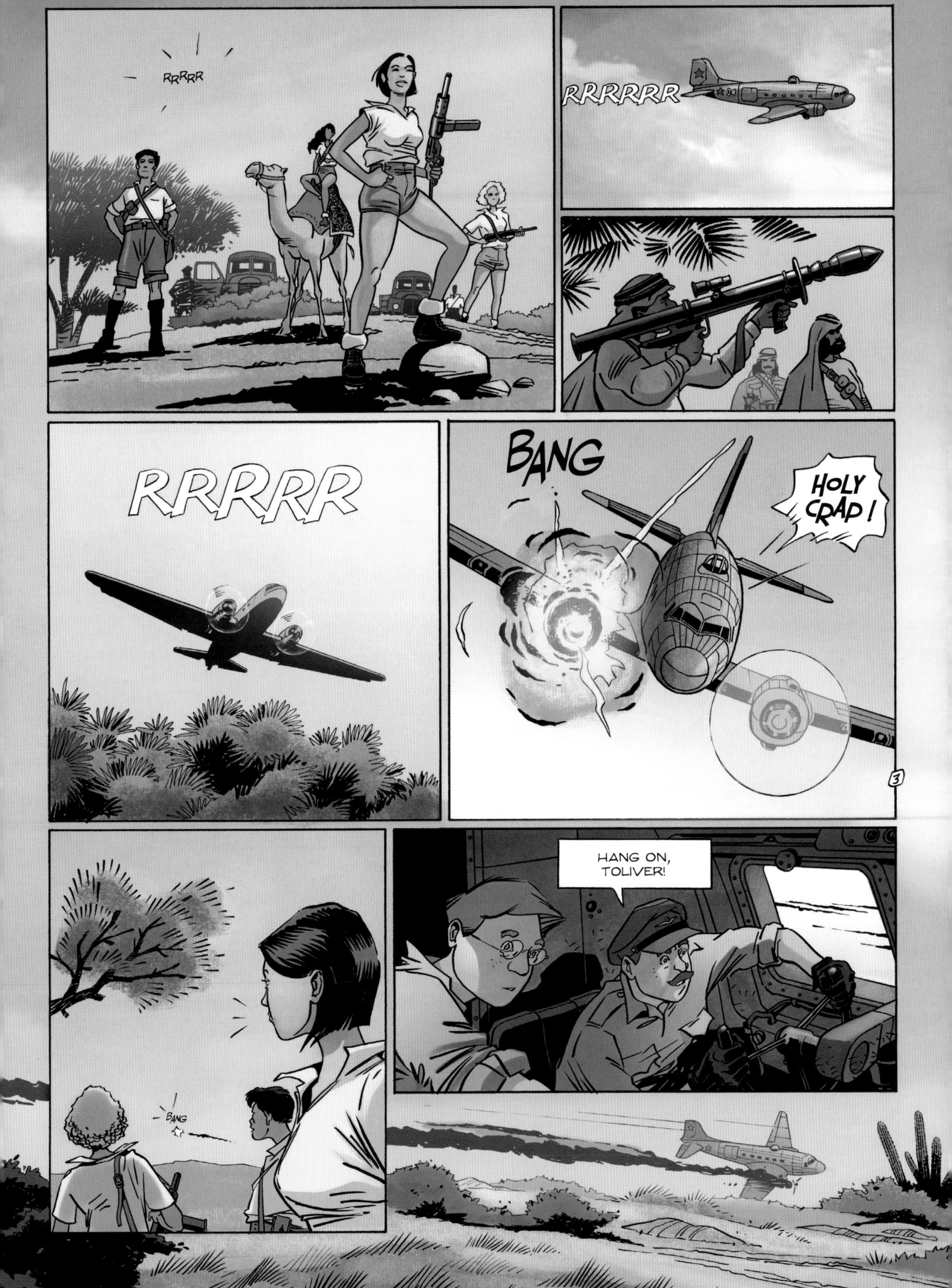
RRRRR
RRRRRR
RRRRR
BANG
HOLY CRAP!
3
HANG ON, TOLIVER!
BANG

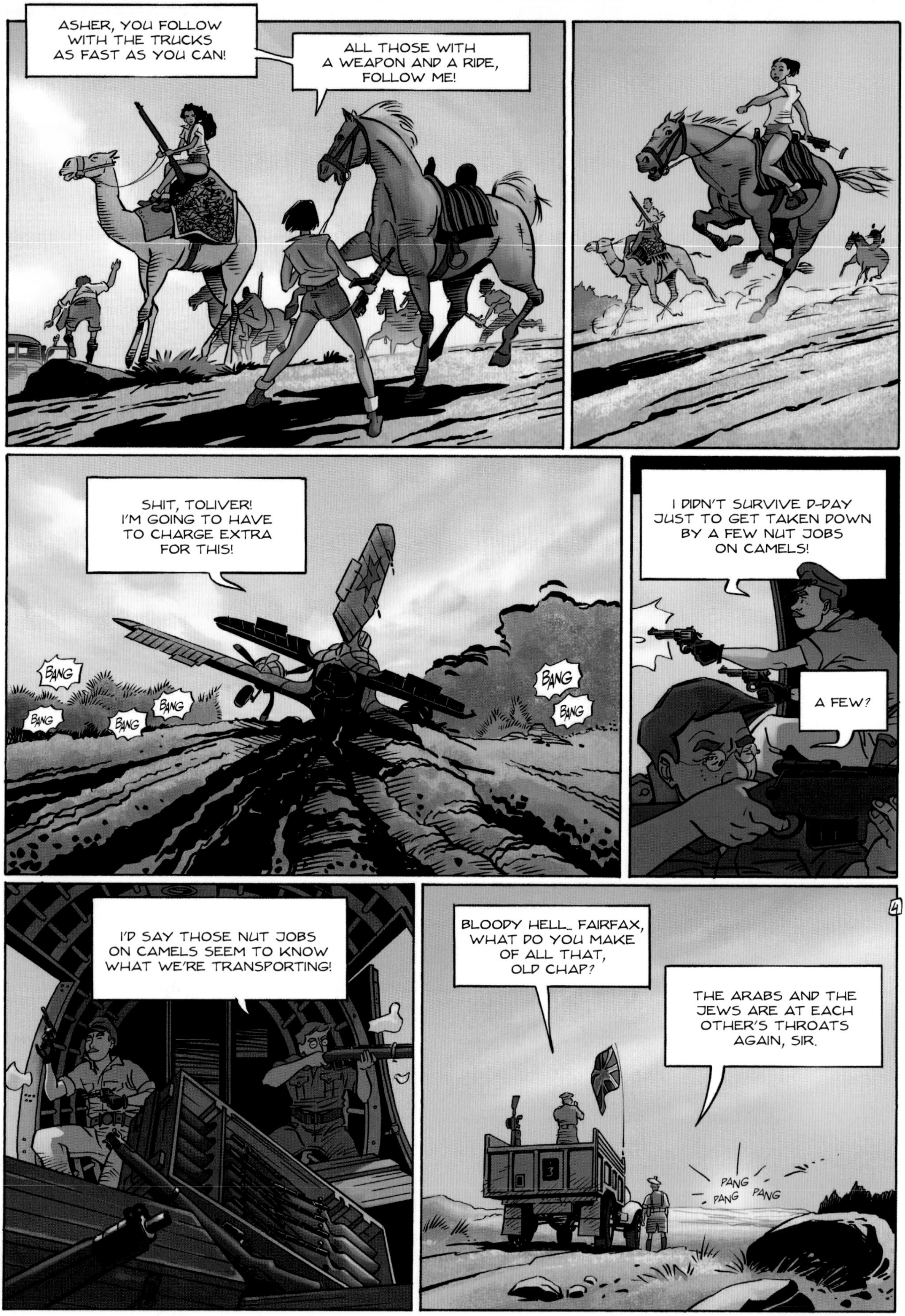
ASHER, YOU FOLLOW WITH THE TRUCKS AS FAST AS YOU CAN!
ALL THOSE WITH A WEAPON AND A RIDE, FOLLOW ME!
SHIT, TOLIVER! I'M GOING TO HAVE TO CHARGE EXTRA FOR THIS!
BANG
BANG
BANG
BANG
BANG
BANG
I DIDN'T SURVIVE D-DAY JUST TO GET TAKEN DOWN BY A FEW NUT JOBS ON CAMELS!
A FEW?
I'D SAY THOSE NUT JOBS ON CAMELS SEEM TO KNOW WHAT WE'RE TRANSPORTING!
BLOODY HELL… FAIRFAX, WHAT DO YOU MAKE OF ALL THAT, OLD CHAP?
THE ARABS AND THE JEWS ARE AT EACH OTHER'S THROATS AGAIN, SIR.
PANG
PANG
PANG

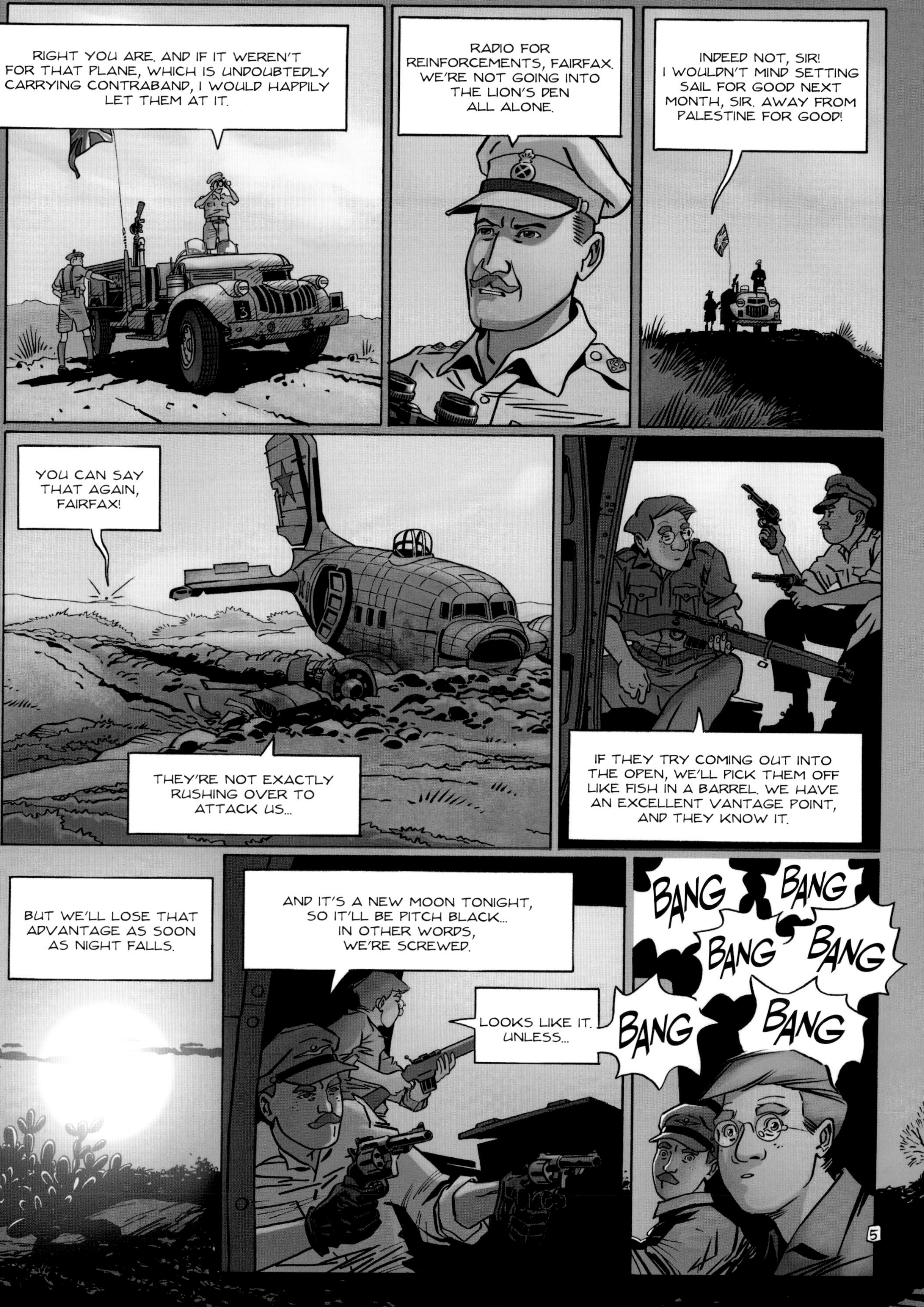
RIGHT YOU ARE. AND IF IT WEREN'T FOR THAT PLANE, WHICH IS UNDOUBTEDLY CARRYING CONTRABAND, I WOULD HAPPILY LET THEM AT IT.
RADIO FOR REINFORCEMENTS, FAIRFAX. WE'RE NOT GOING INTO THE LION'S DEN ALL ALONE.
INDEED NOT, SIR! I WOULDN'T MIND SETTING SAIL FOR GOOD NEXT MONTH, SIR. AWAY FROM PALESTINE FOR GOOD!
YOU CAN SAY THAT AGAIN, FAIRFAX!
THEY'RE NOT EXACTLY RUSHING OVER TO ATTACK US...
IF THEY TRY COMING OUT INTO THE OPEN, WE'LL PICK THEM OFF LIKE FISH IN A BARREL. WE HAVE AN EXCELLENT VANTAGE POINT, AND THEY KNOW IT.
BUT WE'LL LOSE THAT ADVANTAGE AS SOON AS NIGHT FALLS.
AND IT'S A NEW MOON TONIGHT, SO IT'LL BE PITCH BLACK... IN OTHER WORDS, WE'RE SCREWED.
LOOKS LIKE IT. UNLESS...
BANG
BANG
BANG
BANG
BANG
BANG
5

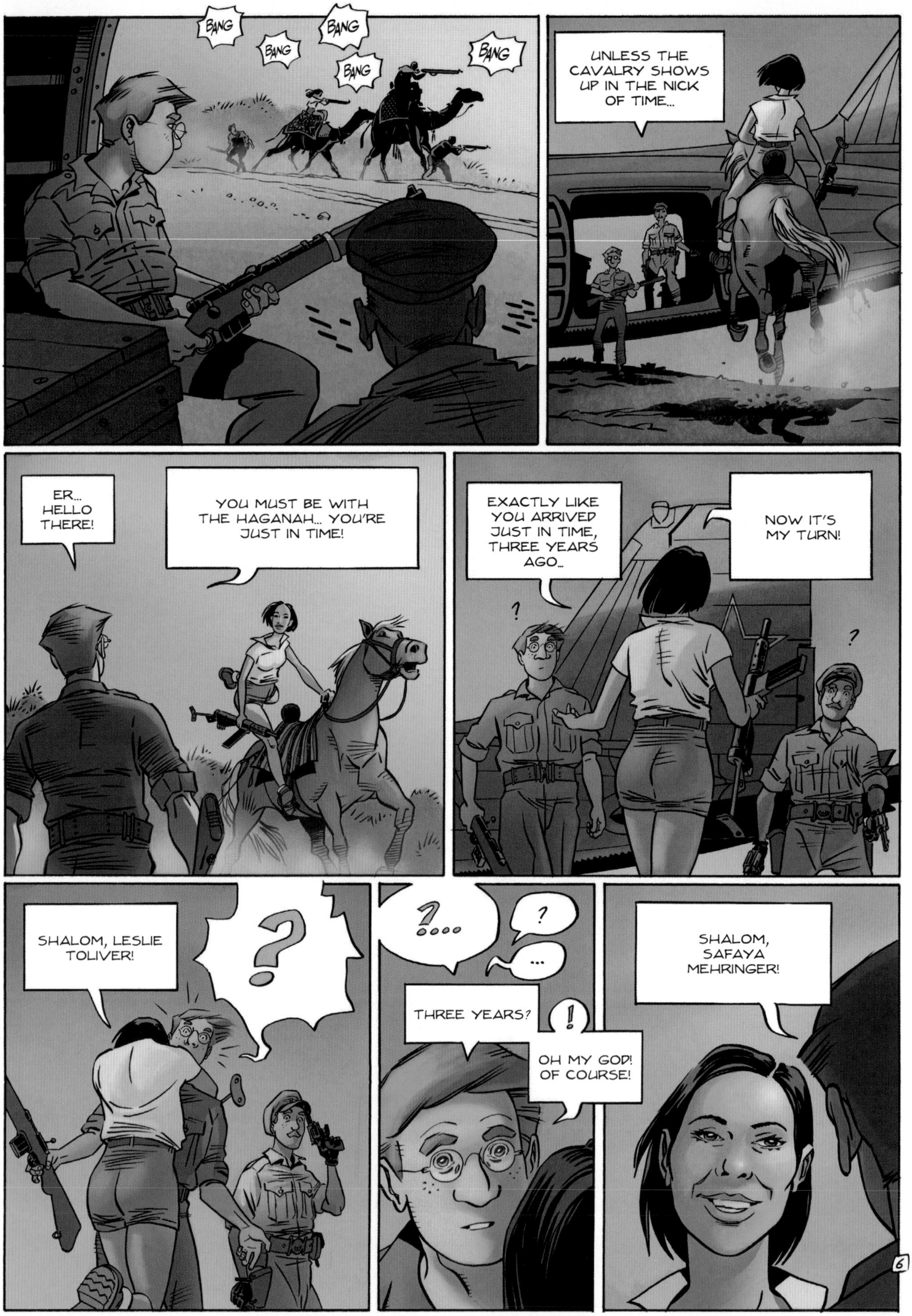
BANG
BANG
BANG
BANG
BANG
UNLESS THE CAVALRY SHOWS UP IN THE NICK OF TIME...
ER... HELLO THERE!
YOU MUST BE WITH THE HAGANAH... YOU'RE JUST IN TIME!
EXACTLY LIKE YOU ARRIVED JUST IN TIME, THREE YEARS AGO...
NOW IT'S MY TURN!
?
?
SHALOM, LESLIE TOLIVER!
?
?...
?
...
THREE YEARS?
!
OH MY GOD! OF COURSE!
SHALOM, SAFAYA MEHRINGER!
6

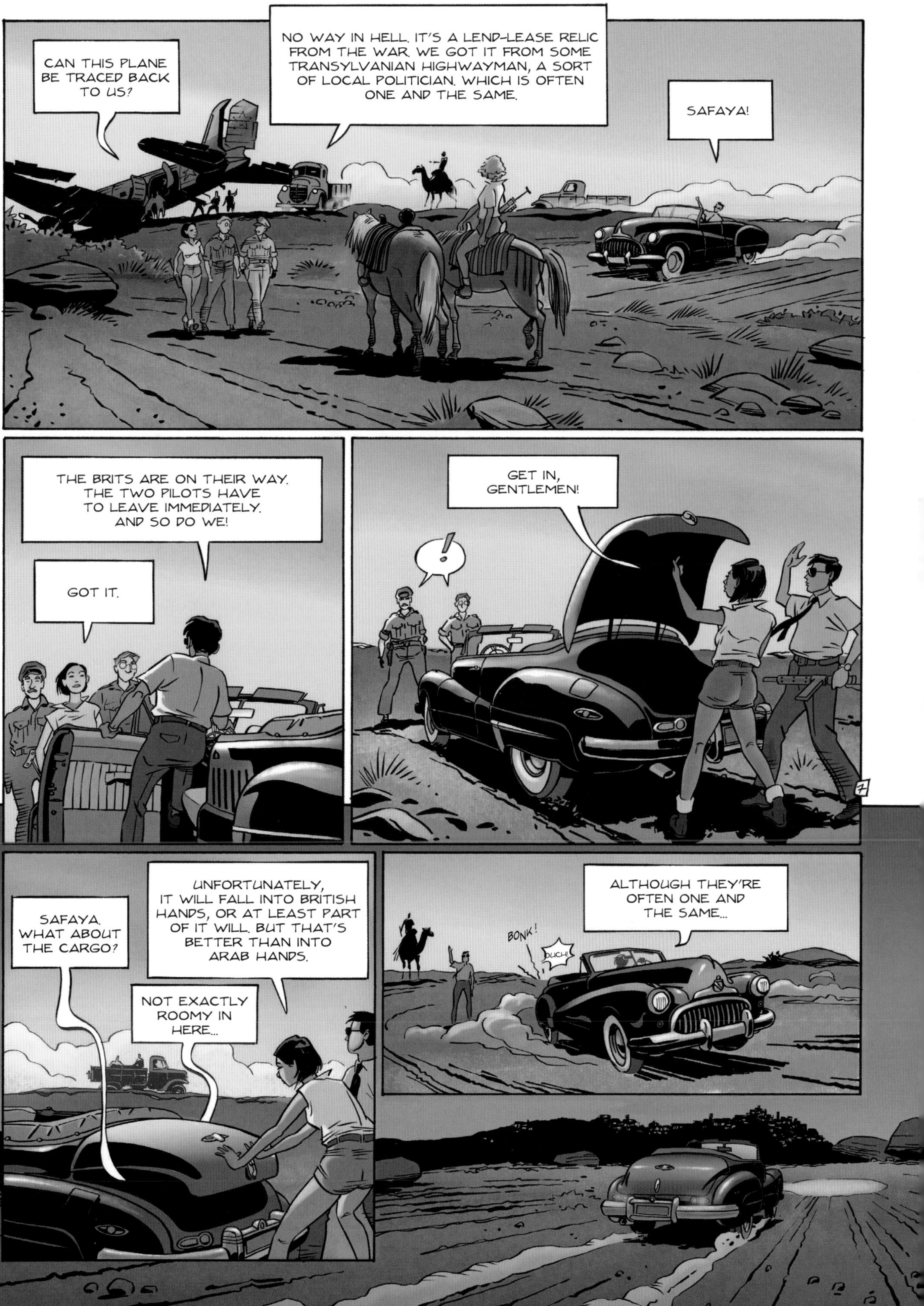
CAN THIS PLANE BE TRACED BACK TO US?
NO WAY IN HELL. IT'S A LEND-LEASE RELIC FROM THE WAR. WE GOT IT FROM SOME TRANSYLVANIAN HIGHWAYMAN, A SORT OF LOCAL POLITICIAN. WHICH IS OFTEN ONE AND THE SAME.
SAFAYA!
THE BRITS ARE ON THEIR WAY. THE TWO PILOTS HAVE TO LEAVE IMMEDIATELY. AND SO DO WE!
GOT IT.
GET IN, GENTLEMEN!
!
SAFAYA. WHAT ABOUT THE CARGO?
UNFORTUNATELY, IT WILL FALL INTO BRITISH HANDS, OR AT LEAST PART OF IT WILL. BUT THAT'S BETTER THAN INTO ARAB HANDS.
NOT EXACTLY ROOMY IN HERE...
ALTHOUGH THEY'RE OFTEN ONE AND THE SAME...
BONK!
OUCH!

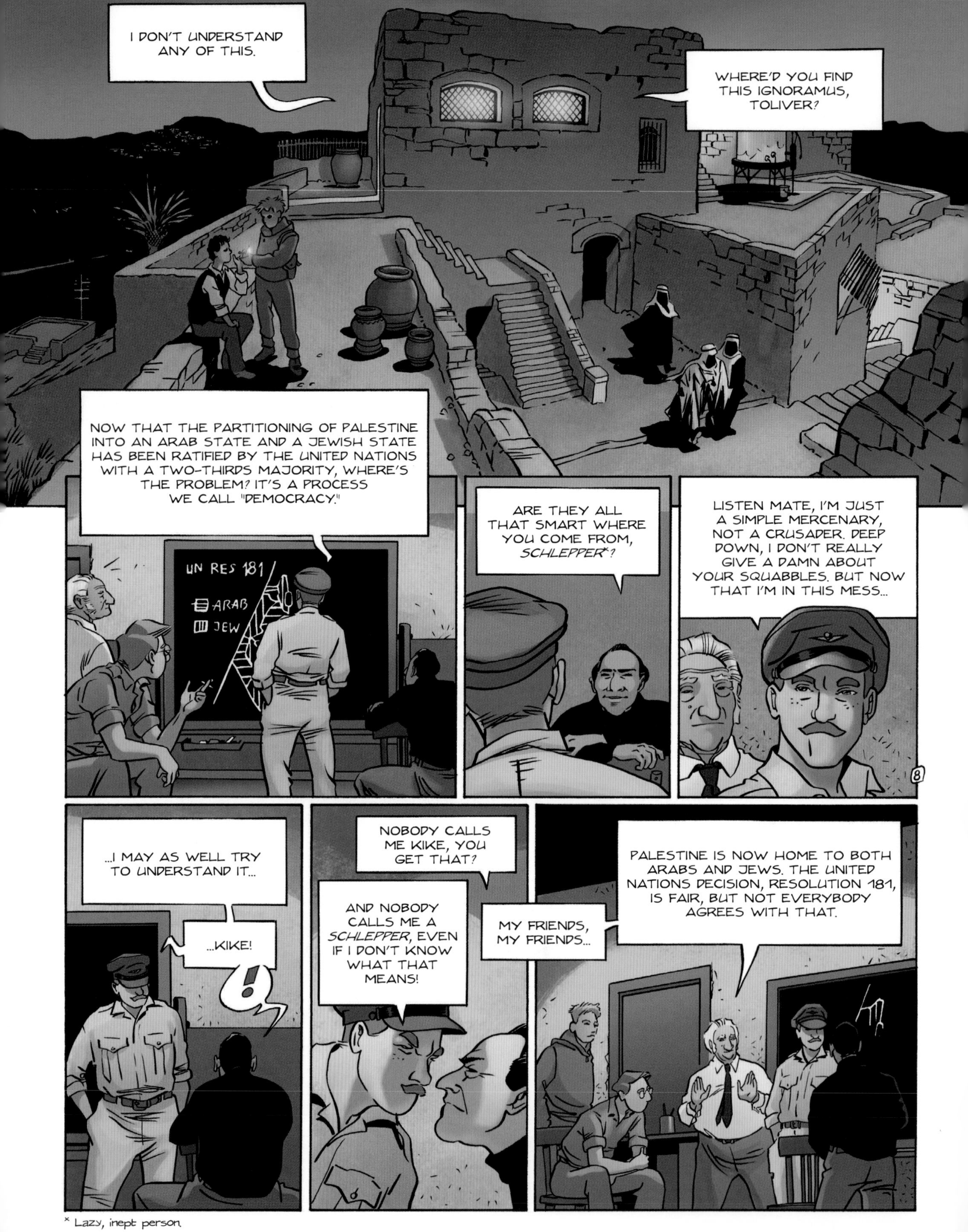
I DON'T UNDERSTAND ANY OF THIS.
WHERE'D YOU FIND THIS IGNORAMUS, TOLIVER?
NOW THAT THE PARTITIONING OF PALESTINE INTO AN ARAB STATE AND A JEWISH STATE HAS BEEN RATIFIED BY THE UNITED NATIONS WITH A TWO-THIRDS MAJORITY, WHERE'S THE PROBLEM? IT'S A PROCESS WE CALL "DEMOCRACY."
UN RES 181
ARAB
JEW
ARE THEY ALL THAT SMART WHERE YOU COME FROM, SCHLEPPER*?
LISTEN MATE, I'M JUST A SIMPLE MERCENARY, NOT A CRUSADER. DEEP DOWN, I DON'T REALLY GIVE A DAMN ABOUT YOUR SQUABBLES. BUT NOW THAT I'M IN THIS MESS...
8
...I MAY AS WELL TRY TO UNDERSTAND IT...
...KIKE!
!
NOBODY CALLS ME KIKE, YOU GET THAT?
AND NOBODY CALLS ME A SCHLEPPER, EVEN IF I DON'T KNOW WHAT THAT MEANS!
MY FRIENDS, MY FRIENDS...
PALESTINE IS NOW HOME TO BOTH ARABS AND JEWS. THE UNITED NATIONS DECISION, RESOLUTION 181, IS FAIR, BUT NOT EVERYBODY AGREES WITH THAT.

* Lazy, inept person.

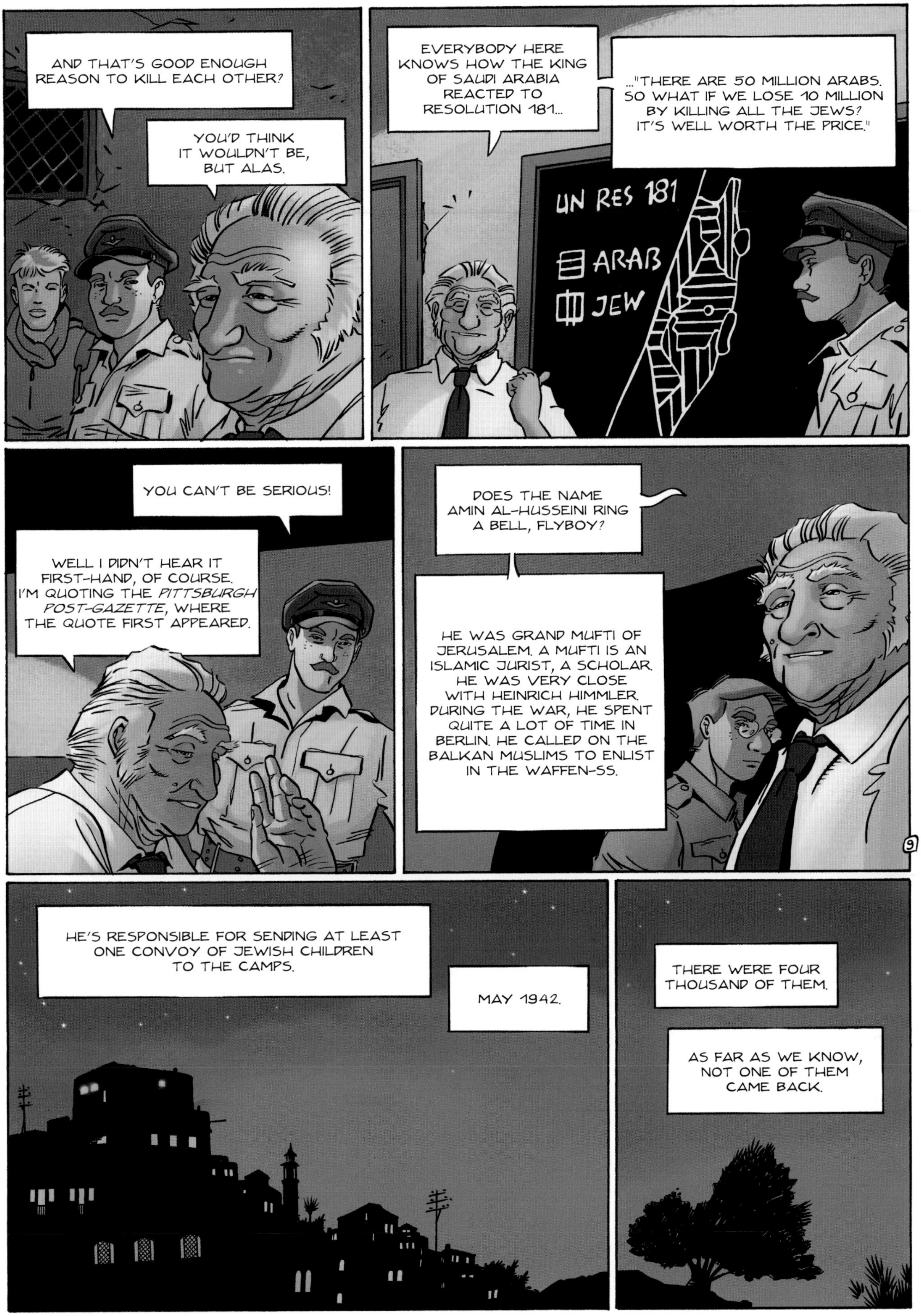
AND THAT'S GOOD ENOUGH REASON TO KILL EACH OTHER?
YOU'D THINK IT WOULDN'T BE, BUT ALAS.
EVERYBODY HERE KNOWS HOW THE KING OF SAUDI ARABIA REACTED TO RESOLUTION 181...
..."THERE ARE 50 MILLION ARABS. SO WHAT IF WE LOSE 10 MILLION BY KILLING ALL THE JEWS? IT'S WELL WORTH THE PRICE."
UN RES 181
ARAB
JEW
YOU CAN'T BE SERIOUS!
WELL I DIDN'T HEAR IT FIRST-HAND, OF COURSE. I'M QUOTING THE *PITTSBURGH POST-GAZETTE*, WHERE THE QUOTE FIRST APPEARED.
DOES THE NAME AMIN AL-HUSSEINI RING A BELL, FLYBOY?
HE WAS GRAND MUFTI OF JERUSALEM. A MUFTI IS AN ISLAMIC JURIST, A SCHOLAR. HE WAS VERY CLOSE WITH HEINRICH HIMMLER. DURING THE WAR, HE SPENT QUITE A LOT OF TIME IN BERLIN. HE CALLED ON THE BALKAN MUSLIMS TO ENLIST IN THE WAFFEN-SS.
9
HE'S RESPONSIBLE FOR SENDING AT LEAST ONE CONVOY OF JEWISH CHILDREN TO THE CAMPS.
MAY 1942.
THERE WERE FOUR THOUSAND OF THEM.
AS FAR AS WE KNOW, NOT ONE OF THEM CAME BACK.

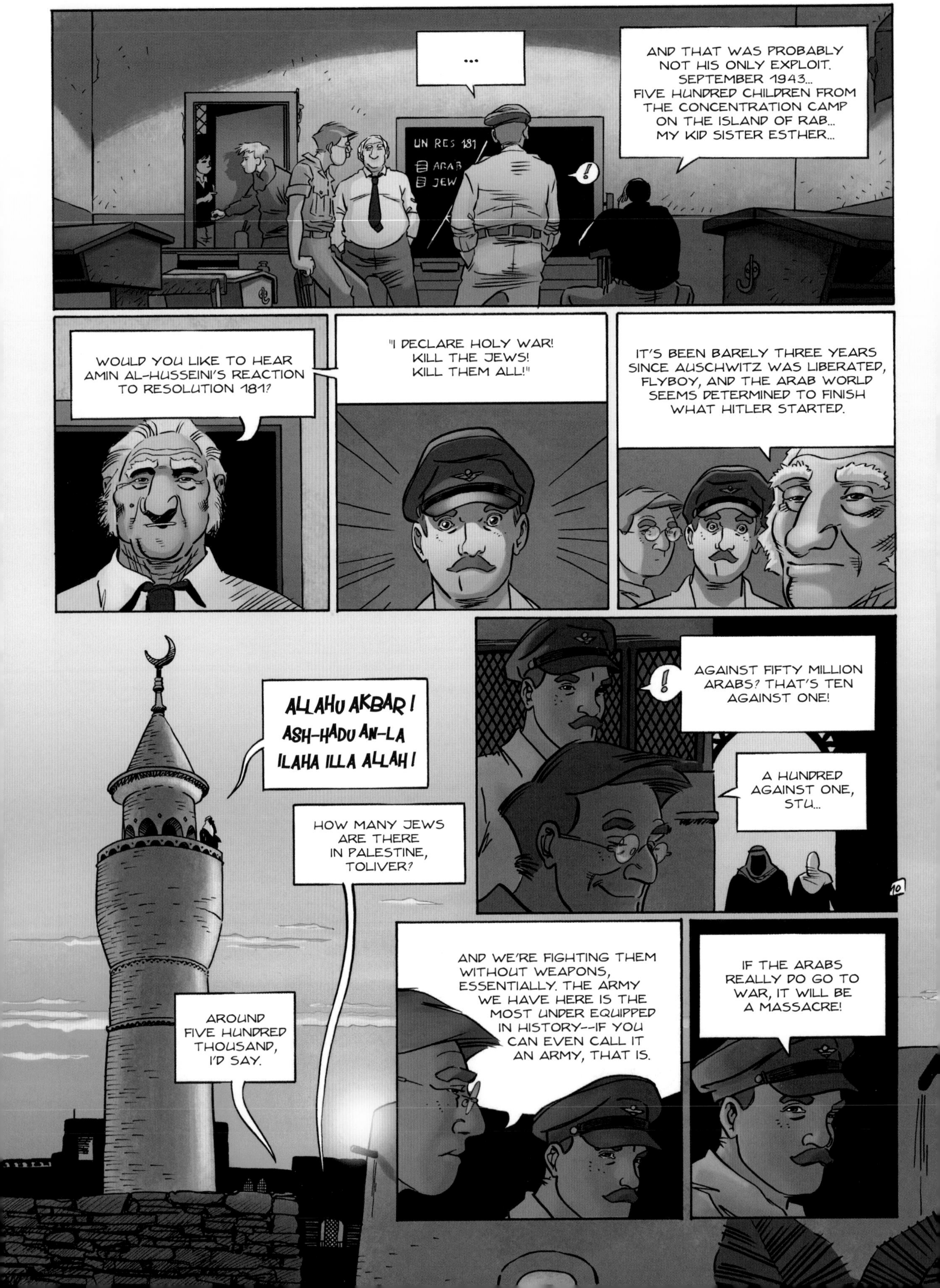
...
AND THAT WAS PROBABLY NOT HIS ONLY EXPLOIT. SEPTEMBER 1943... FIVE HUNDRED CHILDREN FROM THE CONCENTRATION CAMP ON THE ISLAND OF RAB... MY KID SISTER ESTHER...
UN RES 181
ARAB
JEW
!
WOULD YOU LIKE TO HEAR AMIN AL-HUSSEINI'S REACTION TO RESOLUTION 181?
"I DECLARE HOLY WAR! KILL THE JEWS! KILL THEM ALL!"
IT'S BEEN BARELY THREE YEARS SINCE AUSCHWITZ WAS LIBERATED, FLYBOY, AND THE ARAB WORLD SEEMS DETERMINED TO FINISH WHAT HITLER STARTED.
ALLAHU AKBAR! ASH-HADU AN-LA ILAHA ILLA ALLAH!
HOW MANY JEWS ARE THERE IN PALESTINE, TOLIVER?
AROUND FIVE HUNDRED THOUSAND, I'D SAY.
!
AGAINST FIFTY MILLION ARABS? THAT'S TEN AGAINST ONE!
A HUNDRED AGAINST ONE, STU...
10
AND WE'RE FIGHTING THEM WITHOUT WEAPONS, ESSENTIALLY. THE ARMY WE HAVE HERE IS THE MOST UNDER EQUIPPED IN HISTORY--IF YOU CAN EVEN CALL IT AN ARMY, THAT IS.
IF THE ARABS REALLY DO GO TO WAR, IT WILL BE A MASSACRE!

OH, MAKE NO MISTAKE, THEY **WILL** GO TO WAR.

SO WHY DON'T YOU GET OUT OF HERE? YOU'RE NOT JEWISH!

MY MOTHER WAS PART JEWISH. OR AT LEAST JEWISH ENOUGH TO GET GASSED AT SOBIBOR.

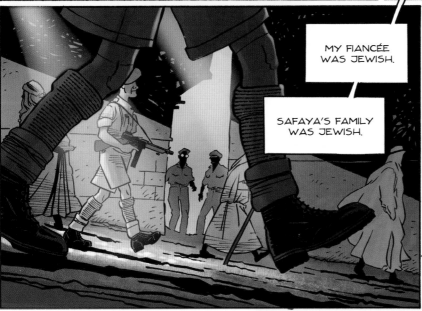

MY FIANCÉE WAS JEWISH.

SAFAYA'S FAMILY WAS JEWISH.

MORE THAN SIX MILLION INNOCENT PEOPLE SHAMEFULLY MURDERED WERE JEWISH.

YEAH, WELL... I'M **NOT** JEWISH!

AND I WOULD LIKE TO GET BACK TO EUROPE ASAP. I FOUND A GIG AS A PILOT FOR A CHARTER COMPANY. JOBS ARE HARD TO COME BY, THESE DAYS. I WANT TO FORGET ABOUT THE WAR, AND THE MEDIEVAL BARBARITY OF IT ALL! RENAISSANCE, HERE I COME! A GOLDEN AGE IS WAITING FOR ME SOMEWHERE... BUT NOT HERE! NOT IN PALESTINE!

THAT'S EXACTLY WHAT THE SURVIVORS ARE HOPING: THAT A GOLDEN AGE AWAITS THEM HERE, IN PALESTINE.

A GOLDEN AGE? A HUNDRED YEARS OF WAR, YOU MEAN! MARK MY WORDS.

THAT MAY BE... BUT WITHOUT GAS CHAMBERS, AT ANY RATE. IN THE FUTURE, JEWS WILL FIGHT BACK WITH EVERYTHING THEY'VE GOT.

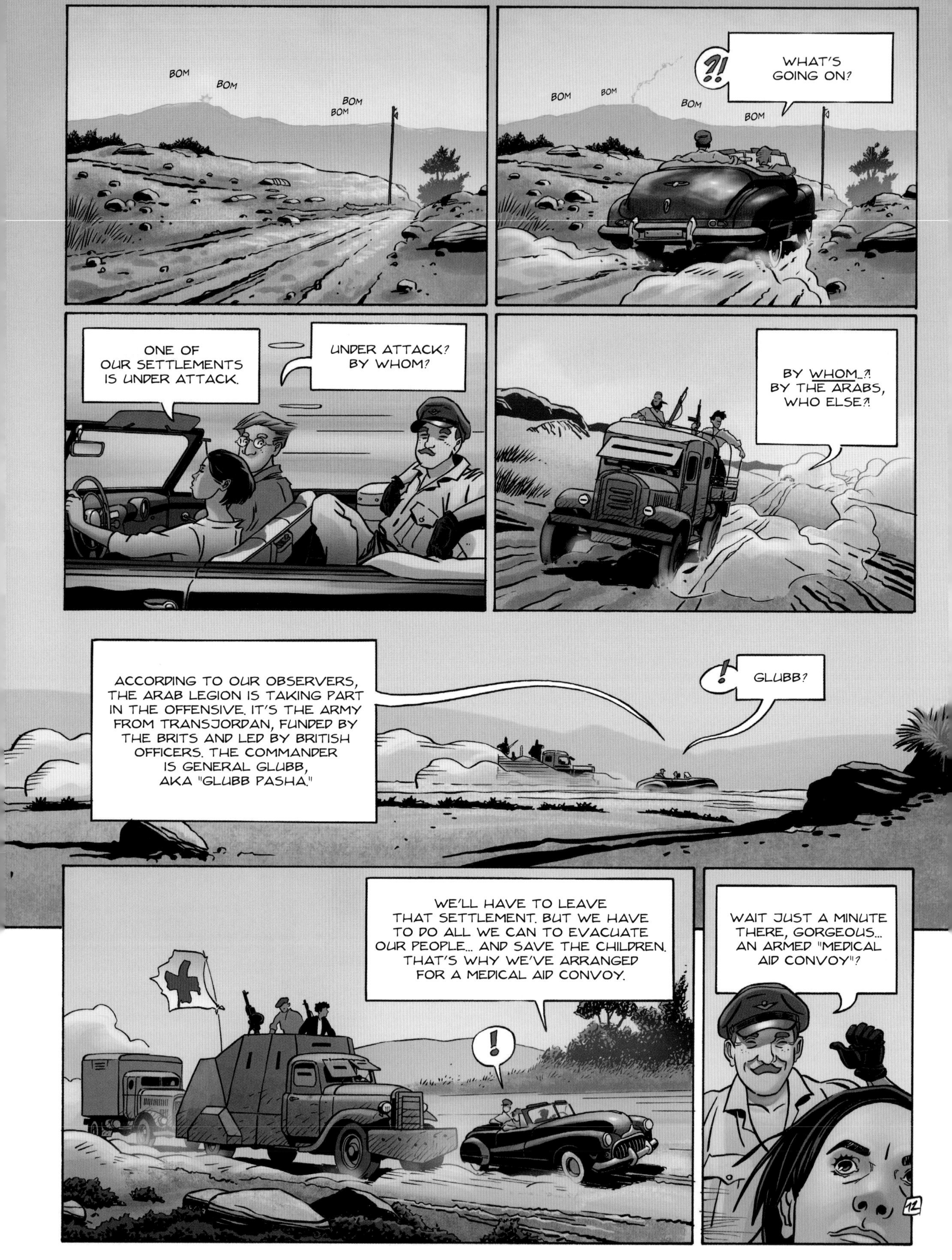
BOM
BOM
BOM
BOM
?!
WHAT'S GOING ON?
BOM
BOM
BOM
BOM
ONE OF OUR SETTLEMENTS IS UNDER ATTACK.
UNDER ATTACK? BY WHOM?
BY WHOM...?! BY THE ARABS, WHO ELSE?!
ACCORDING TO OUR OBSERVERS, THE ARAB LEGION IS TAKING PART IN THE OFFENSIVE. IT'S THE ARMY FROM TRANSJORDAN, FUNDED BY THE BRITS AND LED BY BRITISH OFFICERS. THE COMMANDER IS GENERAL GLUBB, AKA "GLUBB PASHA."
!
GLUBB?
WE'LL HAVE TO LEAVE THAT SETTLEMENT. BUT WE HAVE TO DO ALL WE CAN TO EVACUATE OUR PEOPLE... AND SAVE THE CHILDREN. THAT'S WHY WE'VE ARRANGED FOR A MEDICAL AID CONVOY.
!
WAIT JUST A MINUTE THERE, GORGEOUS... AN ARMED "MEDICAL AID CONVOY"?

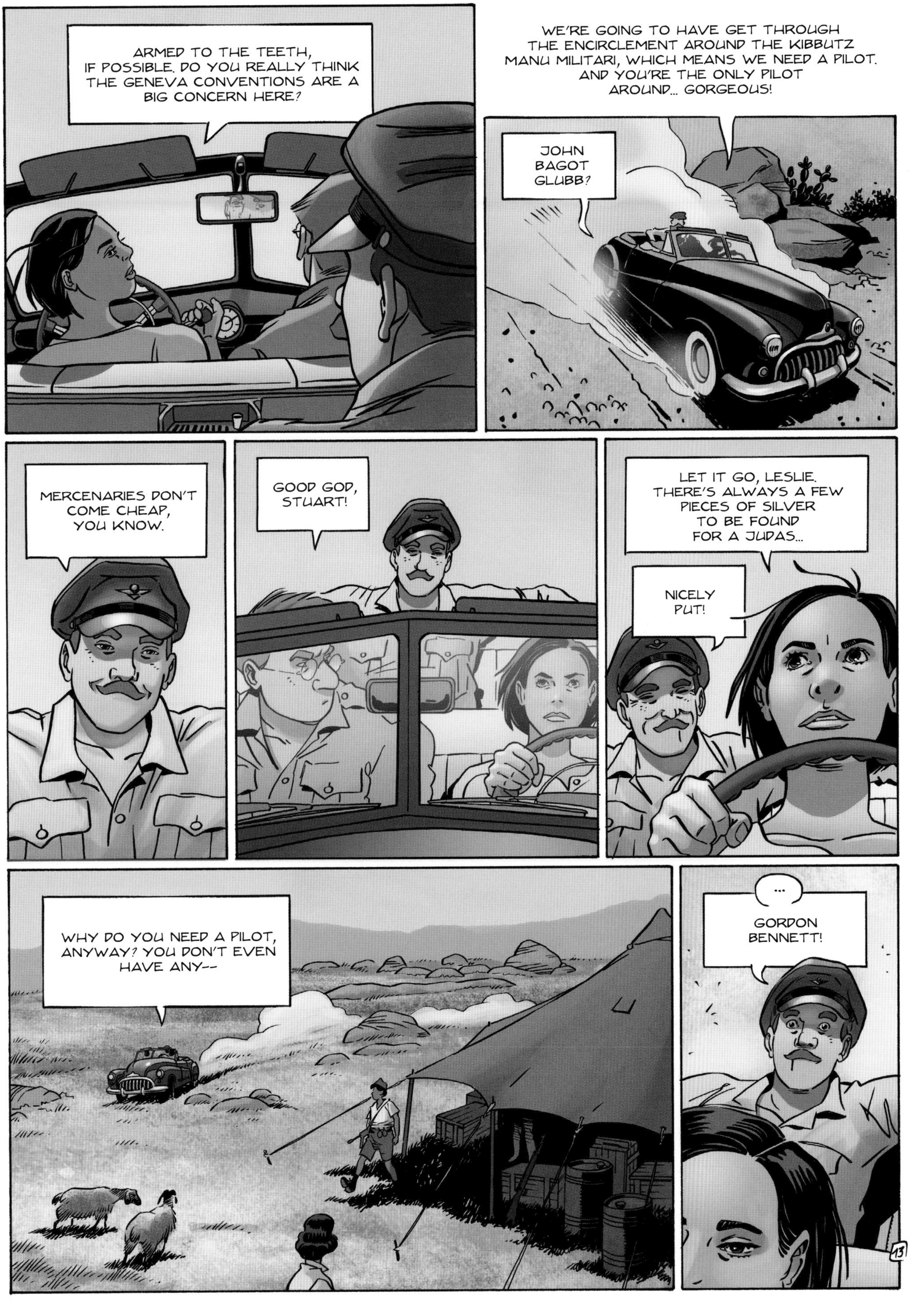
ARMED TO THE TEETH, IF POSSIBLE. DO YOU REALLY THINK THE GENEVA CONVENTIONS ARE A BIG CONCERN HERE?
WE'RE GOING TO HAVE GET THROUGH THE ENCIRCLEMENT AROUND THE KIBBUTZ MANU MILITARI, WHICH MEANS WE NEED A PILOT. AND YOU'RE THE ONLY PILOT AROUND... GORGEOUS!
JOHN BAGOT GLUBB?
MERCENARIES DON'T COME CHEAP, YOU KNOW.
GOOD GOD, STUART!
LET IT GO, LESLIE. THERE'S ALWAYS A FEW PIECES OF SILVER TO BE FOUND FOR A JUDAS...
NICELY PUT!
WHY DO YOU NEED A PILOT, ANYWAY? YOU DON'T EVEN HAVE ANY--
...
GORDON BENNETT!
13

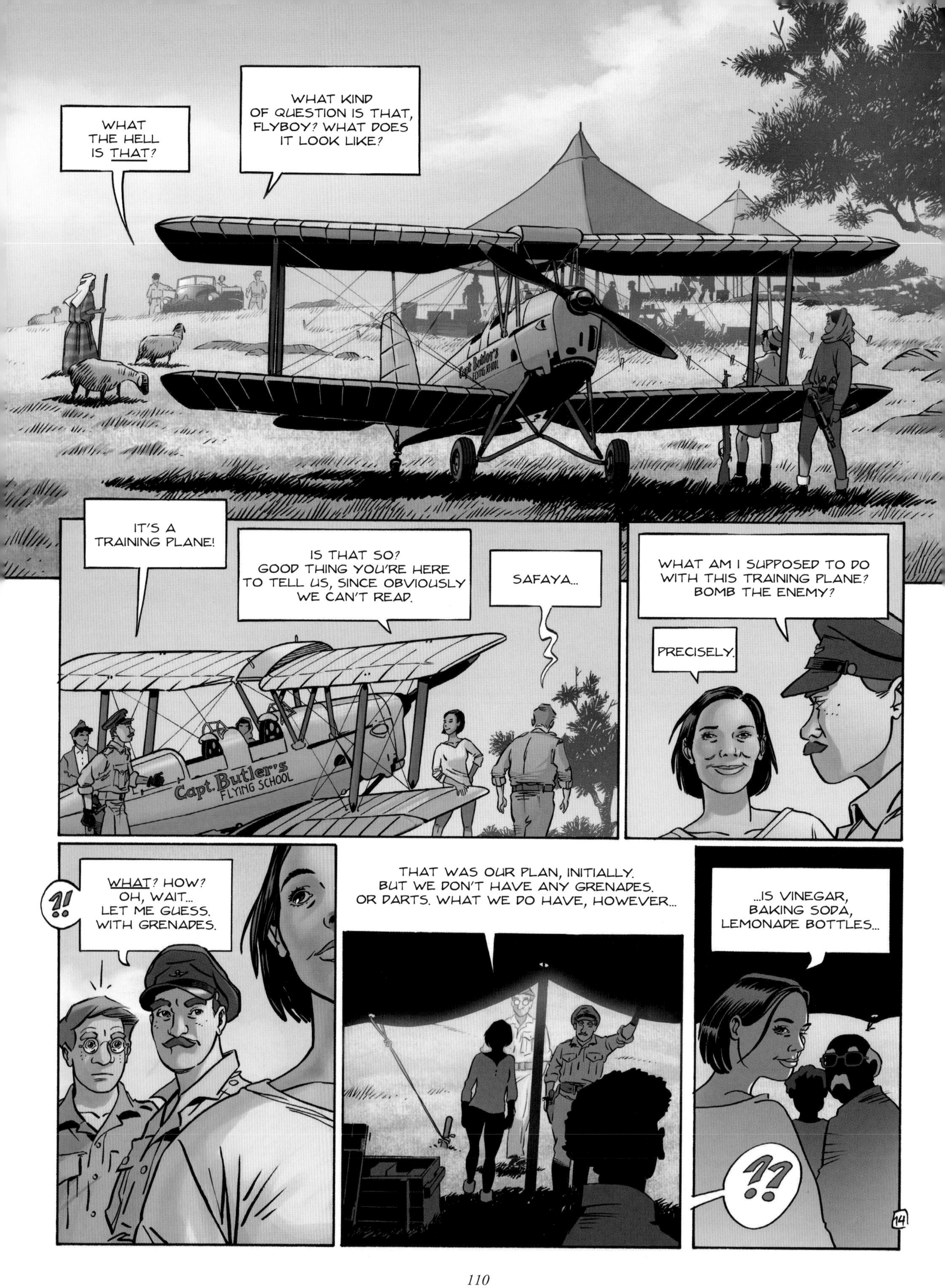
WHAT THE HELL IS THAT?
WHAT KIND OF QUESTION IS THAT, FLYBOY? WHAT DOES IT LOOK LIKE?
Capt. Butler's FLYING SCHOOL
IT'S A TRAINING PLANE!
IS THAT SO? GOOD THING YOU'RE HERE TO TELL US, SINCE OBVIOUSLY WE CAN'T READ.
SAFAYA...
Capt. Butler's FLYING SCHOOL
WHAT AM I SUPPOSED TO DO WITH THIS TRAINING PLANE? BOMB THE ENEMY?
PRECISELY.
?!
WHAT? HOW? OH, WAIT... LET ME GUESS. WITH GRENADES.
THAT WAS OUR PLAN, INITIALLY. BUT WE DON'T HAVE ANY GRENADES. OR DARTS. WHAT WE DO HAVE, HOWEVER...
...IS VINEGAR, BAKING SODA, LEMONADE BOTTLES...
??
14

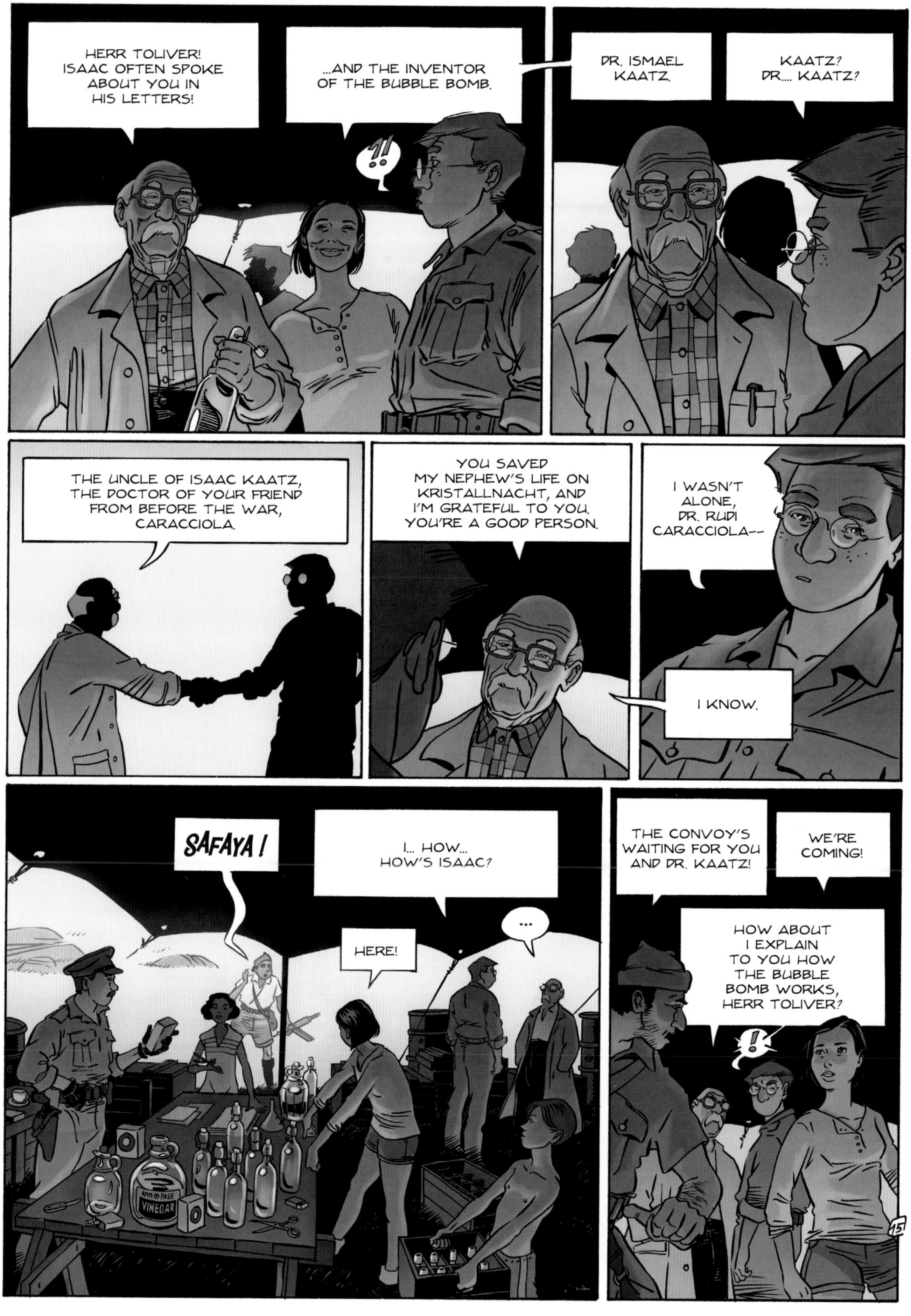
HERR TOLIVER! ISAAC OFTEN SPOKE ABOUT YOU IN HIS LETTERS!
...AND THE INVENTOR OF THE BUBBLE BOMB.
?!!
DR. ISMAEL KAATZ.
KAATZ? DR.... KAATZ?
THE UNCLE OF ISAAC KAATZ, THE DOCTOR OF YOUR FRIEND FROM BEFORE THE WAR, CARACCIOLA.
YOU SAVED MY NEPHEW'S LIFE ON KRISTALLNACHT, AND I'M GRATEFUL TO YOU. YOU'RE A GOOD PERSON.
I WASN'T ALONE, DR. RUDI CARACCIOLA--
I KNOW.
SAFAYA!
I... HOW... HOW'S ISAAC?
HERE!
...
VINEGAR
THE CONVOY'S WAITING FOR YOU AND DR. KAATZ!
WE'RE COMING!
HOW ABOUT I EXPLAIN TO YOU HOW THE BUBBLE BOMB WORKS, HERR TOLIVER?
!
15

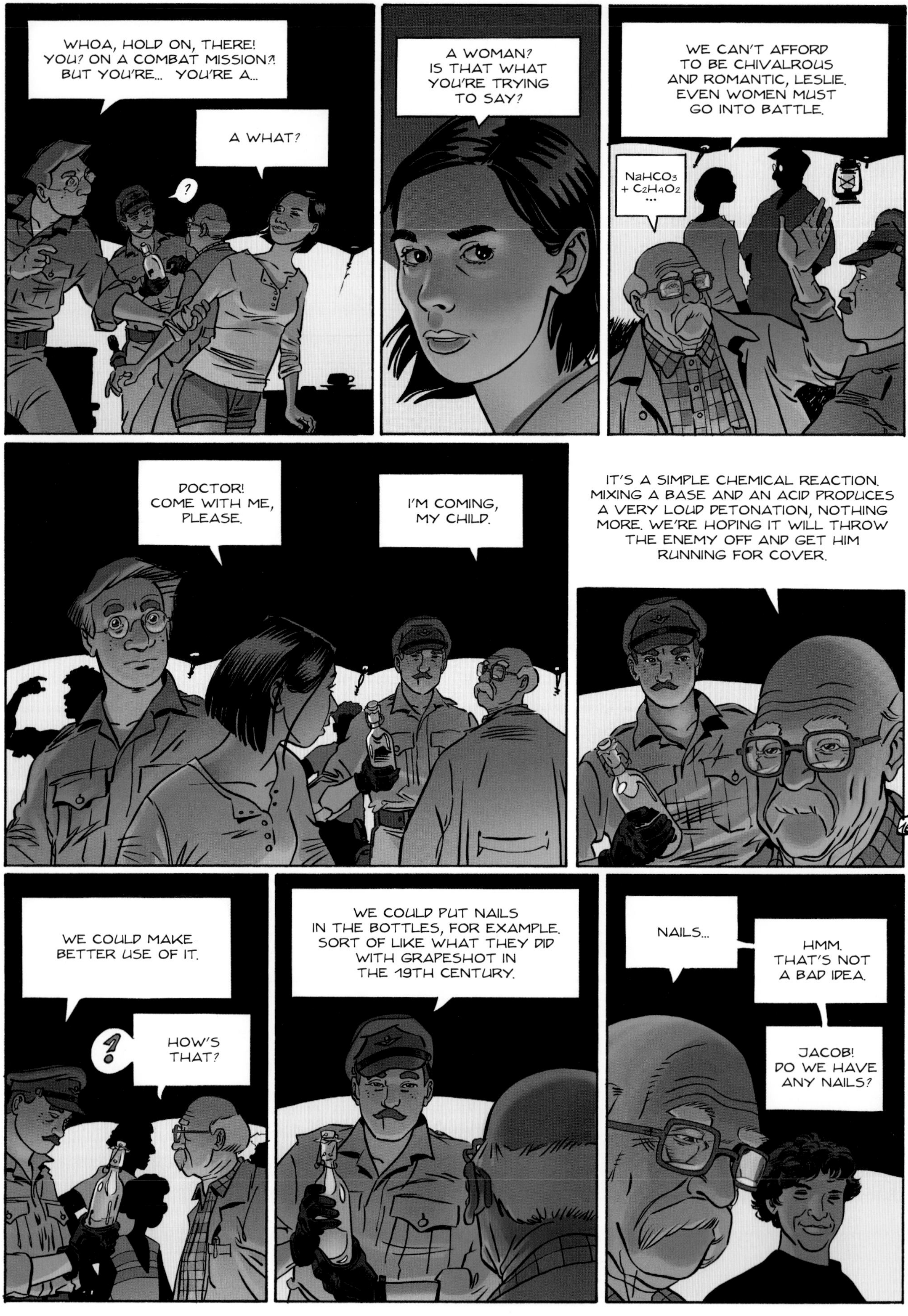
WHOA, HOLD ON, THERE! YOU? ON A COMBAT MISSION?! BUT YOU'RE... YOU'RE A...
?
A WHAT?
A WOMAN? IS THAT WHAT YOU'RE TRYING TO SAY?
WE CAN'T AFFORD TO BE CHIVALROUS AND ROMANTIC, LESLIE. EVEN WOMEN MUST GO INTO BATTLE.
$NaHCO_3$ + $C_2H_4O_2$ ...
DOCTOR! COME WITH ME, PLEASE.
I'M COMING, MY CHILD.
IT'S A SIMPLE CHEMICAL REACTION. MIXING A BASE AND AN ACID PRODUCES A VERY LOUD DETONATION, NOTHING MORE. WE'RE HOPING IT WILL THROW THE ENEMY OFF AND GET HIM RUNNING FOR COVER.
16
WE COULD MAKE BETTER USE OF IT.
?
HOW'S THAT?
WE COULD PUT NAILS IN THE BOTTLES, FOR EXAMPLE. SORT OF LIKE WHAT THEY DID WITH GRAPESHOT IN THE 19TH CENTURY.
NAILS...
HMM. THAT'S NOT A BAD IDEA.
JACOB! DO WE HAVE ANY NAILS?

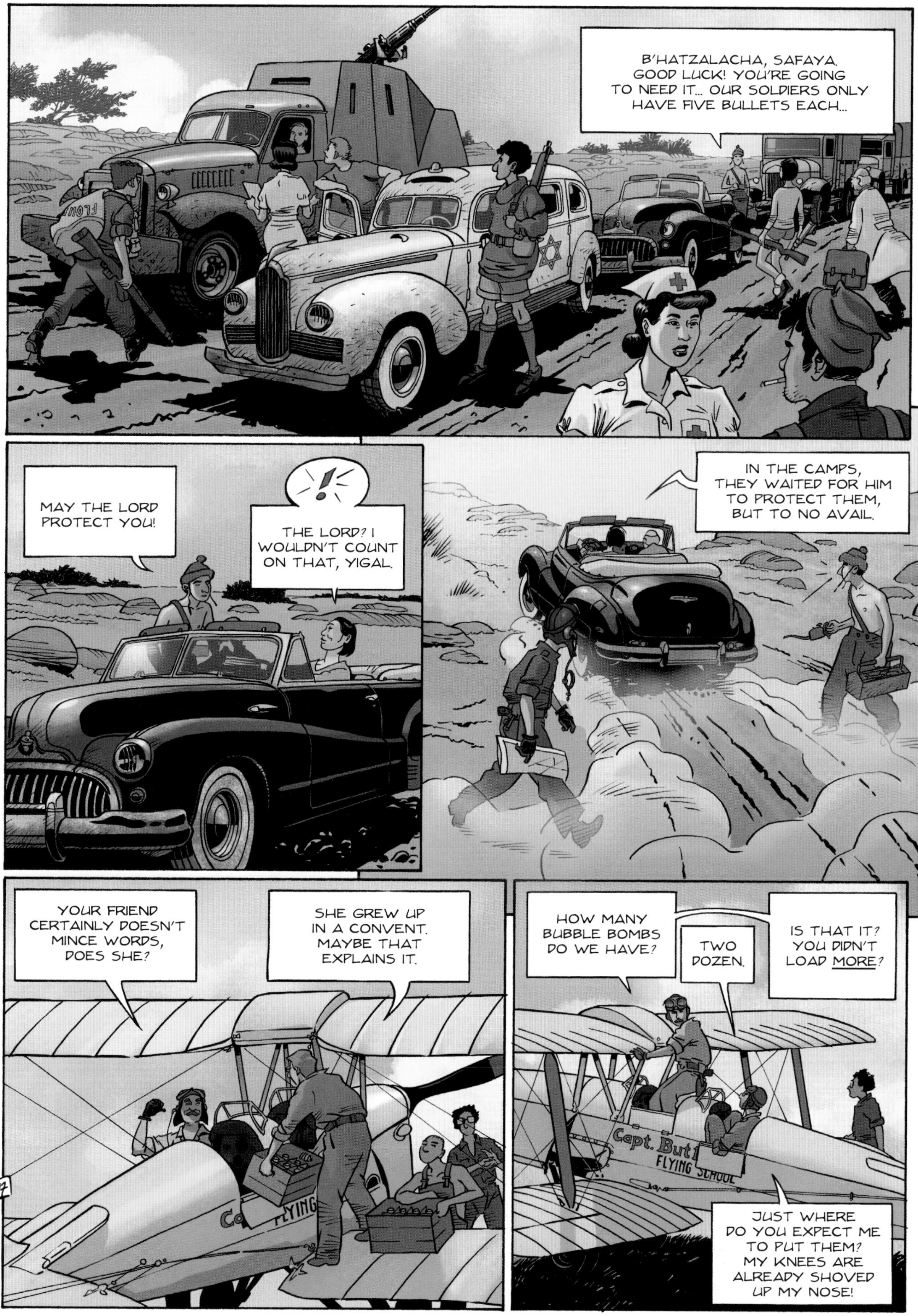
B'HATZALACHA, SAFAYA. GOOD LUCK! YOU'RE GOING TO NEED IT... OUR SOLDIERS ONLY HAVE FIVE BULLETS EACH...
MAY THE LORD PROTECT YOU!
!
THE LORD? I WOULDN'T COUNT ON THAT, YIGAL.
IN THE CAMPS, THEY WAITED FOR HIM TO PROTECT THEM, BUT TO NO AVAIL.
YOUR FRIEND CERTAINLY DOESN'T MINCE WORDS, DOES SHE?
SHE GREW UP IN A CONVENT. MAYBE THAT EXPLAINS IT.
HOW MANY BUBBLE BOMBS DO WE HAVE?
TWO DOZEN.
IS THAT IT? YOU DIDN'T LOAD MORE?
Capt. But
FLYING SCHOOL
JUST WHERE DO YOU EXPECT ME TO PUT THEM? MY KNEES ARE ALREADY SHOVED UP MY NOSE!

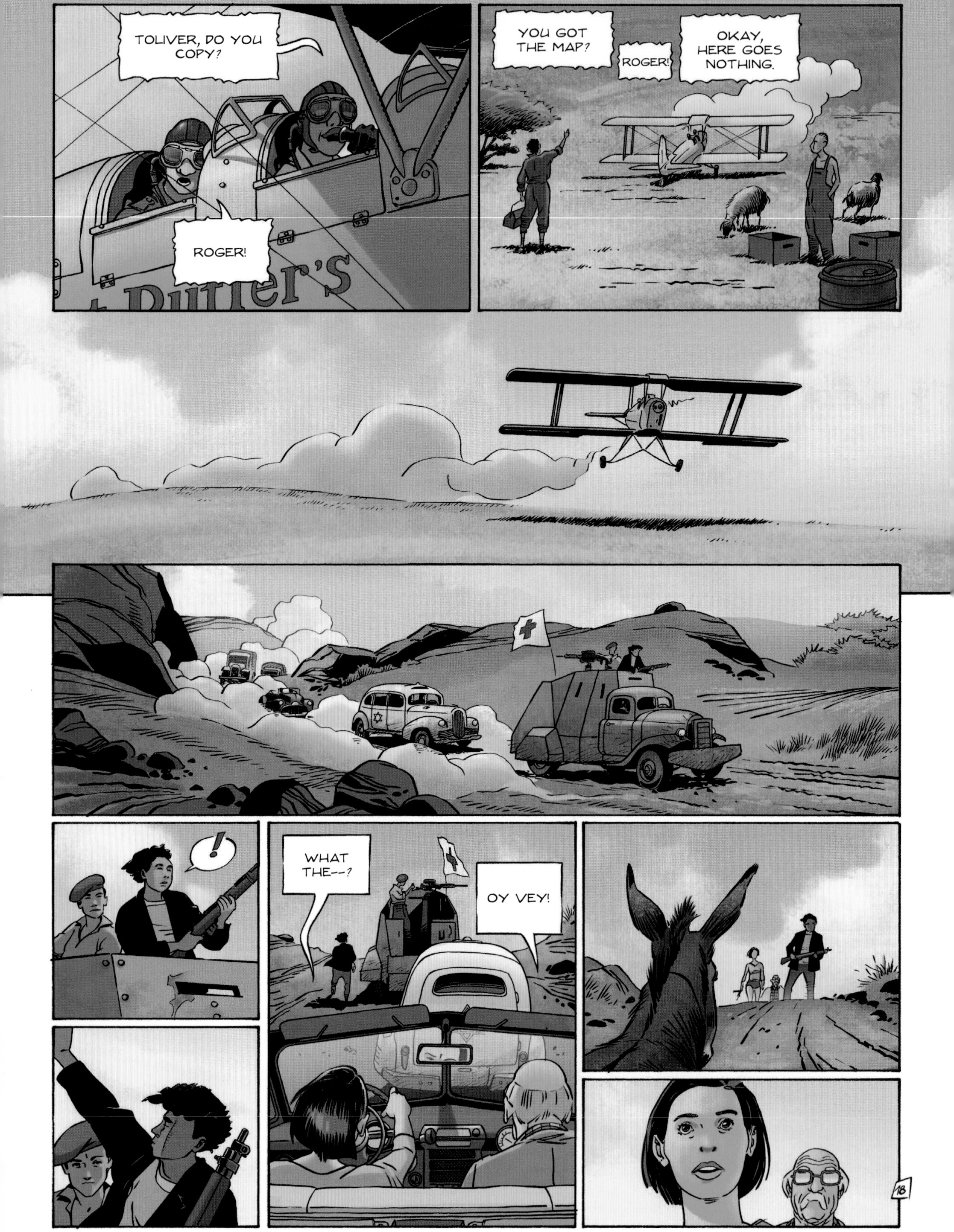
TOLIVER, DO YOU COPY?
ROGER!
YOU GOT THE MAP?
ROGER!
OKAY, HERE GOES NOTHING.
!
WHAT THE--?
OY VEY!
18

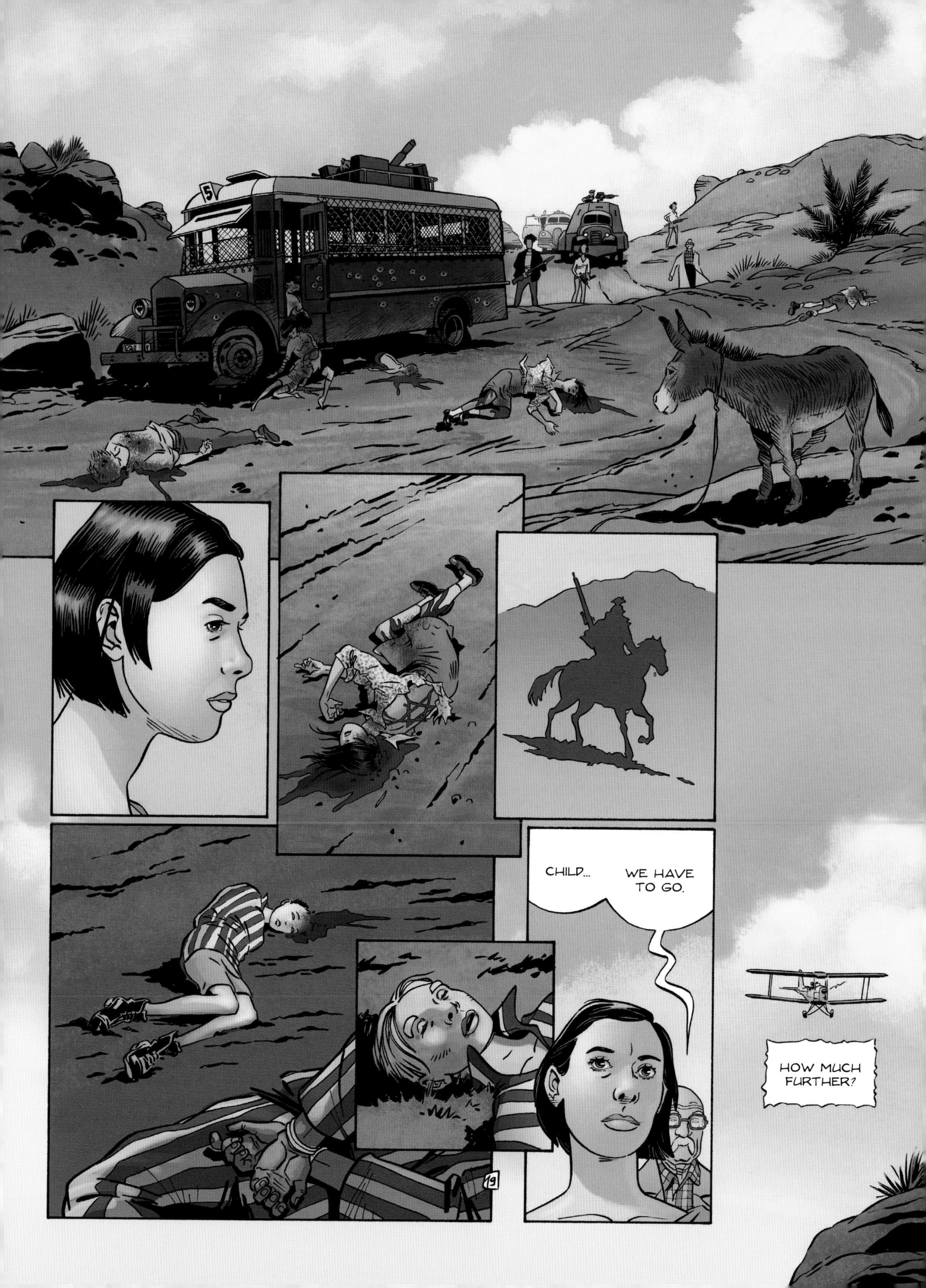
CHILD...
WE HAVE TO GO.
HOW MUCH FURTHER?
19

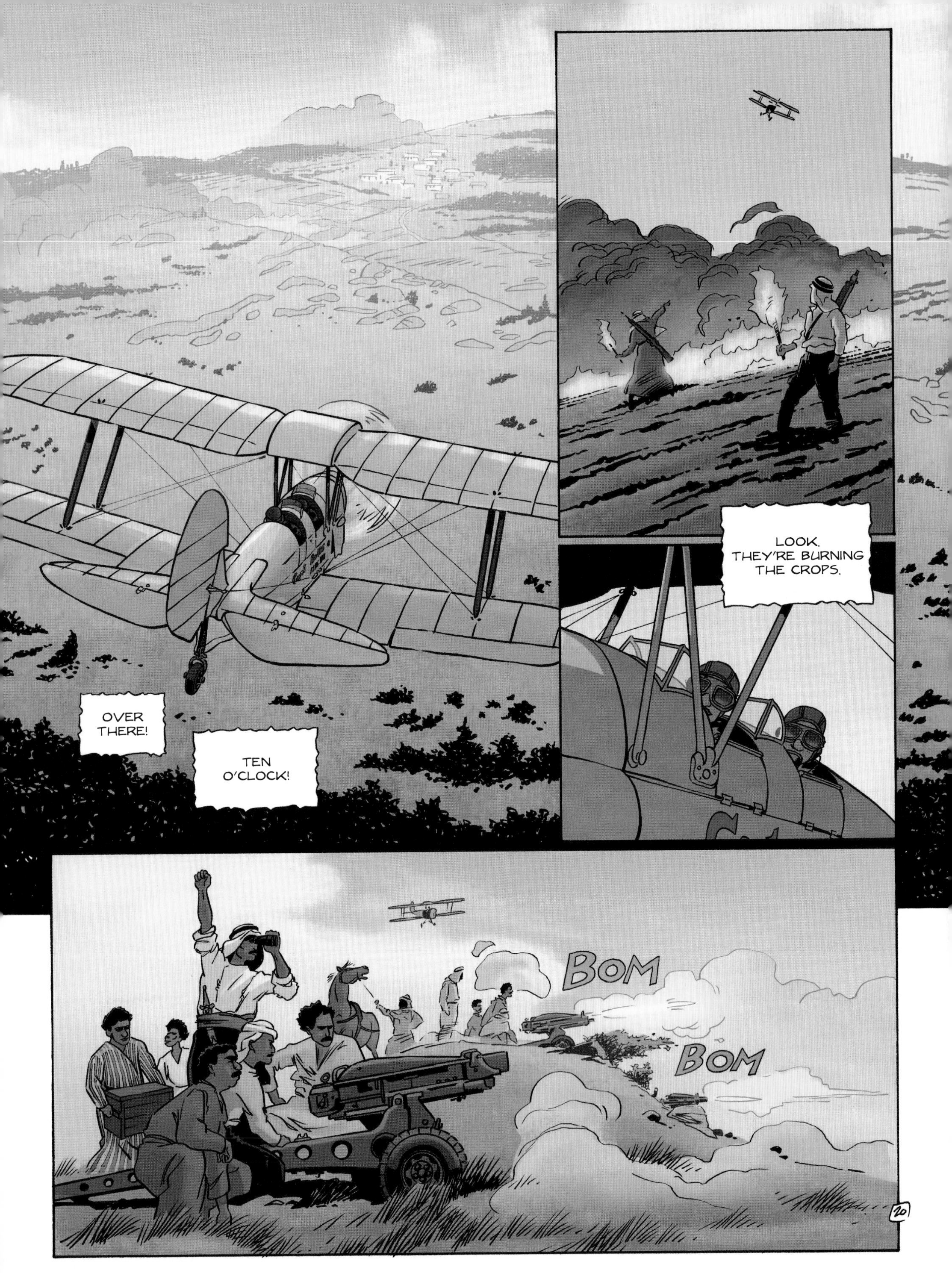
OVER THERE!
TEN O'CLOCK!
LOOK. THEY'RE BURNING THE CROPS.
BOM
BOM
20

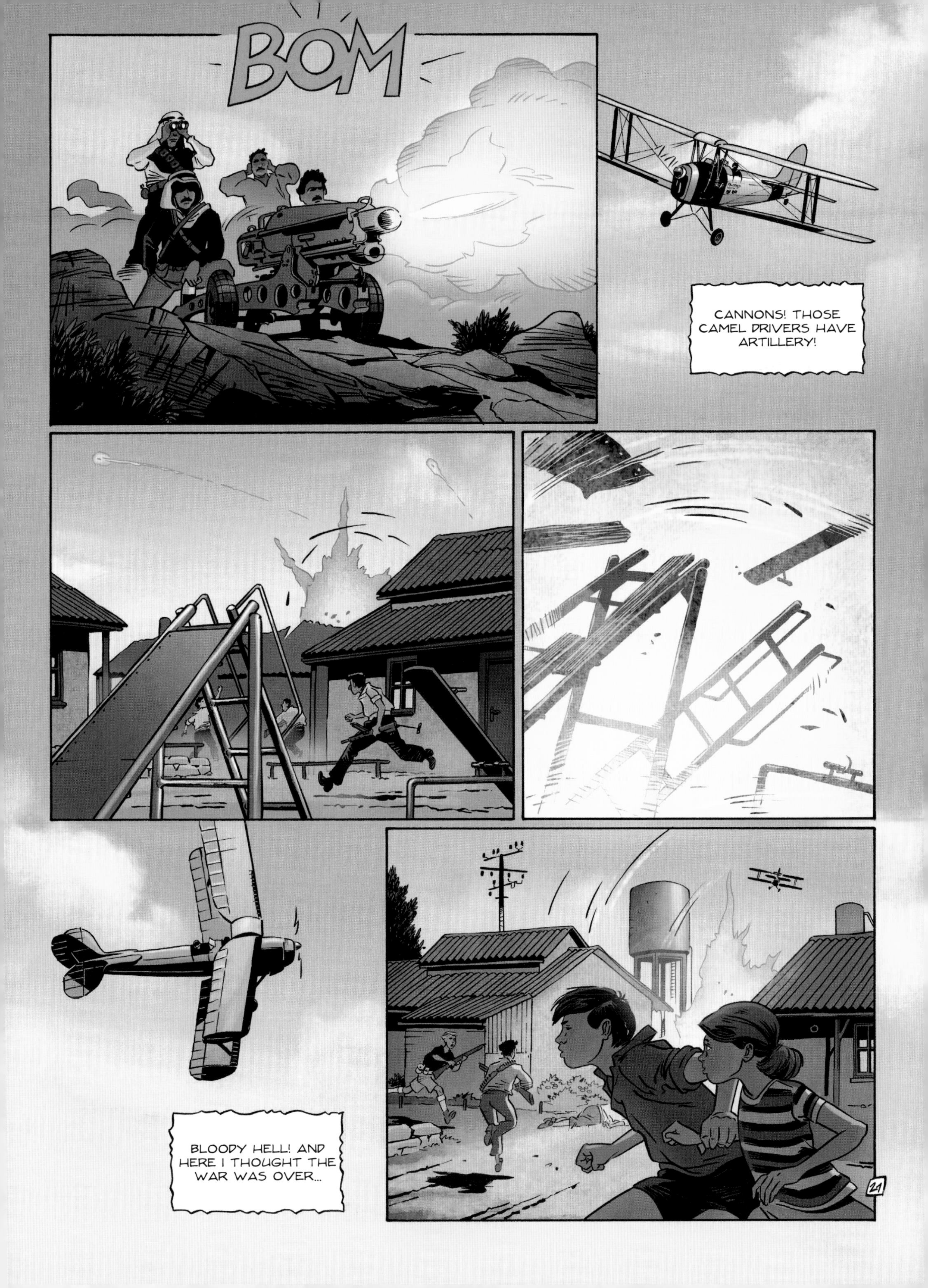
BOM
CANNONS! THOSE CAMEL DRIVERS HAVE ARTILLERY!
BLOODY HELL! AND HERE I THOUGHT THE WAR WAS OVER...
21

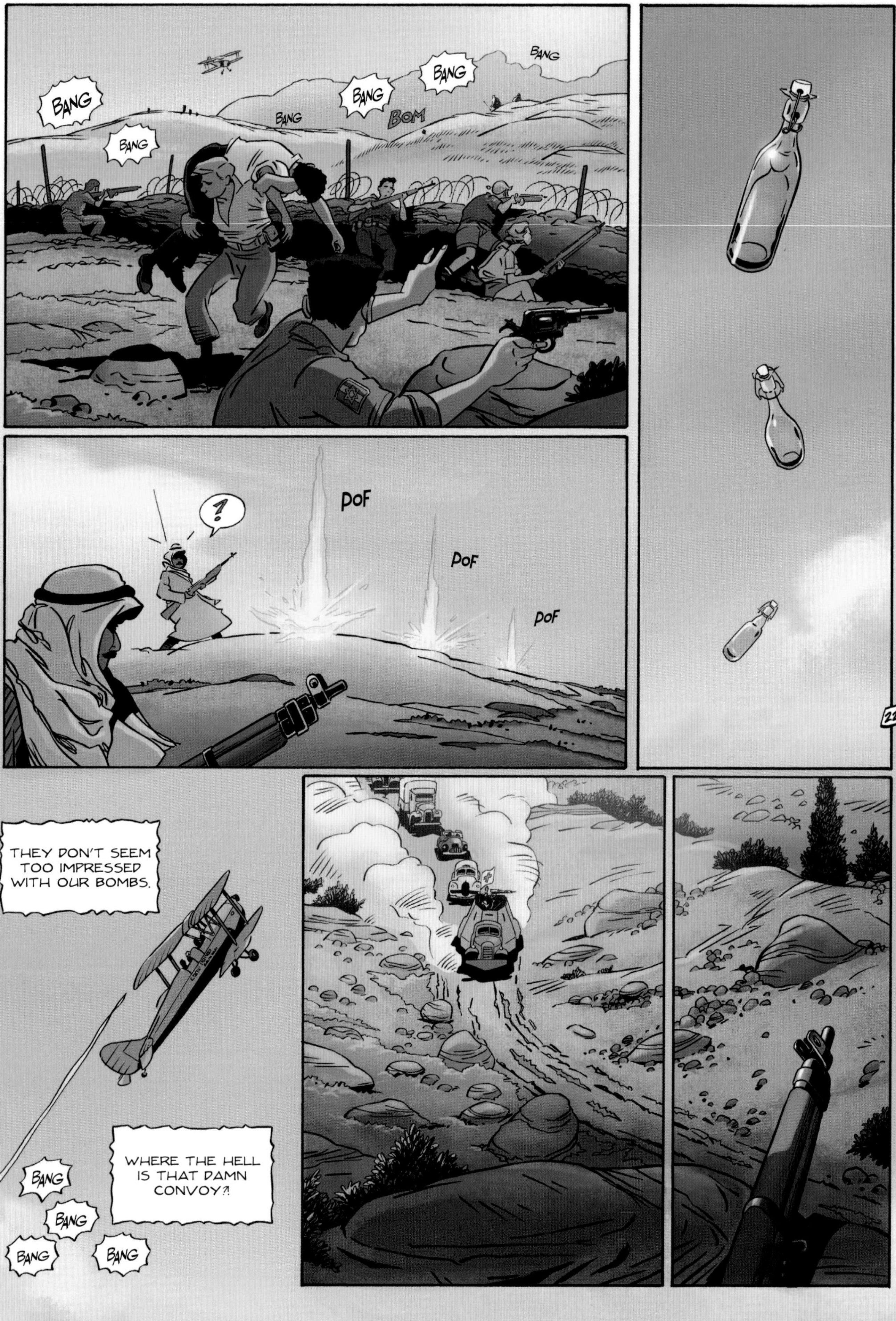

BANG
BANG
BANG
BANG
BANG
BOM
BANG
BANG
?
POF
POF
POF
22
THEY DON'T SEEM TOO IMPRESSED WITH OUR BOMBS.
WHERE THE HELL IS THAT DAMN CONVOY?!
BANG
BANG
BANG
BANG

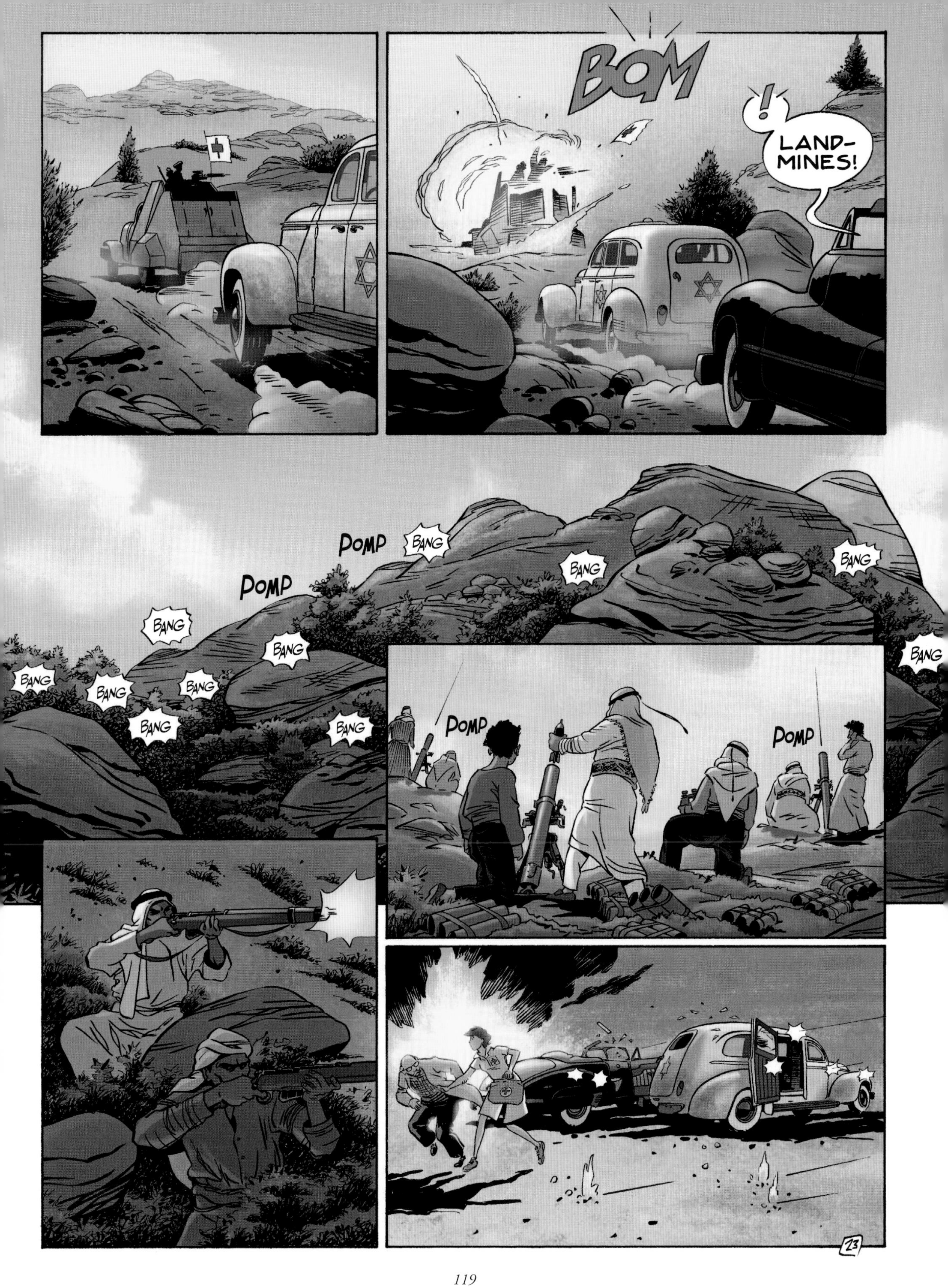
BOM
!
LAND-
MINES!
POMP
BANG
POMP
BANG
BANG
BANG
BANG
BANG
BANG
BANG
BANG
BANG
BANG
POMP
POMP
23

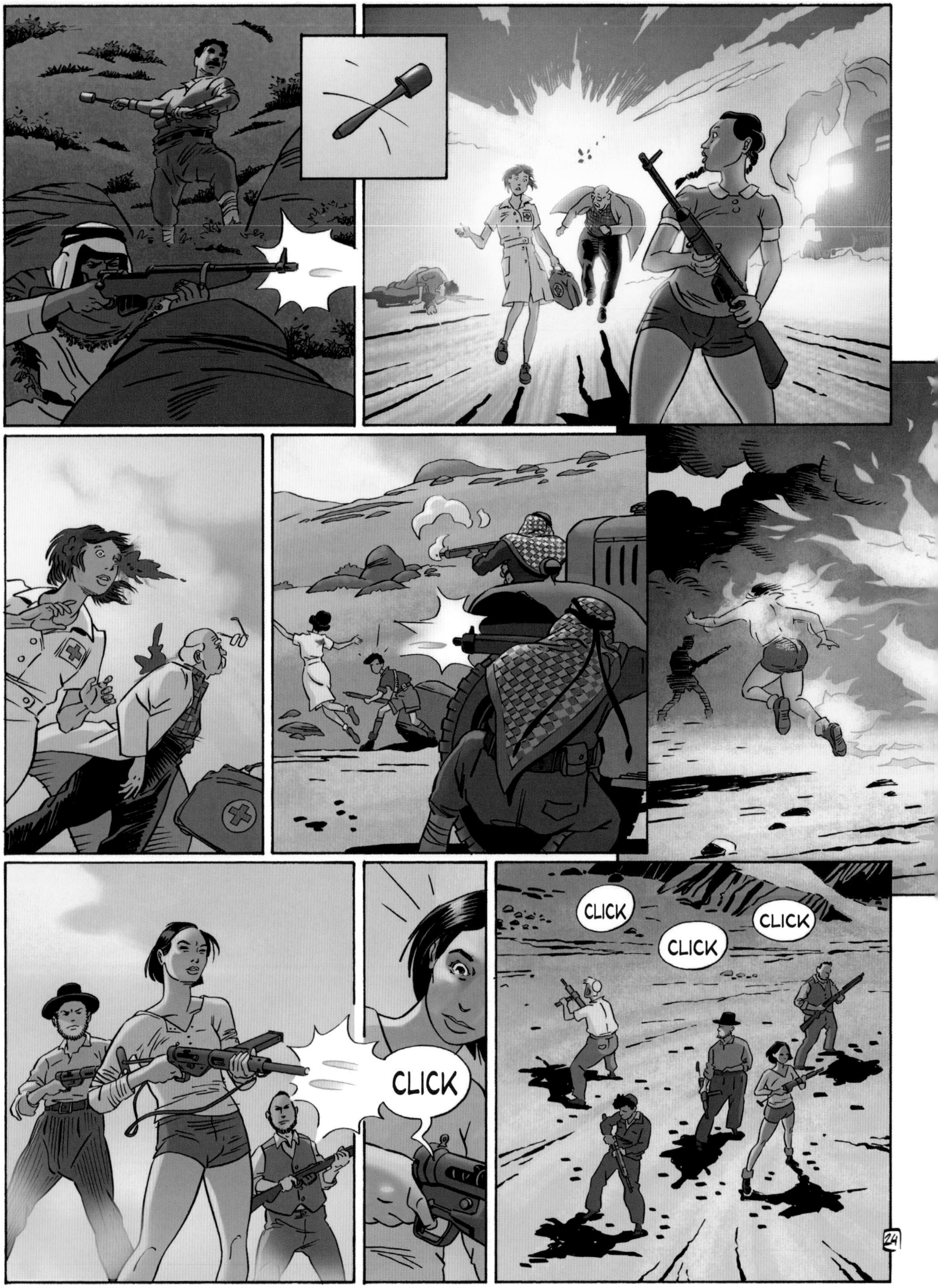
CLICK
CLICK
CLICK
CLICK
24

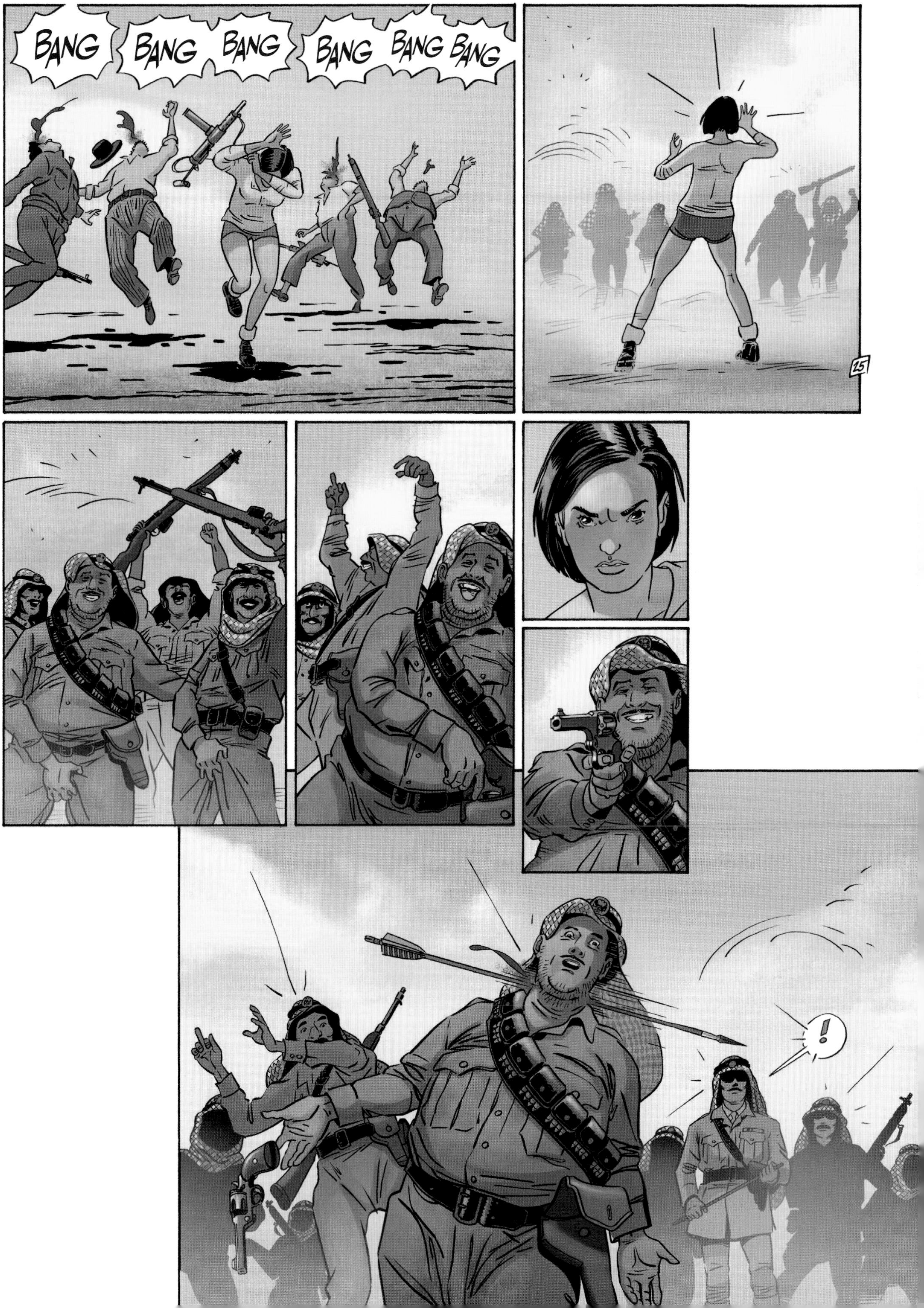
BANG
BANG
BANG
BANG
BANG
BANG
25
!

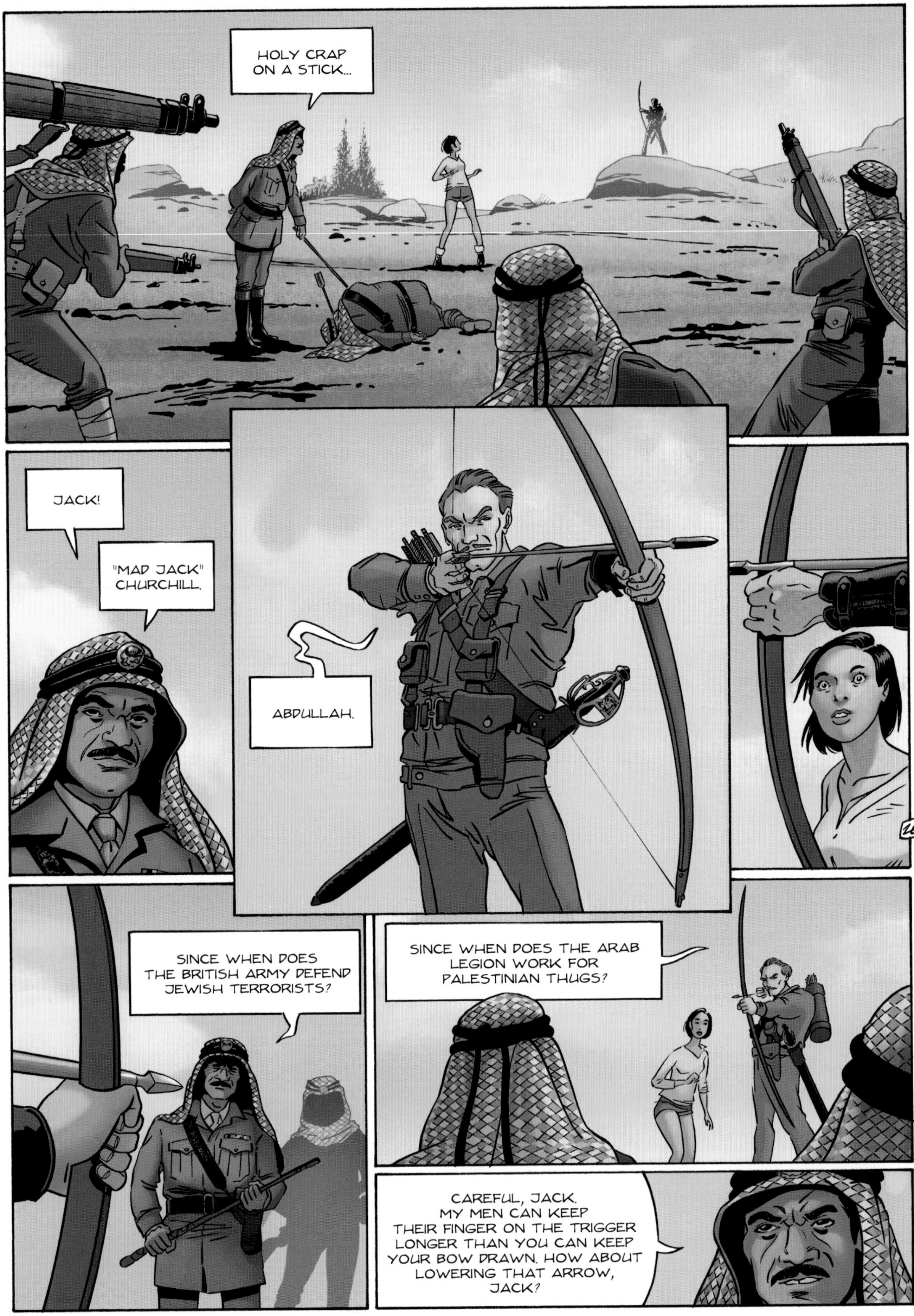
HOLY CRAP ON A STICK...
JACK!
"MAD JACK" CHURCHILL.
ABDULLAH.
26
SINCE WHEN DOES THE BRITISH ARMY DEFEND JEWISH TERRORISTS?
SINCE WHEN DOES THE ARAB LEGION WORK FOR PALESTINIAN THUGS?
CAREFUL, JACK. MY MEN CAN KEEP THEIR FINGER ON THE TRIGGER LONGER THAN YOU CAN KEEP YOUR BOW DRAWN. HOW ABOUT LOWERING THAT ARROW, JACK?

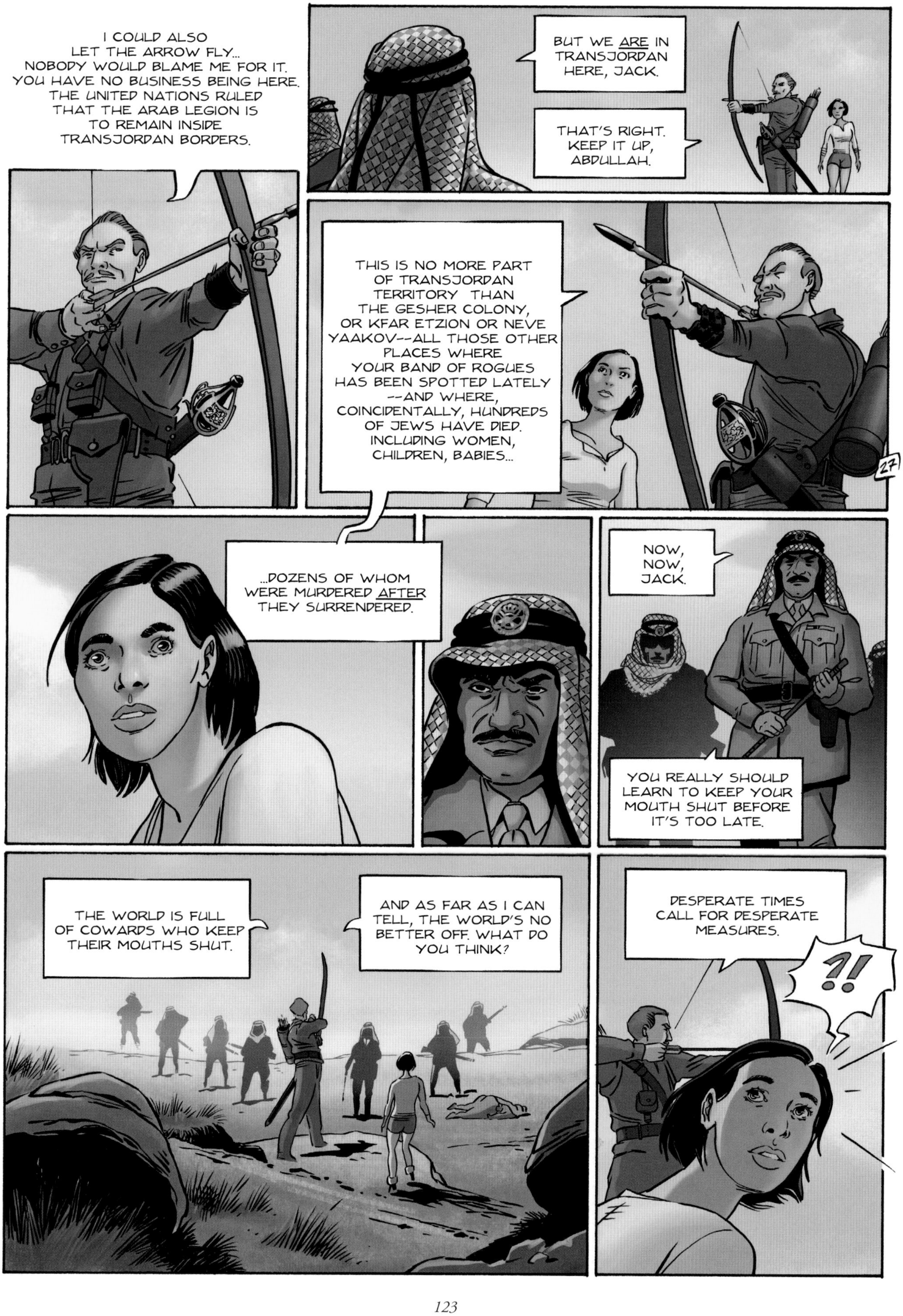
I COULD ALSO LET THE ARROW FLY... NOBODY WOULD BLAME ME FOR IT. YOU HAVE NO BUSINESS BEING HERE. THE UNITED NATIONS RULED THAT THE ARAB LEGION IS TO REMAIN INSIDE TRANSJORDAN BORDERS.
BUT WE ARE IN TRANSJORDAN HERE, JACK.
THAT'S RIGHT. KEEP IT UP, ABDULLAH.
THIS IS NO MORE PART OF TRANSJORDAN TERRITORY THAN THE GESHER COLONY, OR KFAR ETZION OR NEVE YAAKOV--ALL THOSE OTHER PLACES WHERE YOUR BAND OF ROGUES HAS BEEN SPOTTED LATELY --AND WHERE, COINCIDENTALLY, HUNDREDS OF JEWS HAVE DIED. INCLUDING WOMEN, CHILDREN, BABIES...
27
...DOZENS OF WHOM WERE MURDERED AFTER THEY SURRENDERED.
NOW, NOW, JACK.
YOU REALLY SHOULD LEARN TO KEEP YOUR MOUTH SHUT BEFORE IT'S TOO LATE.
THE WORLD IS FULL OF COWARDS WHO KEEP THEIR MOUTHS SHUT.
AND AS FAR AS I CAN TELL, THE WORLD'S NO BETTER OFF. WHAT DO YOU THINK?
DESPERATE TIMES CALL FOR DESPERATE MEASURES.
?!

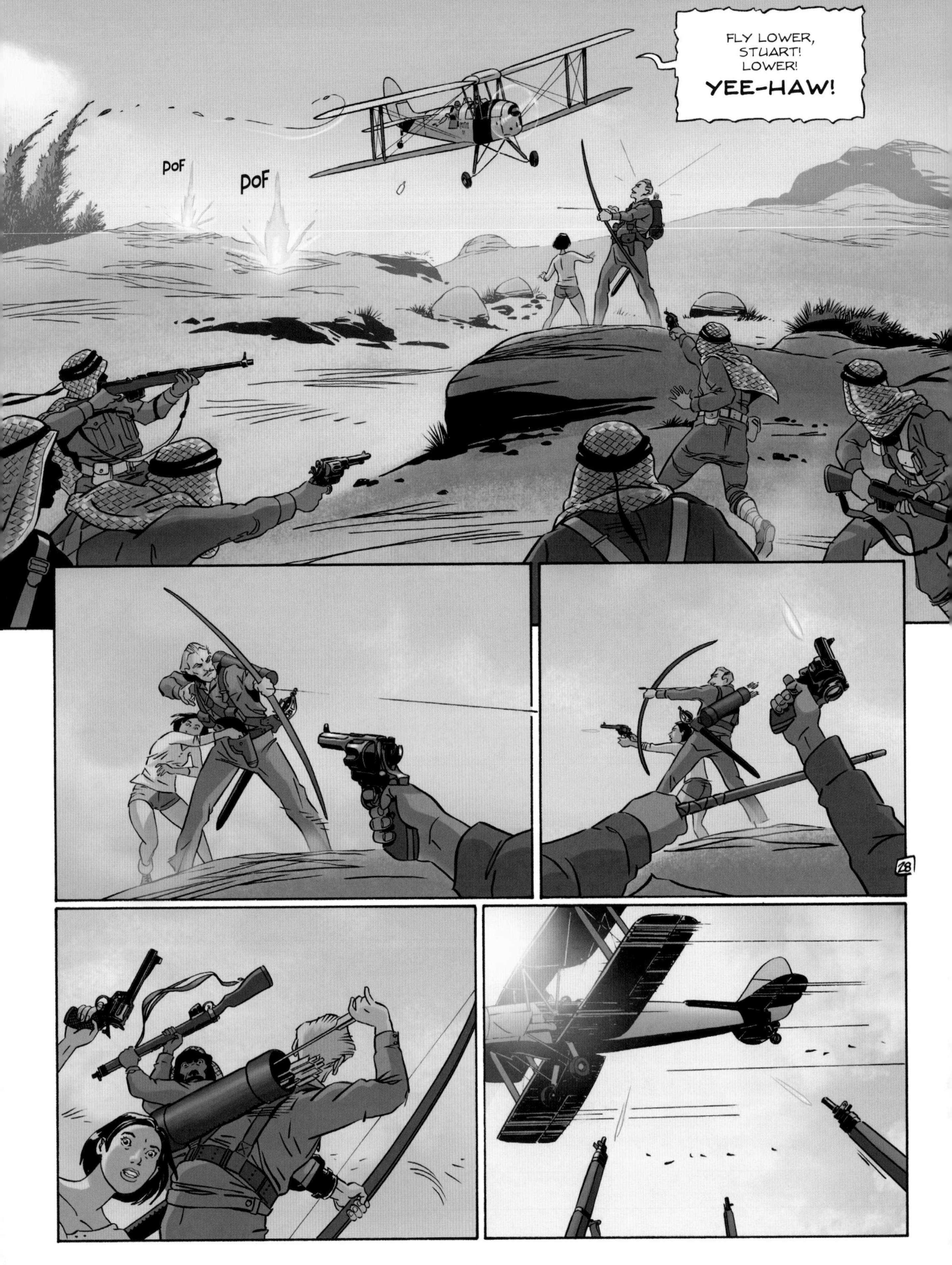
FLY LOWER, STUART! LOWER!
YEE-HAW!
POF
POF
28

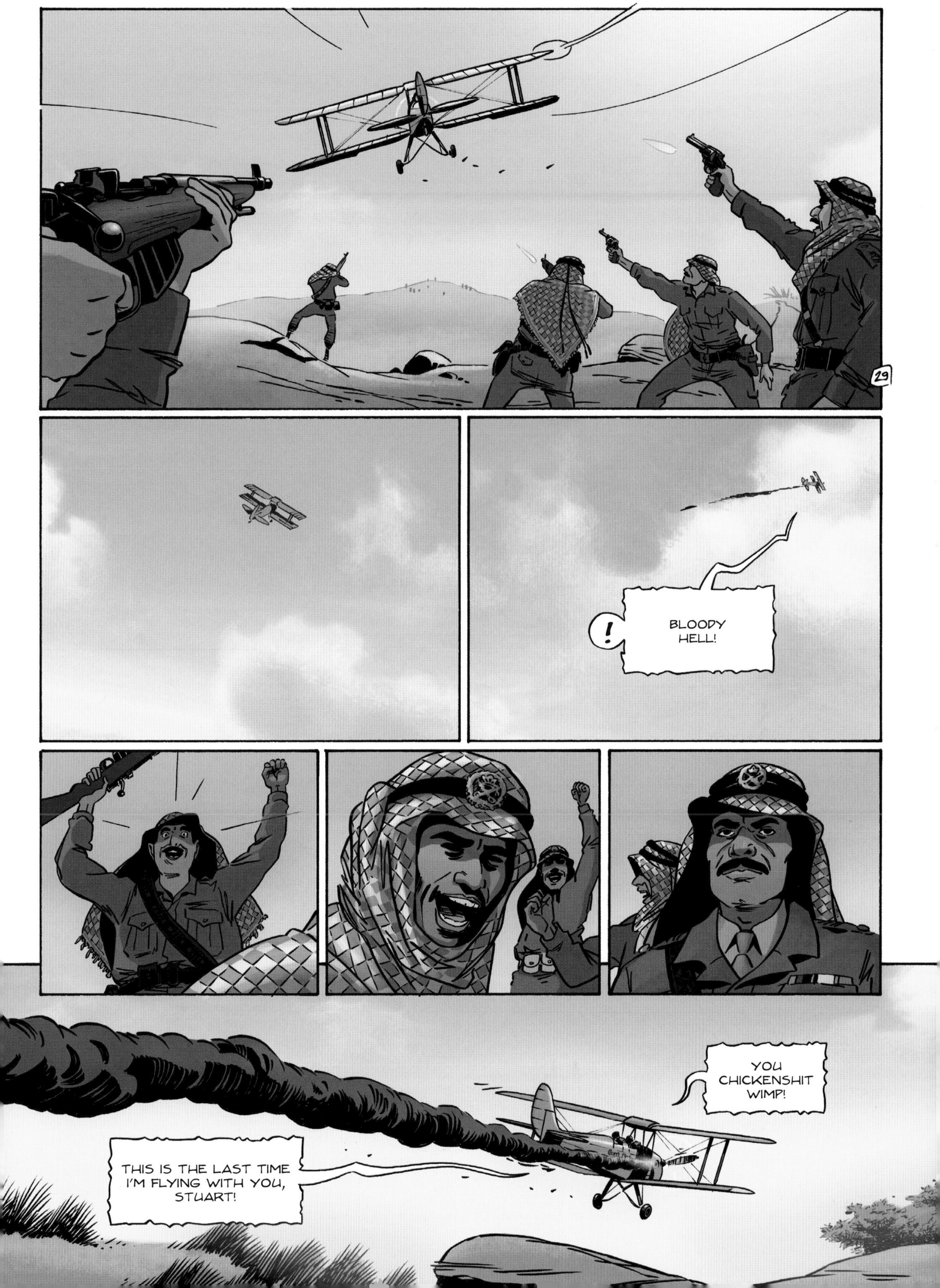
29
!
BLOODY HELL!
YOU CHICKENSHIT WIMP!
THIS IS THE LAST TIME I'M FLYING WITH YOU, STUART!

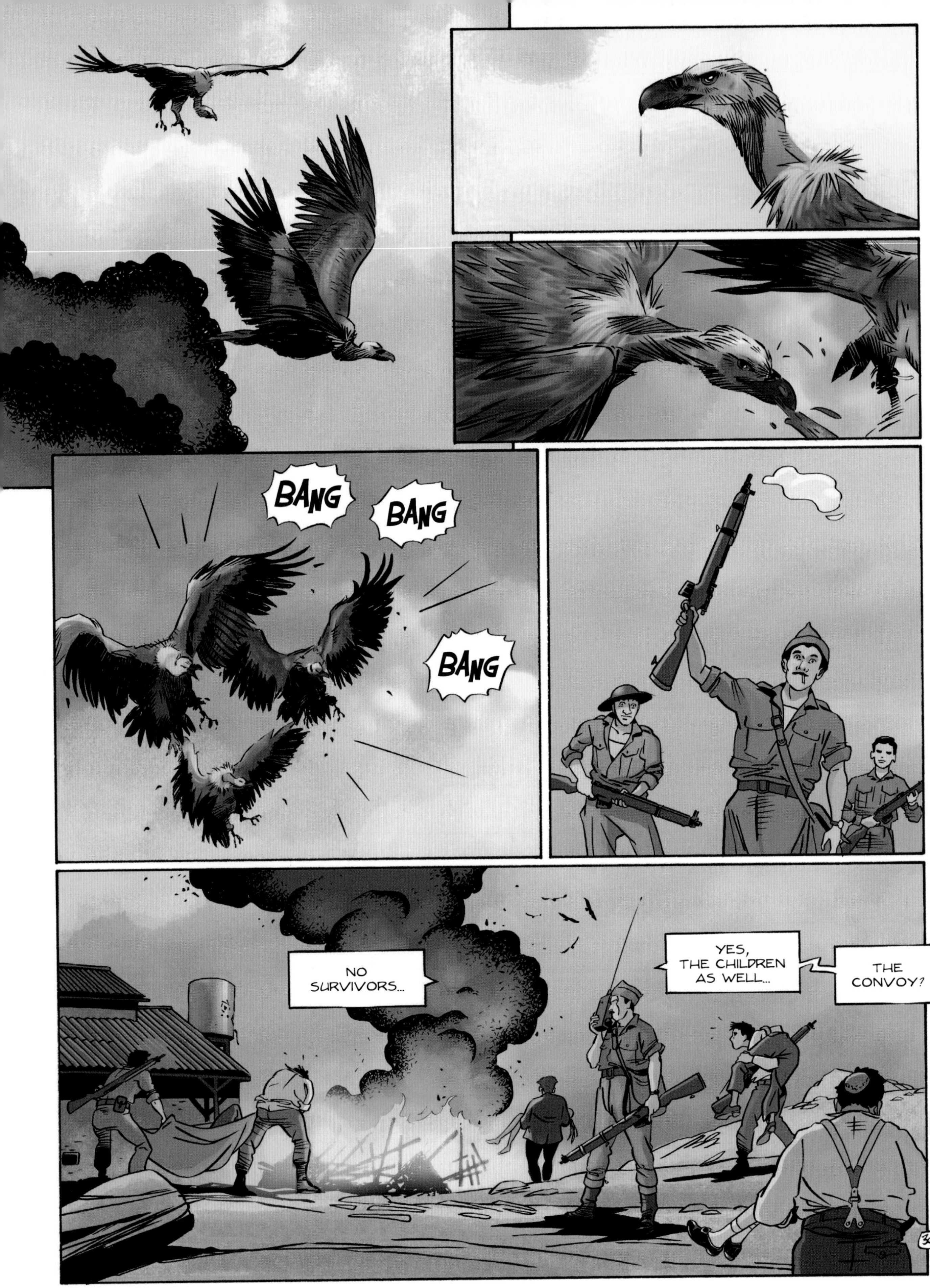
BANG
BANG
BANG
NO SURVIVORS...
THE CONVOY?
YES, THE CHILDREN AS WELL...
30

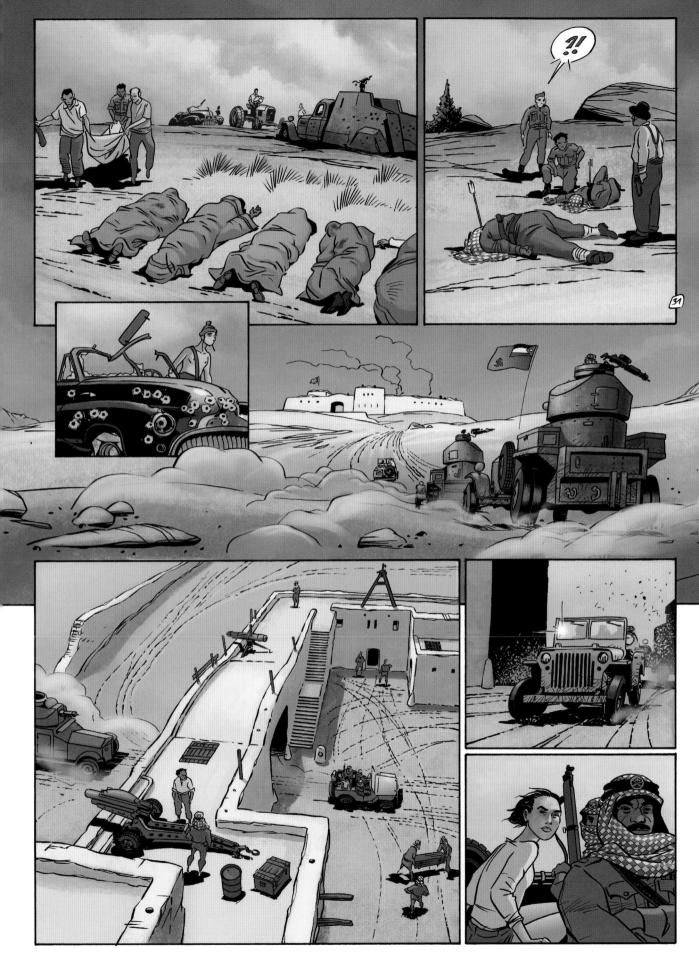

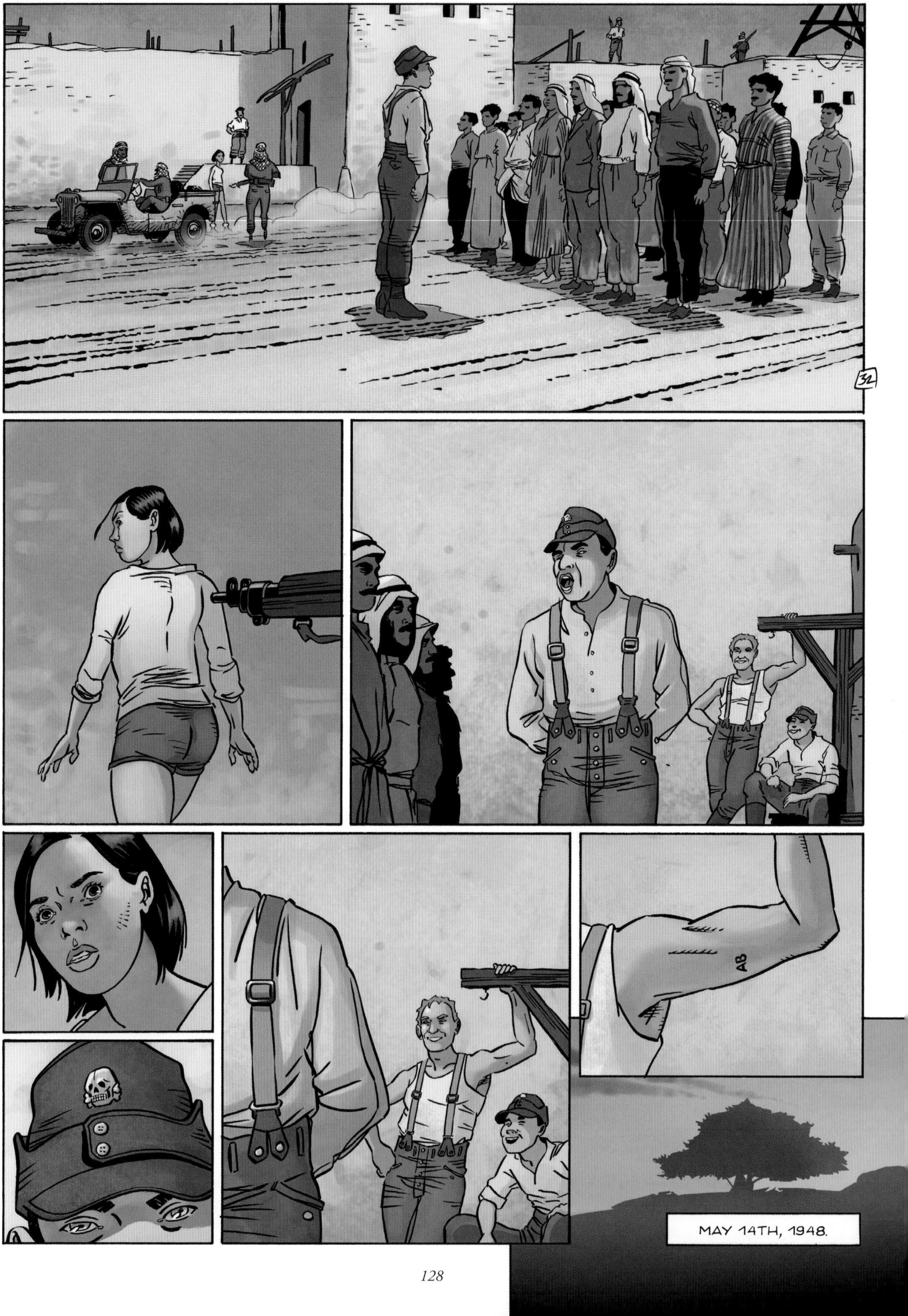
32
AB
MAY 14TH, 1948.

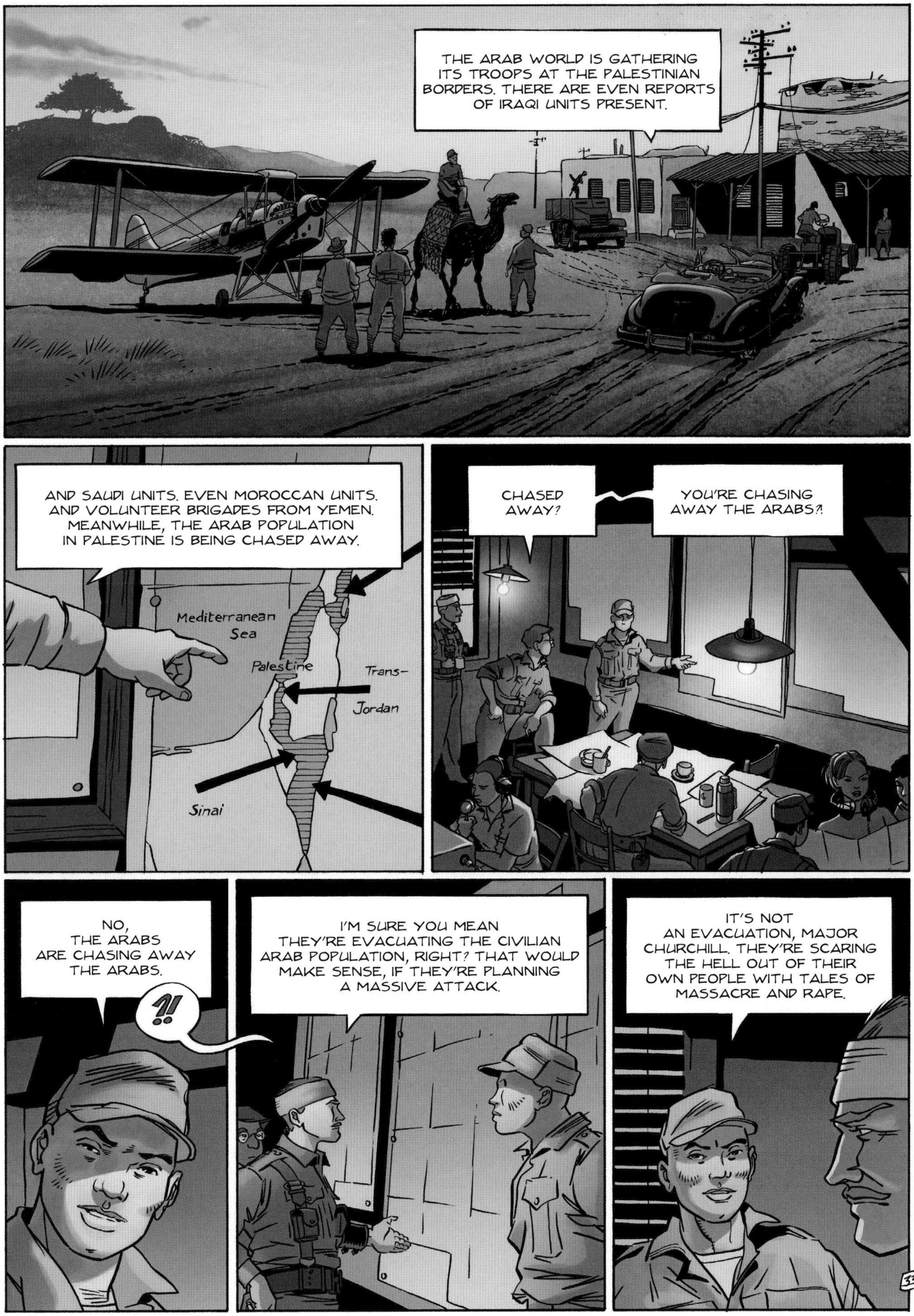
THE ARAB WORLD IS GATHERING ITS TROOPS AT THE PALESTINIAN BORDERS. THERE ARE EVEN REPORTS OF IRAQI UNITS PRESENT.
AND SAUDI UNITS. EVEN MOROCCAN UNITS. AND VOLUNTEER BRIGADES FROM YEMEN. MEANWHILE, THE ARAB POPULATION IN PALESTINE IS BEING CHASED AWAY.
Mediterranean Sea
Palestine
Trans-Jordan
Sinai
CHASED AWAY?
YOU'RE CHASING AWAY THE ARABS?!
NO, THE ARABS ARE CHASING AWAY THE ARABS.
?!
I'M SURE YOU MEAN THEY'RE EVACUATING THE CIVILIAN ARAB POPULATION, RIGHT? THAT WOULD MAKE SENSE, IF THEY'RE PLANNING A MASSIVE ATTACK.
IT'S NOT AN EVACUATION, MAJOR CHURCHILL. THEY'RE SCARING THE HELL OUT OF THEIR OWN PEOPLE WITH TALES OF MASSACRE AND RAPE.

SPEAKING OF WHICH... SAFAYA TOLD ME ABOUT THE ATTACK THAT A FEW JEWISH MILITIA LAUNCHED ON SOME VILLAGE OR OTHER.

DEIR YASSIN, YES. IT WAS RAZED BY THE IRGUN AND ITS BASTARD OFFSPRING, THE LEHI. THOSE TWO GROUPS REFUSE TO SUBMIT TO ANY JOINT CHAIN OF COMMAND.

HAH! SO MUCH FOR UNITY AMONG THE JEWISH PEOPLE! YET THERE IS STRENGTH IN UNITY, EVEN THE BELGIANS KNOW THAT.

TO HELL WITH THE IRGUN AND THE LEHI! THEY GAVE THE ARABS A POWERFUL PROPAGANDA TOOL. WORSE STILL, THEY GAVE THEM AN IDEA.

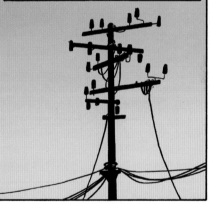

TENS OF THOUSANDS OF ARABS ARE FLEEING, DESPITE THE JEWS' ATTEMPT TO PUT A STOP TO THE EXODUS.

SOME ARAB LEADERS ARE DELIBERATELY ADDING FUEL TO THE FIRE. THEY'RE TRYING TO CREATE A REFUGEE PROBLEM THEY CAN USE TO THEIR POLITICAL ADVANTAGE LATER ON.

AN ALL-OUT WAR... THIS IS GOING TO TURN INTO AN ALL-OUT WAR...

SAFAYA...

WHEN I CAME TO, SHE WAS GONE. I KNOW ABDULLAH. WE WORKED TOGETHER QUITE A BIT, LAST YEAR. HE'S A SMART MAN, HE'LL HAVE UNDERSTOOD THAT IT'S BEST NOT TO LET THE SITUATION DETERIORATE AND HE'LL HAVE TAKEN THE YOUNG WOMAN UNDER HIS PROTECTION.

"UNDER HIS PROTECTION"? WHAT DOES "UNDER HIS PROTECTION" MEAN, EXACTLY?

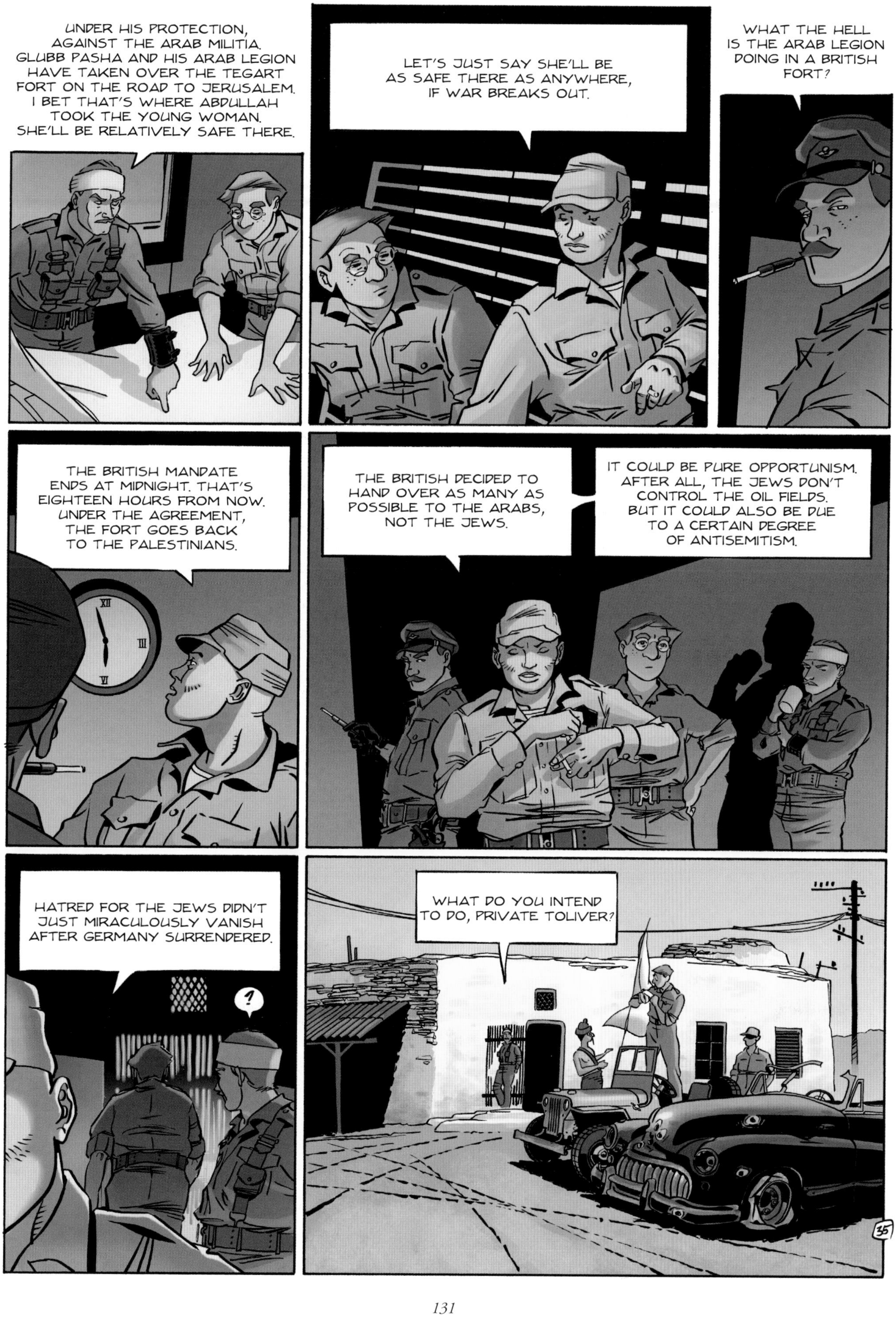
UNDER HIS PROTECTION, AGAINST THE ARAB MILITIA. GLUBB PASHA AND HIS ARAB LEGION HAVE TAKEN OVER THE TEGART FORT ON THE ROAD TO JERUSALEM. I BET THAT'S WHERE ABDULLAH TOOK THE YOUNG WOMAN. SHE'LL BE RELATIVELY SAFE THERE.
LET'S JUST SAY SHE'LL BE AS SAFE THERE AS ANYWHERE, IF WAR BREAKS OUT.
WHAT THE HELL IS THE ARAB LEGION DOING IN A BRITISH FORT?
THE BRITISH MANDATE ENDS AT MIDNIGHT. THAT'S EIGHTEEN HOURS FROM NOW. UNDER THE AGREEMENT, THE FORT GOES BACK TO THE PALESTINIANS.
THE BRITISH DECIDED TO HAND OVER AS MANY AS POSSIBLE TO THE ARABS, NOT THE JEWS.
IT COULD BE PURE OPPORTUNISM. AFTER ALL, THE JEWS DON'T CONTROL THE OIL FIELDS. BUT IT COULD ALSO BE DUE TO A CERTAIN DEGREE OF ANTISEMITISM.
HATRED FOR THE JEWS DIDN'T JUST MIRACULOUSLY VANISH AFTER GERMANY SURRENDERED.
?
WHAT DO YOU INTEND TO DO, PRIVATE TOLIVER?
35

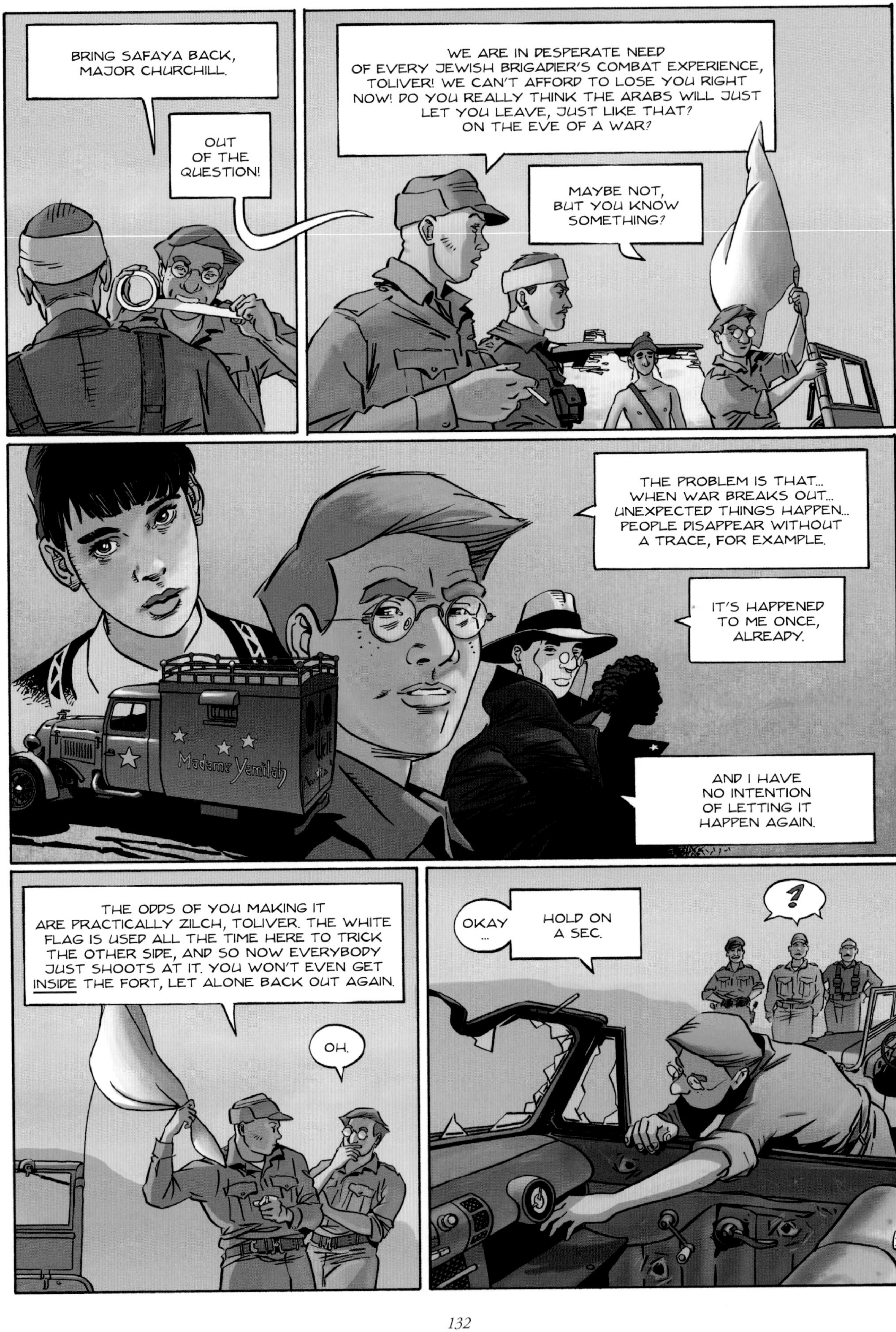
BRING SAFAYA BACK, MAJOR CHURCHILL.
OUT OF THE QUESTION!
WE ARE IN DESPERATE NEED OF EVERY JEWISH BRIGADIER'S COMBAT EXPERIENCE, TOLIVER! WE CAN'T AFFORD TO LOSE YOU RIGHT NOW! DO YOU REALLY THINK THE ARABS WILL JUST LET YOU LEAVE, JUST LIKE THAT? ON THE EVE OF A WAR?
MAYBE NOT, BUT YOU KNOW SOMETHING?
THE PROBLEM IS THAT... WHEN WAR BREAKS OUT... UNEXPECTED THINGS HAPPEN... PEOPLE DISAPPEAR WITHOUT A TRACE, FOR EXAMPLE.
IT'S HAPPENED TO ME ONCE, ALREADY.
Madame Yamilah
AND I HAVE NO INTENTION OF LETTING IT HAPPEN AGAIN.
THE ODDS OF YOU MAKING IT ARE PRACTICALLY ZILCH, TOLIVER. THE WHITE FLAG IS USED ALL THE TIME HERE TO TRICK THE OTHER SIDE, AND SO NOW EVERYBODY JUST SHOOTS AT IT. YOU WON'T EVEN GET INSIDE THE FORT, LET ALONE BACK OUT AGAIN.
OH.
OKAY...
HOLD ON A SEC.
?
36

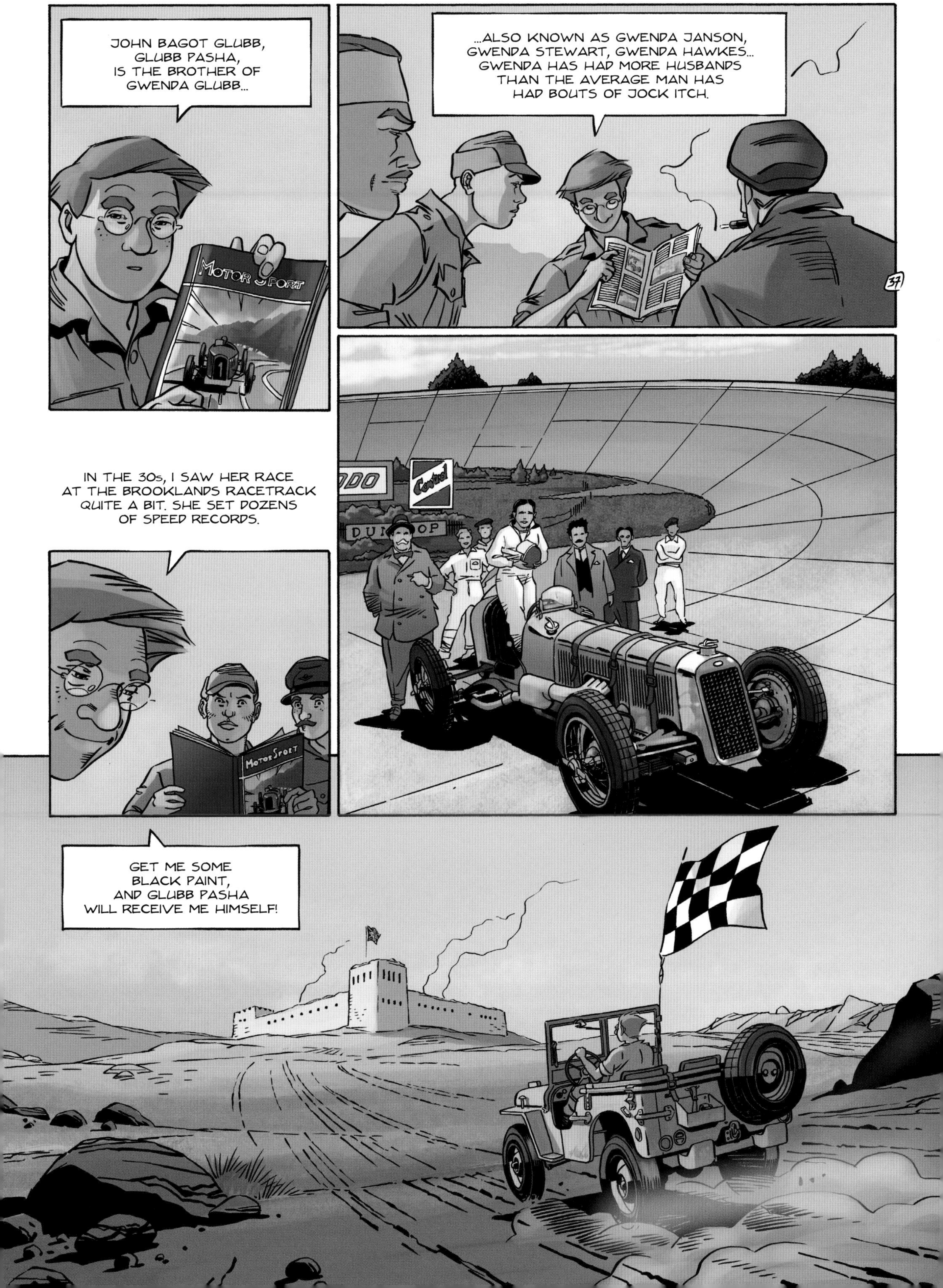
JOHN BAGOT GLUBB, GLUBB PASHA, IS THE BROTHER OF GWENDA GLUBB...
MOTOR SPORT
...ALSO KNOWN AS GWENDA JANSON, GWENDA STEWART, GWENDA HAWKES... GWENDA HAS HAD MORE HUSBANDS THAN THE AVERAGE MAN HAS HAD BOUTS OF JOCK ITCH.
37
Castrol
DUNLOP
IN THE 30s, I SAW HER RACE AT THE BROOKLANDS RACETRACK QUITE A BIT. SHE SET DOZENS OF SPEED RECORDS.
MOTOR SPORT
GET ME SOME BLACK PAINT, AND GLUBB PASHA WILL RECEIVE ME HIMSELF!

WELL... A DESPERATE PLOY IF I EVER SAW ONE.

DESPERATE?

"WE CAN STILL HOPE EVEN TODAY THAT A WRATHFUL GOD MAY STILL HAVE MERCY ON US."

?

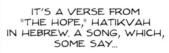

IT'S A VERSE FROM "THE HOPE," HATIKVAH IN HEBREW. A SONG, WHICH, SOME SAY...

...WAS SUNG EVEN IN THE GAS CHAMBERS.

38

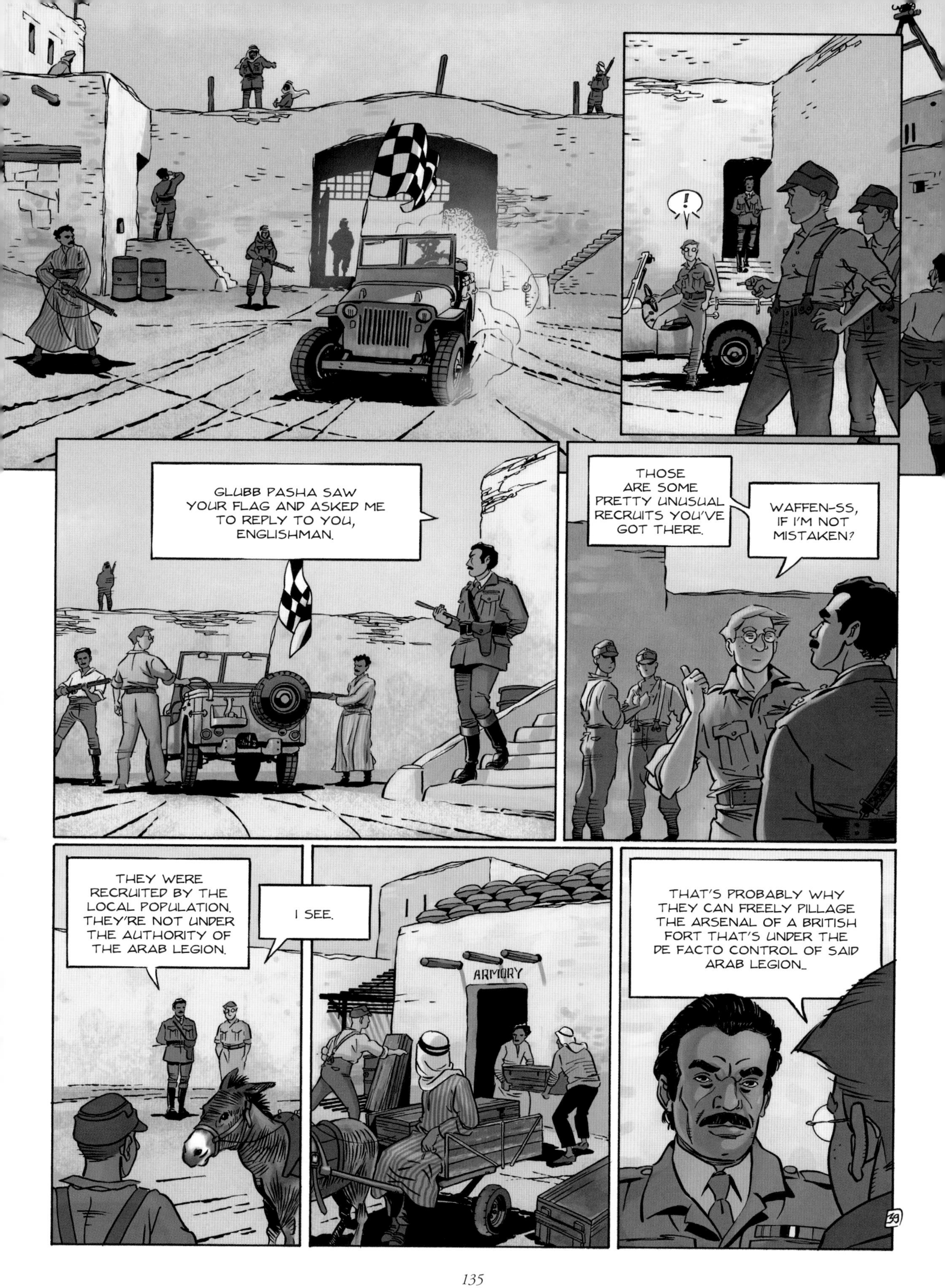
!
GLUBB PASHA SAW YOUR FLAG AND ASKED ME TO REPLY TO YOU, ENGLISHMAN.
THOSE ARE SOME PRETTY UNUSUAL RECRUITS YOU'VE GOT THERE.
WAFFEN-SS, IF I'M NOT MISTAKEN?
THEY WERE RECRUITED BY THE LOCAL POPULATION. THEY'RE NOT UNDER THE AUTHORITY OF THE ARAB LEGION.
I SEE.
ARMORY
THAT'S PROBABLY WHY THEY CAN FREELY PILLAGE THE ARSENAL OF A BRITISH FORT THAT'S UNDER THE DE FACTO CONTROL OF SAID ARAB LEGION...
39

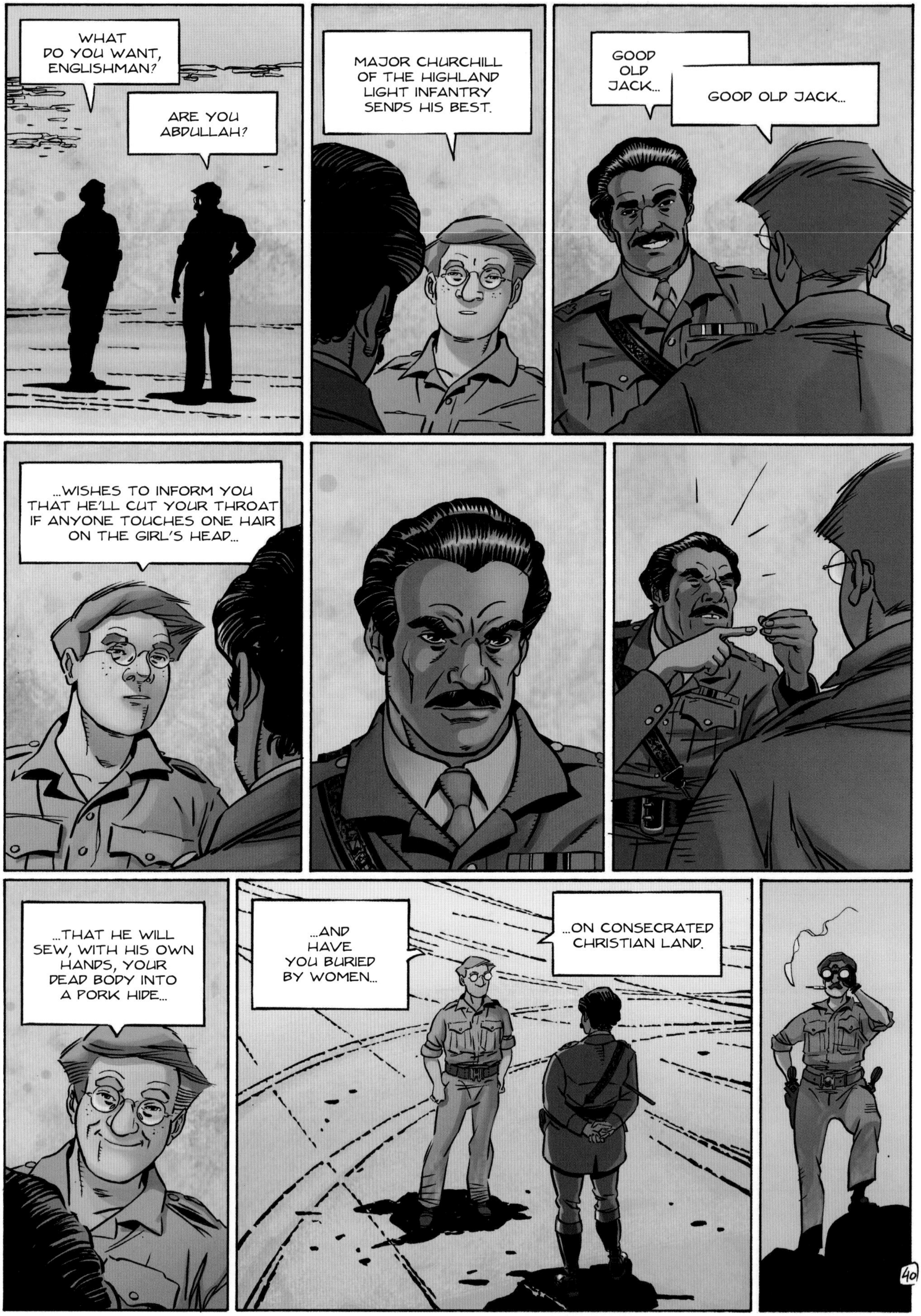
WHAT DO YOU WANT, ENGLISHMAN?
ARE YOU ABDULLAH?
MAJOR CHURCHILL OF THE HIGHLAND LIGHT INFANTRY SENDS HIS BEST.
GOOD OLD JACK...
GOOD OLD JACK...
...WISHES TO INFORM YOU THAT HE'LL CUT YOUR THROAT IF ANYONE TOUCHES ONE HAIR ON THE GIRL'S HEAD...
...THAT HE WILL SEW, WITH HIS OWN HANDS, YOUR DEAD BODY INTO A PORK HIDE...
...AND HAVE YOU BURIED BY WOMEN...
...ON CONSECRATED CHRISTIAN LAND.
40

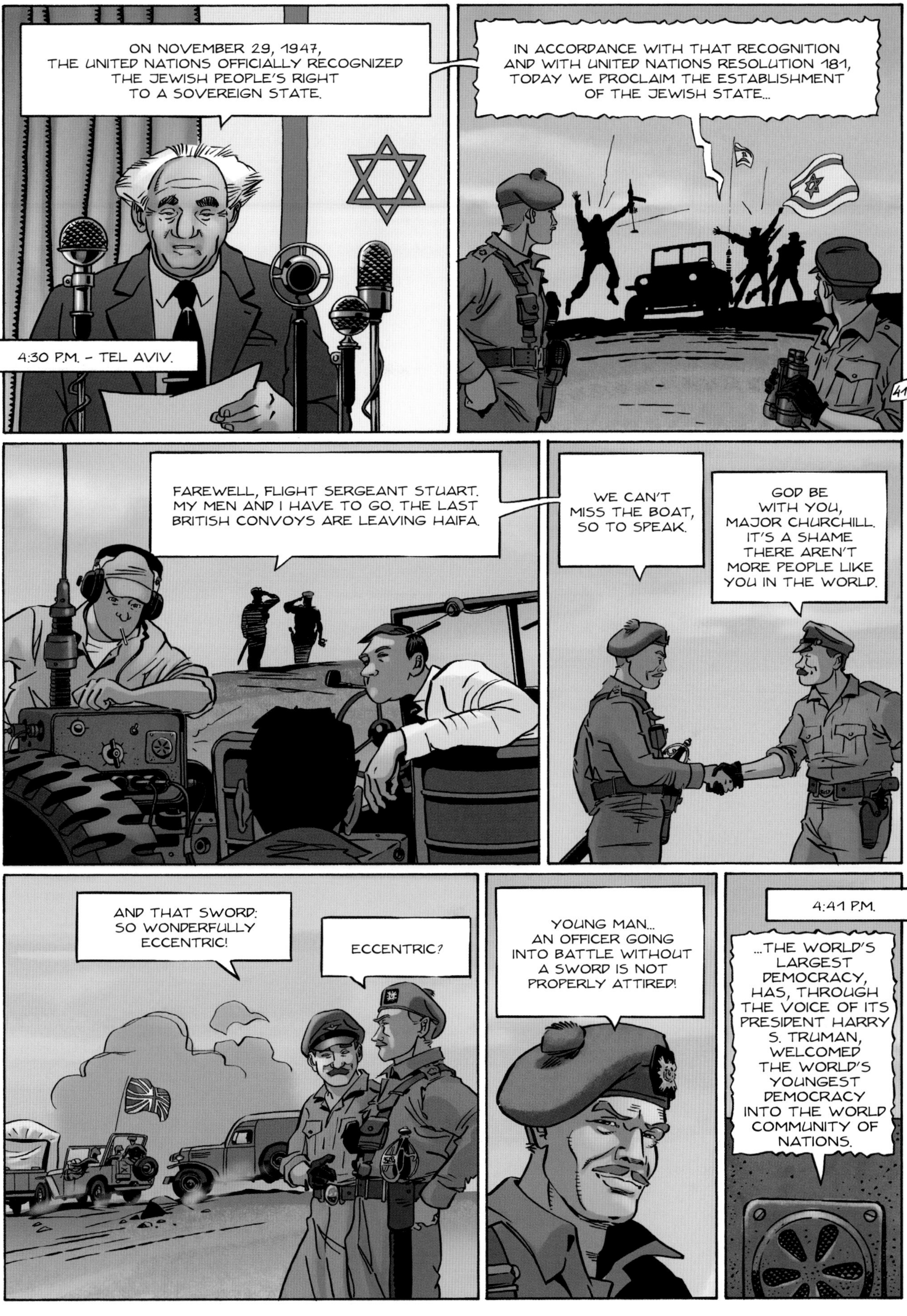
ON NOVEMBER 29, 1947, THE UNITED NATIONS OFFICIALLY RECOGNIZED THE JEWISH PEOPLE'S RIGHT TO A SOVEREIGN STATE.
4:30 P.M. - TEL AVIV.
IN ACCORDANCE WITH THAT RECOGNITION AND WITH UNITED NATIONS RESOLUTION 181, TODAY WE PROCLAIM THE ESTABLISHMENT OF THE JEWISH STATE...
41
FAREWELL, FLIGHT SERGEANT STUART. MY MEN AND I HAVE TO GO. THE LAST BRITISH CONVOYS ARE LEAVING HAIFA.
WE CAN'T MISS THE BOAT, SO TO SPEAK.
GOD BE WITH YOU, MAJOR CHURCHILL. IT'S A SHAME THERE AREN'T MORE PEOPLE LIKE YOU IN THE WORLD.
AND THAT SWORD: SO WONDERFULLY ECCENTRIC!
ECCENTRIC?
YOUNG MAN... AN OFFICER GOING INTO BATTLE WITHOUT A SWORD IS NOT PROPERLY ATTIRED!
4:41 P.M.
...THE WORLD'S LARGEST DEMOCRACY, HAS, THROUGH THE VOICE OF ITS PRESIDENT HARRY S. TRUMAN, WELCOMED THE WORLD'S YOUNGEST DEMOCRACY INTO THE WORLD COMMUNITY OF NATIONS.

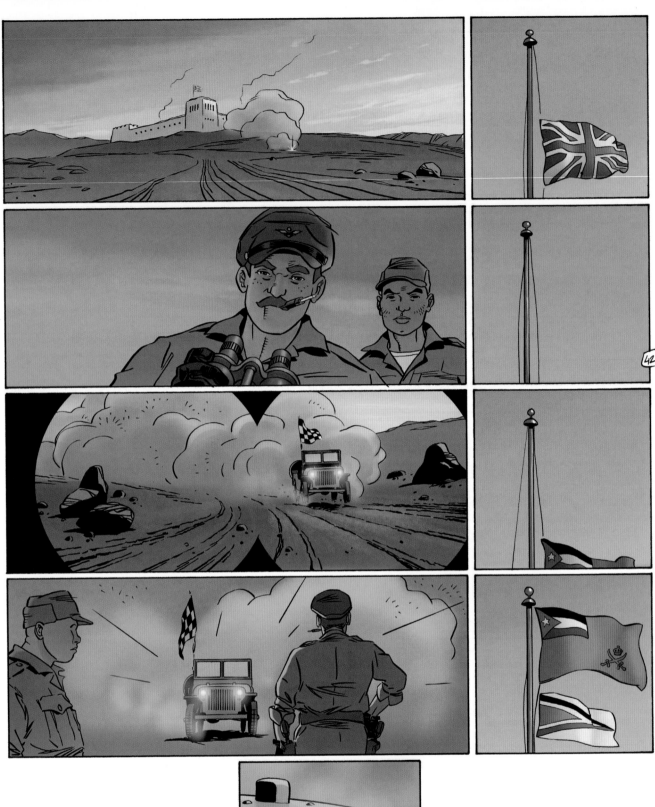

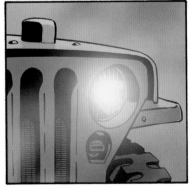

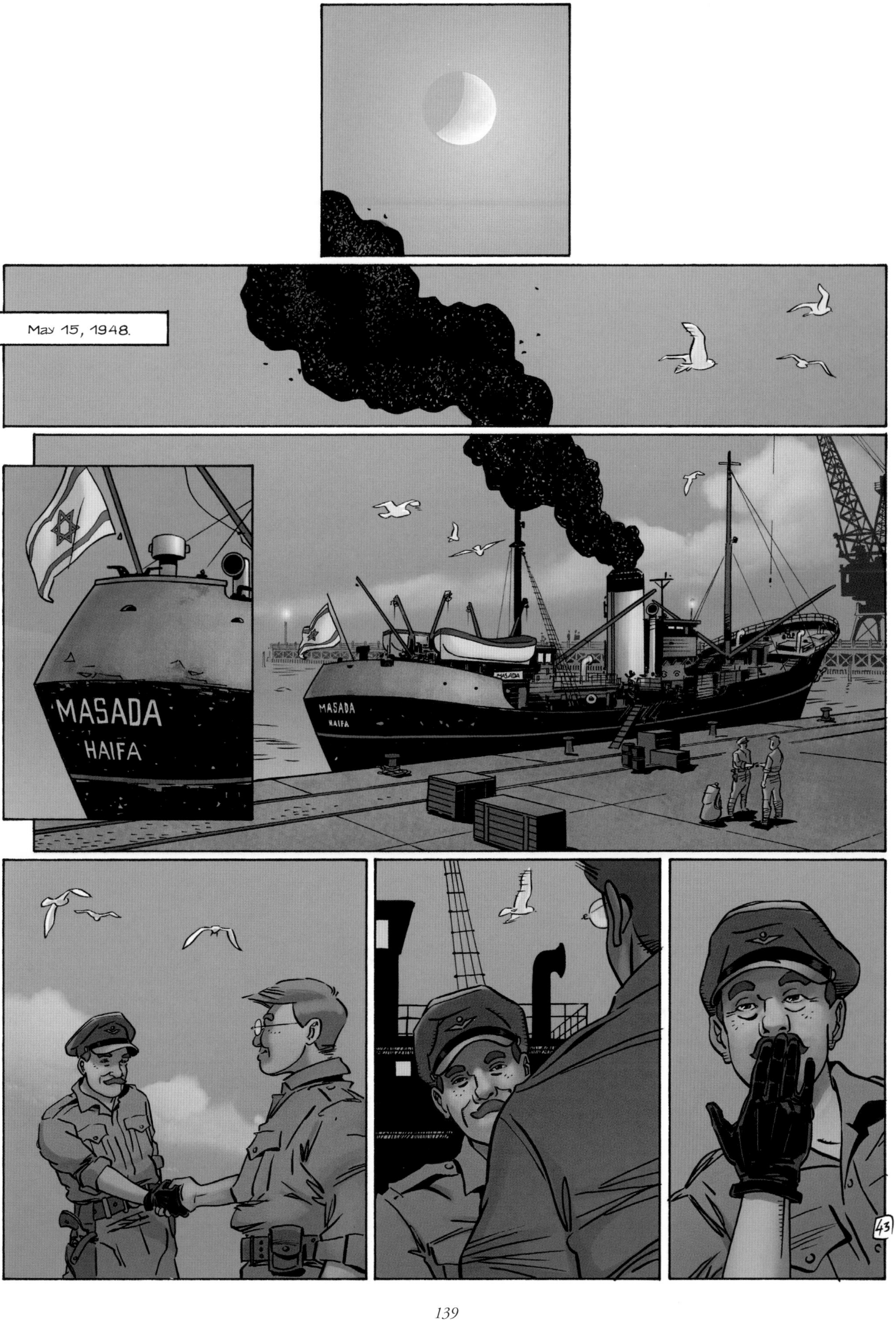
May 15, 1948.
MASADA
HAIFA
MASADA
HAIFA
MASADA
43

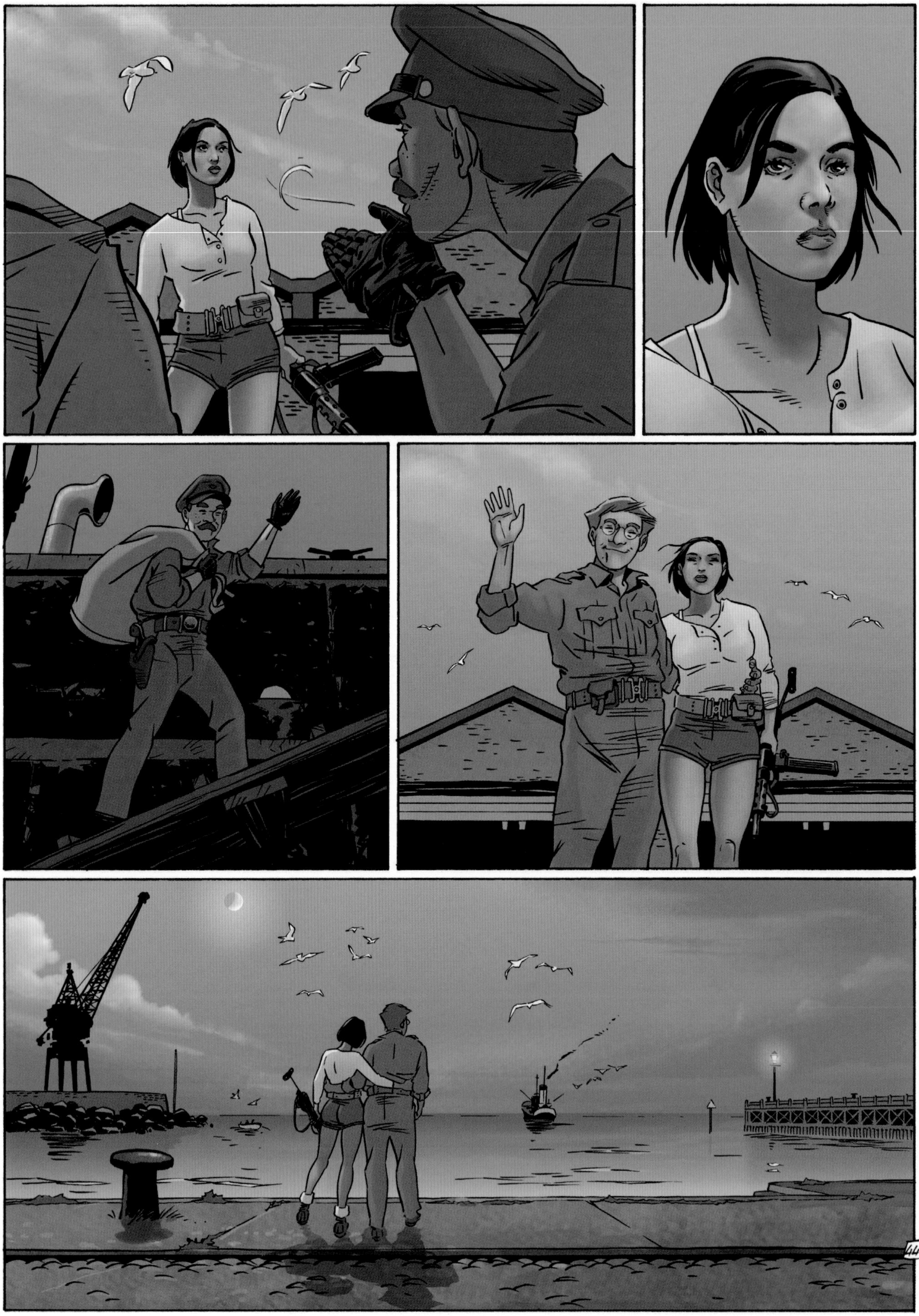
44

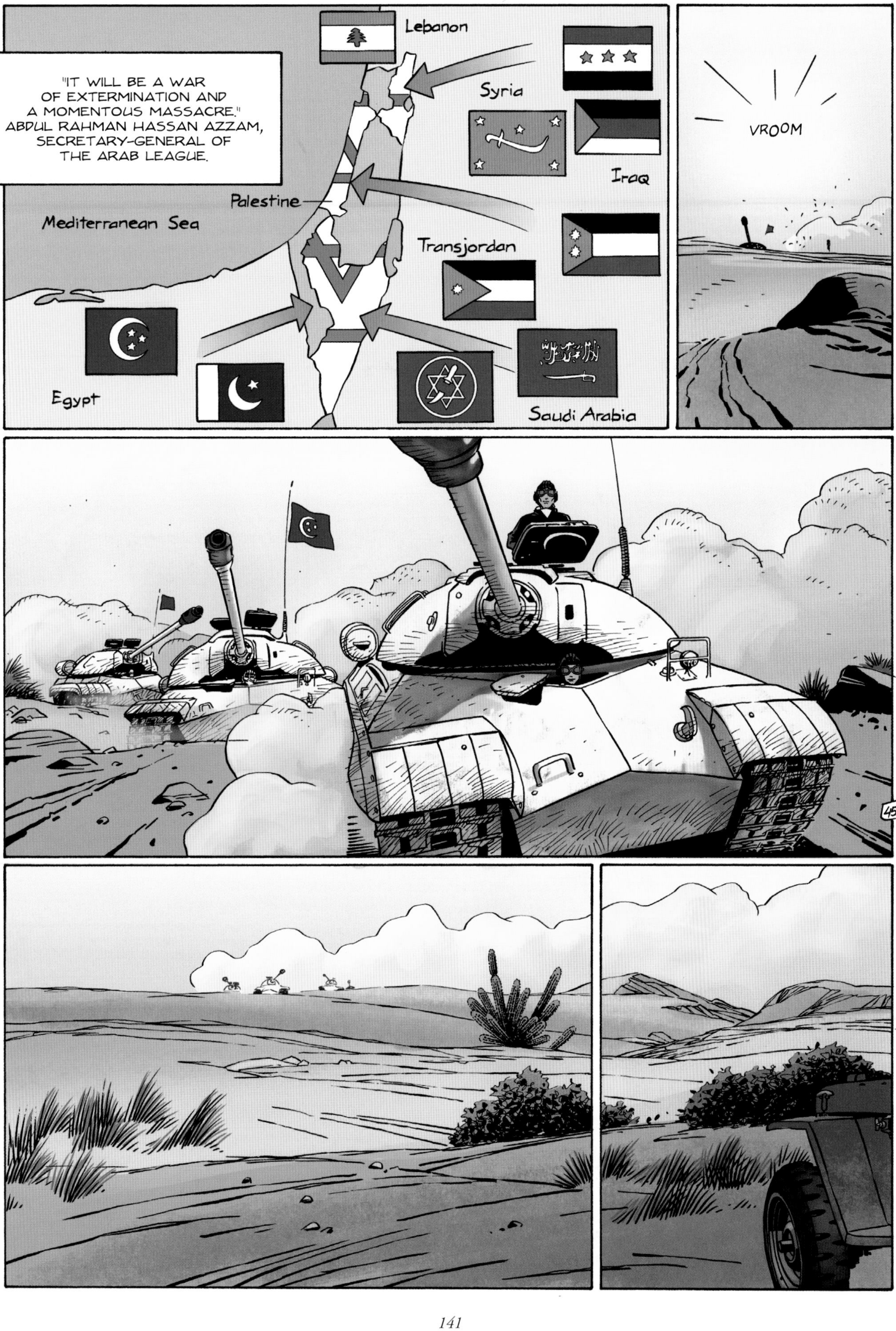
"IT WILL BE A WAR OF EXTERMINATION AND A MOMENTOUS MASSACRE." ABDUL RAHMAN HASSAN AZZAM, SECRETARY-GENERAL OF THE ARAB LEAGUE.
Lebanon
Syria
Iraq
Palestine
Mediterranean Sea
Transjordan
Egypt
Saudi Arabia
VROOM
45

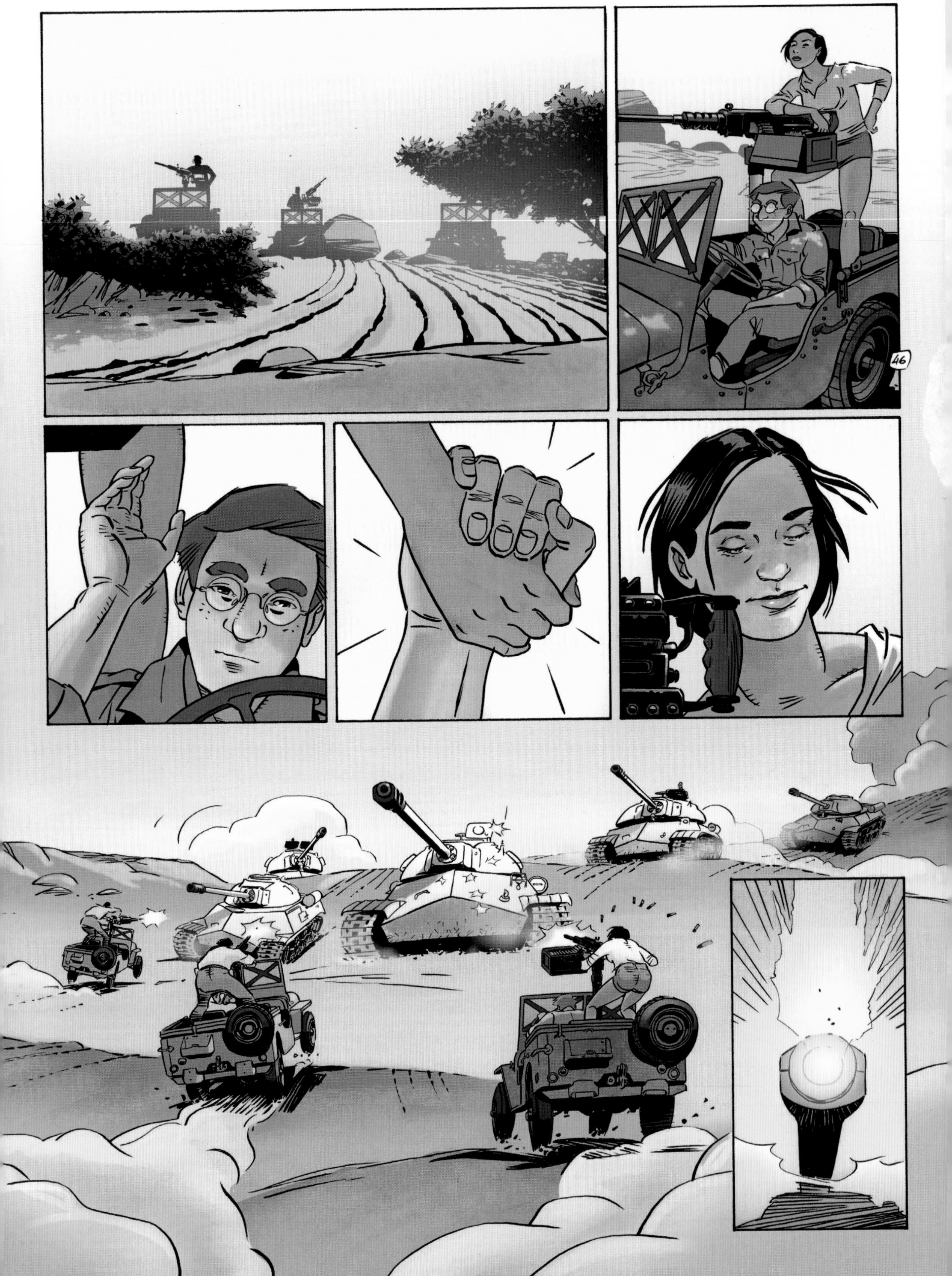
46